SCOTLAND'S
First WAR of
INDEPENDENCE

To Philip

without whom it would not have been possible

Overleaf: *Scottish silver penny from the reign of King Robert the Bruce; c.1320.*

SCOTLAND'S
First WAR of
INDEPENDENCE

SARAH CROME

AUCH✤BOOKS

First Published in 1999.
New photographs copyright © Auch Books
Text copyright © Sarah Crome
First published in the United Kingdom 1999 by
Auch Books, 17 Commercial Road,
Alford, Lincolnshire, LN13 9EY

British Library Cataloguing-in-Publication Data.
A CIP catalogue record for this book
is available from the British Library.

ISBN 0-9536316-0-5

Designed by The S S Crome, Alford, Lincolnshire.
Maps by Bray Design
Production by Nicholas Russell, Cambridge.
Printed in the UK by Jarrold Book Printing Ltd, Thetford

CONTENTS

FOREWORD

By Nigel Tranter

I have pleasure in expressing my esteem and admiration for this most ambitious, accurate and extraordinarily-detailed account of one of the most dramatic and significant periods in the history of both Scotland and England. The author is to be congratulated on the conception and on the execution of this notable and indeed daunting project, on all the deep research necessary, and on the excellence, relevance and abundance of the illustrations.

As one who has himself been much engaged in the study and concern for this highly important chapter in our island's story, I commend this book to all discerning readers. History is the memory of the races, and a nation which loses its memory is sad indeed, and not worthy to be called a nation. Here is an enthralling account of one of the most tumultuous and momentous forty years of *two* nations. I salute the author.

Nigel Tranter

INTRODUCTION

Standing silently beneath the lighthouse at Turnberry golfcourse are the remains of a great castle. The earthworks and surviving masonry go largely unnoticed by the golfers as they come and go, and only the hole known as *"Bruce's Castle"* gives away its significant past. Such is the fate of many anonymous locations from the most tumultuous era in Scottish history. On the face of it, there is very little hard evidence that survives from Scotland's Wars of Independence, fought in the late thirteenth and early fourteenth centuries. Ironically, so much of the heritage was destroyed by both English invasion and the Scots' own scorched earth policy. But there is, in fact, much to remind us of those turbulent years and it is largely through the landscape of Scotland itself, which provided the stage, that we associate the war. It is also thanks to the monument builders who later commemorated the remarkable deeds of those who participated in the conflict.

My first visit to Scotland in 1987 made me realise that I had completely missed out on an area of British history. I knew nothing about the subject of this book, simply because I had not been to Scotland before. My own awareness of Scottish history was affected by all the stereotypes portrayed through television, advertising and products, but I soon realised that this was not entirely my fault. Having worked within the field of interpreting Scotland's heritage, I learned that it was partly how Scotland presented itself to the world and how it promoted its image abroad that prejudiced people's opinions.

Perhaps unsurprisingly, Scotland's wars with England have never been in the forefront of the tourism agenda, even after the film 'Braveheart' proved it had wide international appeal. The pursuit of 'right against might' by those selfless people who, against the odds, achieved their objective is a story understood by many other cultures in every corner of the world. Now, at last, outwith Scotland, William Wallace is the household name he deserves to be. But despite the 'Braveheart' phenomenon, or perhaps because of it, there is still a reluctance to talk openly about this proud era of history at home. Perhaps there is an underlying national feeling that it may stir up resentment within the present United Kingdom. But discouraging knowlege of history only fuels misunderstandings of the past which, in some ways, brings about greater conflict. We owe our present to the events of the past and we should all feel detached enough from the events of 700 years ago to learn from them without becoming too deeply involved.

The recent Devolution referendum resulted in Scotland confidently voting yes to its first Parliament for 300 years. Contrary to popular opinion before the vote, Scots did not lose their nerve over home rule, and dispelled the myth of the Scottish 'cringe', the idea that as a nation, the Scots lack confidence. The quality of debate on the issue of home rule, particularly amongst the English, has revealed a massive hole in people's understanding of the history of the British Isles. This book may help to explain the origin of many attitudes and correct the misconception that Scotland has, somehow, always been 'under the thumb' of England. There are parallels between attitudes of people today and of those living 700 years ago, but much has happened in the intervening centuries to distort people's ideas of the rights and wrongs of Scottish home rule.

Until recently, education throughout the United Kingdom taught British history from an English perspective and consequently many misunderstand the path of Scottish history. The Norman Conquest of *England* in 1066 features so prominently in the presentation of the past that it is impossible for many to realise that there were other countries in the British Isles at that time with their own agendas. When Edward I of England invaded Scotland in 1296, the Scots, who had been ruled under a continuous line of Celtic kings since the Dark Ages, had enjoyed centuries of prosperity, independence and peace with their neighbours. When, after the death of the last king of this line, the Scots decided to fight back, it was not for the sake of rebellion against England who considered themselves the natural rulers of Scotland, but for the rightful defence of their freedom.

Above: The Queen arrives in a open-topped carriage to open Scotland's first Parliament for nearly 300 years.

It is important for us to perceive the people of England and Scotland in the context of that age. The culture of England's nobility, and to a large extent Scotland's, was fundamentally Norman French, the Conquest having occured only 200 years previously. The diverse peoples of both countries were led by this élite.

From the English point of view, we should particularly take note of how we were used. We (the English) are supposed to admire Edward I for his strength and there are examples of his generosity towards common people; for example, in order to help small towns flourish, many were awarded market charters. My own town received its charter in 1283. But however a fair king he is portrayed to the English, the reality is that his military campaigns bore a heavy burden on us economically, in the name of expanding our territory ever wider. Year after year, men were torn away from their homes and livelihoods to fight, not in defence, but in an aggressive campaign to assimilate other

nations. No doubt they were encouraged by the anti-Scots propaganda issued by such holy places as Lanercost Priory. Only later, when Scots retaliated, were English called upon to defend their lives.

Although we associate this period of history with the birth of Scottish nationalism, it is interesting that towards the end of the thirteenth century, before the conflict began, Scotland was very much an out-going, internationally minded nation, while England was undergoing a rising tide of nationalism encouraged by King Edward I himself. He took much more power on to his own shoulders and, in 1290, with the support of many of his people, expelled all Jews from the country. At the same time, Edward used his subjects in any way he could to achieve his aims. He even took away goods from tradesmen and resold them as his own in Europe to raise money for his military campaigns. It is not surprising that today in England, we too are not taught much about this era from our past.

It is also important to emphasise, at the risk of revealing how the story ends, that this war was won by the Scots. Once again, there seems to be a popular misconception that, although the Battle of Bannockburn saw a decisive victory for Scotland, the English subjugated the Scots anyway. This is to deny centuries of subsequent history which saw the rise of the House of Stewart. From 1371, when Robert II ascended the throne, until 1714 on the death of Queen Anne, the Stewarts ruled Scotland and then both Scotland and England as a United Kingdom. It should be recognised that it was not conquest that brought Scotland into a united kingdom with England, but a Treaty of Union 400 years after Robert the Bruce won permanent recognition for Scotland's sovereignty.

In writing this book, I am not presenting new facts apart from recent developments, notably excavations on the alleged Bruce's heart and the return of the Stone of Destiny to Scotland. Nor am I complicating the events by presenting many different theories about how things happened. I am, however, hopefully providing a unique chronological view of the story in a thorough account which weaves together the story of this forty-year conflict with the images that we can associate with it. In order to help understand this period fully, one needs to draw together the wealth of landscape, built heritage and artefacts. Most of the landscape features associated with those times are still there and little changed. For example, the Pass of Brander saw plenty of action 700 years ago and, today, road and railway share the route taken by Robert Bruce when he defeated the MacDougalls. Such is the scale of mountain and loch, that modern development does not remove the historical environment and, with a little imagination, one can envisage the conflict unfolding down the pass. Of Scotland's built heritage, there is very little that survives from before 1300 simply because of the extent of destruction. Where remains survive, even as part of a later building, I have tried to illustrate them here. Most of Edinburgh Castle was dismantled by Robert the Bruce so that the English could never re-occupy it, but he did save St. Margaret's Chapel at the very top of the castle.

Few of us today can imagine the horrors of medieval warfare and, to explain further the scale of the conflict, I have recreated some contemporary battle scenes and provided illustrated maps. Presenting the story in visual as well as written form has enabled me to put across the sheer scale of the task, and the ground covered by those involved. Although I have featured all the key locations, it has not been possible to illustrate every site connected with the War. For the sake of continuity, I have kept pictures that are relevant to the text on the same page.

To explain further the structure of the book: the events of the War can be clearly defined in stages, and for the purposes of interpreting events, this book presents them in four parts. Part 1, *The End of a Golden Age*, leads us from the death of Alexander III, King of Scots in 1286 to the defeat of King John Balliol by Edward I ten years later. Part 2, *Fighting for a Lost Cause*, is marked by the beginning of resistance to English occupation by William Wallace until his death in 1305. Part 3, *Turning the Tide*, shows how Robert Bruce renewed the fight for freedom and how this ultimately led to the greatest battle fought on Scottish soil. Part 4, *The Price of Freedom*, begins with the Battle of Bannockburn in 1314. It continues with the long and desperate struggle with England for international recognition of Scotland's independence, which came at last with the Treaty of Edinburgh in 1328.

Retention of their independence seemed an impossible task for the Scots. They spent much of that time merely surviving, during which they built up their strength, confidence and international influence to eventually win the day. The characters of Wallace and Bruce have often been biographised separately to the extent that we tend to disassociate the achievements of the two. We should not forget that the fight begun by William Wallace was continued and won by King Robert the Bruce. This book presents the continuity of their failures and triumphs and the legacy of the Scotland that they left behind, in a positive light.

Sarah Crome
August 1999

LOCATION MAP

showing principal locations in Scotland and northern England. Each place name is followed by a brief description of buildings, monuments or other features that can be seen there.

SCOTLAND

Aberdeen: Statue of Wallace, Union Street.

Annan: Small town.

Arbroath: Abbey ruins.

Ayr: Wallace Tower, St. John's Tower.

Banff: Coastal town.

Bannockburn: Battlefield Heritage Centre.

Biggar: Small town.

Birgham: Plaque commemorating Treaty.

Brechin: Cathedral; Stracathro church.

Caerlaverock: Castle ruins.

Castle Tioram: Castle ruins.

Dail Righ: St. Fillan's church.

Douglas: Castle mound; St. Bride's kirk.

Dumbarton: Castle; Cardross (Vale of Leven).

Dumfries: Town and Dervorguilla's Bridge.

Dunaverty: Site of castle.

Dunbar: Town and castle ruins.

Dunfermline: Palace and Abbey.

Dunnottar Castle: Cliff-top castle ruins.

Dunstaffnage Castle: Castle ruins.

Edinburgh: Castle and St. Margaret's Chapel; Holyrood Abbey.

Elderslie: Monument to Wallace.

Elgin: Cathedral ruins.

Falkirk: Battle site; Parish churchyard monuments to Graeme and Stewart.

Glasgow: Cathedral; Robroyston monument and well to Wallace.

Glenluce: Abbey ruins.

Glen Trool: Battle site.

Inverlochy: Castle ruins.

Inverness: Castle and town.

Inverurie: The Bass (motte and bailey castle); Old Meldrum battle site.

Irvine: Plaque commemorating 'Capitulation'.

Jedburgh: Abbey ruins and site of castle.

Kildrummy: Castle ruins.

Kinghorn: Monument to Alexander III.

Kinloss: Abbey ruins.

Kirkwall: St. Magnus' cathedral and Bishop's Palace ruins.

Kisimul Castle: Island castle ruins.

Lanark: St. Kentigern's church ruins; Parish church and plaque to Wallace's house.

Largs: Monument to battle of 1263.

Linlithgow: Palace; St. Michael's church.

Loch Doon: Castle ruins.

Lochindorb: Island castle ruins.

Lochmaben: Castle ruins and town.

Loudoun Hill: Prominent landscape feature.

Lumphanan: Peel Ring castle site.

Melrose: Abbey ruins and town.

Methven: Battle site nearby.

Paisley: Abbey and town.

Pass of Brander: Battle site.

Peebles: The cross Kirk; St. Andrew's Tower and site of castle.

Perth: City and Royal Burgh.

Roxburgh: Castle ruins and landscape features.

Scone: Palace, Moot Hill and abbey.

Selkirk: Site of former abbey and castle.

Slioch: Battle site.

St. Andrews: Cathedral and castle ruins.

Stirling: Town and castle; battle site and National Wallace Monument.

Stobo: Parish church; medieval keep.

Tain: St. Duthac's chapel ruins.

Turnberry: Castle ruins.

Upsettlington: Border village.

Urquhart Castle: Castle ruins.

Whithorn: Priory ruins and chapel.

ENGLAND

Alnwick: Castle and town.

Bamburgh: Castle.

Berwick upon Tweed: Castle ruins and town.

Beverley: Minster.

Boroughbridge: Plaque on bridge.

Burgh by Sands: Monument to Edward I.

Byland Abbey: Abbey ruins.

Carlisle: Castle and city.

Corbridge: Roman ruins.

Durham: Cathedral and castle.

Haltwhistle: Town and church.

Harbottle: Castle ruins.

Hexham: Abbey.

Lanercost: Priory and Hadrian's Wall.

Mitford: Castle ruins.

Myton: Battle site.

Newcastle: Castle and Roman ruins.

Norham: Castle ruins.

Northallerton: Town and church.

Rievaulx Abbey: Abbey ruins.

Scarborough: Castle ruins.

Stanhope Park: Village and riverside.

Sutton Bank: Landscape feature.

Wark: Castle ruins.

York: Minster; Ancient walls and castle.

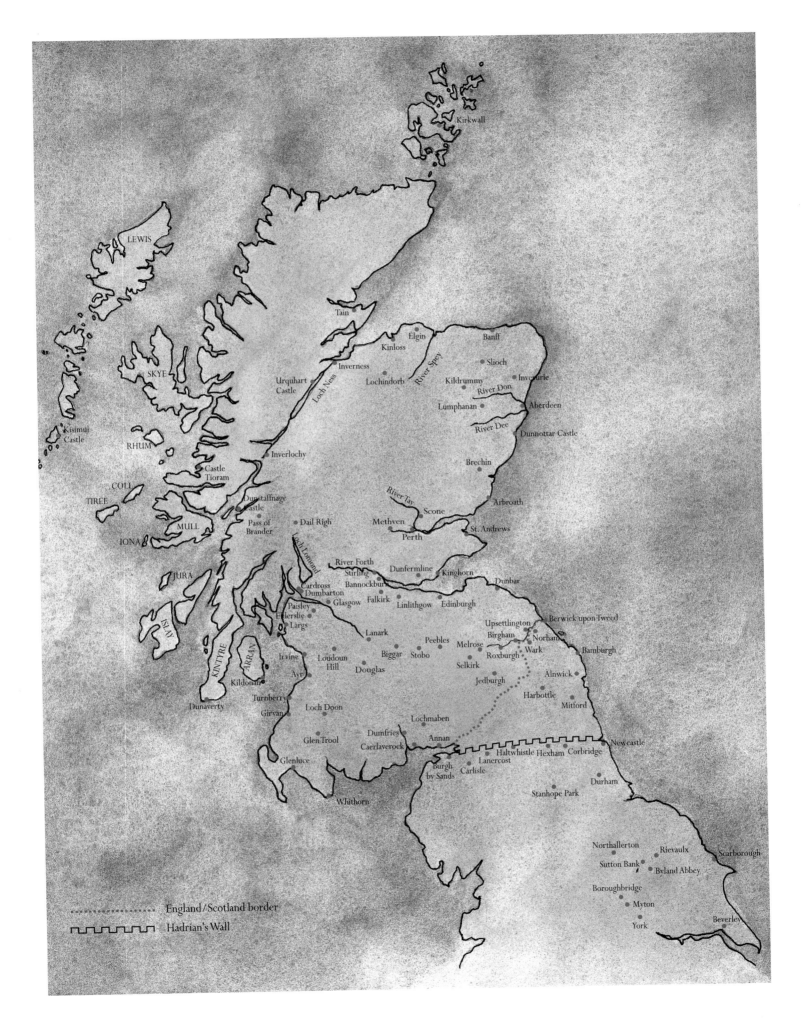

LEWIS

SKYE

Kisimul
Castle

RHUM

COLL

TIREE

IONA

MULL

JURA

ISLAY

KINTYRE

ARRAN

Kirkwall

Tain

Urquhart
Castle

Loch Ness

Inverness

Elgin

Kinloss

Lochindorb

River Spey

Banff

Slioch

Kildrummy

River Don

Inverurie

Lumphanan

Aberdeen

River Dee

Dunnottar Castle

Brechin

Inverlochy

Castle
Tioram

Dunstaffnage
Castle

Pass of
Brander

Dail Righ

River Tay

Scone

Methven

Perth

St. Andrews

Arbroath

Loch Lomond

River Forth

Stirling

Bannockburn

Dunfermline

Kinghorn

Dunbar

Cardross

Dumbarton

Falkirk

Linlithgow

Edinburgh

Glasgow

Paisley

Elderslie

Largs

Lanark

Peebles

Melrose

Upsettlington

Berwick upon Tweed

Birgham

Norham

Roxburgh

Wark

Bamburgh

Biggar

Stobo

Selkirk

Alnwick

Irvine

Loudoun
Hill

Douglas

Jedburgh

Harbottle

Mitford

Ayr

Kildonan

Turnberry

Loch Doon

Lochmaben

Dunaverty

Girvan

Glen Trool

Dumfries

Caerlaverock

Annan

Lochmaben

Burgh
by Sands

Lanercost

Haltwhistle

Hexham

Corbridge

Newcastle

Glenluce

Carlisle

Stanhope Park

Durham

Whithorn

Northallerton

Rievaulx

Scarborough

Sutton Bank

Byland Abbey

Boroughbridge

Myton

York

Beverley

- - - - - - - - - - England / Scotland border

⊓⊔⊓⊔⊓⊔⊓ Hadrian's Wall

CHRONOLOGY

Part 1: The End of a Golden Age

1286
March   King Alexander III falls to his death at Kinghorn, Fife.

April   Six Guardians are elected to govern Scotland.

September   An envoy is sent to King Edward I of England. The Bruce family enters into 'The Turnberry Band' asserting their claims to the throne.

1289
November   **The Treaty of Salisbury** confirms that the 'Maid of Norway' should become the new Queen of Scots.

1290
July   **The Treaty of Birgham** confirms betrothal of the six year-old Maid to the four year-old Prince of Wales.

September   The Maid of Norway dies on her way to Scotland.

December   Edward I's queen, Eleanor of Castile, dies.

1291
May   Anglo-Scottish parliament at Norham.

June   Edward I, with armed host, arbitrates over Scottish throne as long as Scots swear fealty to him.

1292
November   Court of Claims pronounces in favour of Balliol, and against Bruce 'the Competitor' for the Scottish throne. **John Balliol is crowned at Scone** on St. Andrew's Day and pays homage to King Edward.

1293
October   King John is summoned to London, accused of contumacy.

1294
June   War breaks out between England and France. King John is told to provide forces.

September   Revolt in Wales.

1295
July   'Council of Twelve' takes power away from King John.

October   Franco-Scottish Treaty. The Auld Alliance between France and Scotland is renewed.

1296
March   **The Sack of Berwick**. England invades Scotland.

April   Scots are defeated at **The Battle of Dunbar**. Edward marches through Scotland.

July   King John Balliol abdicates.

August   2,000 freeholders pay homage to Edward on the **Ragman Roll**.

September   Edward hands government of Scotland over to John de Warenne, Earl of Surrey.

Key events are shown in bold.

Part 2: Fighting for a Lost Cause

1297
May   **William Wallace kills the Sheriff of Lanark** and overcomes the garrison. He and William Douglas attack the English Justiciar at Scone. Robert Bruce leads a Scots uprising in Carrick.

July   Scots nobles meet English contingent to negotiate peace at the 'Capitulation of Irvine'. Andrew Murray leads rising in Moray.

September   Wallace joins up with Murray at **The Battle of Stirling Bridge**. English Army is defeated.

October   Wallace invades England.

November   Murray dies of Battle wounds. William Lamberton is made Bishop of St. Andrews.

1298
February   Wallace is knighted and appointed Guardian.

July   Edward I crosses the border with armed host. Scots are defeated at **The Battle of Falkirk.**

September   Wallace resigns Guardianship. Bruce and Comyn become joint Guardians.

1299
July   Edward I sends John Balliol to Cambrai.

August   Bishop Lamberton is made third Guardian.

September   Wallace is sent on diplomatic mission to France.

November   The Scots take Stirling Castle.

1300
May   Bruce resigns Guardianship. Ingram de Umfraville appointed in his place.

July   Edward I leads a campaign in Galloway.

October   Truce is agreed for seven months.

November   King Philip of France recommends Wallace to the Pope.

1301
January   John de Soules becomes sole Guardian.

May   Scots delegation visits Pope to defend independence.

September   Edward I campaigns in southwest and takes Bothwell Castle.

1302
February   Bruce submits to Edward I and marries Elizabeth de Burgh.

July   French feudal host defeated at Courtrai.

October   Scots envoys go to France to prevent truce between England and France.

1303
February   English routed at **The Battle of Roslin.**

May   England and France agree peace, Scots excluded.

1304
February   John Comyn submits to Edward I.

April   Robert Bruce, father of the future king, dies.

June   Secret band between Robert Bruce and Lamberton.

July   Stirling Castle falls.

1305
February   Edward I orders new constitution for Scotland.

August   **Wallace is captured and executed.**

September   New ordinance for governing Scotland is proclaimed.

CHRONOLOGY

Part 3: Turning the Tide

1306

February	Robert Bruce murders John Comyn at Dumfries.
March	**Bruce is enthroned at Scone** by Isabel of Buchan.
June	The Scots defeated by Earl of Pembroke at **The Battle of Methven.**
August	King Robert is defeated by MacDougall of Lorne at **The Battle of Dail Righ.**
September	The king escapes to Dunaverty then Rathlin.
	Nigel Bruce captured at Kildrummy and executed.
	King Robert's wife and Marjorie Bruce are captured at Tain.

1307

February	The king returns to the mainland at Turnberry Castle.
April	His first major victory over the English at **Glen Trool**.
May	King Robert succeeds again at **The Battle of Loudoun Hill**.
July	**King Edward dies** at Burgh on Sands.
December	King Robert falls ill. Skirmish at Slioch.

1308

May	**The Battle of Inverurie.**
August	King Robert defeats MacDougall of Lorne at **The Battle of Brander.**
October	The king assails Urquhart Castle forcing the Earl of Ross to submit.

1309

March	King Robert holds his first parliament at St. Andrews.
August	The king now controls Scotland north of the Tay.

1310

August	King Edward II invades Scotland for the first time.

1311

August	King Robert retaliates and invades northern England.

1312

August	The king again raids northern England.
October	**The Treaty of Inverness** between Scotland and Norway secures the friendship of these two countries.

1313

January	King Robert captures Perth.
February	The king reconquers the southwest and Dumfries.
May	King Robert takes The Isle of Man.
June	Edward Bruce besieges Stirling Castle and gives its English governor one year's respite.

1314

February	James Douglas captures Roxburgh Castle.
March	Thomas Randolph captures Edinburgh Castle.

Part 4: The Price of Freedom

1314

June	**The Battle of Bannockburn.**
November	Parliament at Cambuskenneth Abbey.

1315

April	Act of Succession makes Edward Bruce heir presumptive.
May	Marjorie Bruce marries Walter Stewart.
	Edward Bruce invades Ireland.

1316

May	Edward Bruce is created High King of Ireland.
June	Marjorie Bruce dies giving birth to Robert Stewart.

1317

January	King Robert goes to Ireland to fight with his brother.
May	The king returns home.

1318

April	The Scots retake Berwick upon Tweed.
October	Edward Bruce is killed in Ireland.
	Succession settled on two year-old Robert Stewart.

1319

July	Edward II besieges Berwick upon Tweed.
September	English clergy are routed at 'The Chapter of Myton'.
December	Two year truce is declared.

1320

April	**The Declaration of Arbroath** is sent to Pope John XXII.
August	The Soules conspirators are tried.

1322

August	Edward II's last invasion of Scotland.
October	King Robert pursues Edward II into England and defeats the English at **The Battle of Old Byland.**

1323

January	Andrew Harclay is executed for his 'Treaty' with the Scots.
May	Thirteen-year truce declared.

1324

January	The Pope recognises Robert Bruce as king.
April	Queen Elizabeth gives birth to a boy, named David.

1326

April	**The Treaty of Corbeil** between France and Scotland.
July	Succession settled on David Bruce.

1327

January	Edward II is deposed by Isabella and Roger Mortimer.
February	**Edward III is crowned**. Scots attack Norham castle.
June	The Scots raid County Durham.
August	Douglas and Randolph defeat English at Stanhope Park.
	Bruce invades Northumberland.

1328

March	**The Treaty of Edinburgh** agreed at Holyrood Abbey.
May	The Treaty is ratified in Northampton.
July	Marriage of David Bruce to Joan of the Tower.

1329

June	King Robert the Bruce dies at his manor near Dumbarton.
	The Pope grants Scotland the anointing of kings.

1330

March	James Douglas dies in Spain carrying the king's heart.

Part 1. 1286 – 1296
THE END OF A GOLDEN AGE

"When Alexander our King was dead."

King Alexander III of Scotland had become separated from his guide. The rain and wind were lashing down upon him as he tried desperately in the darkness to keep his horse away from the cliff edge. He was determined to reach his new Queen, Yolande, before the night was out, and his manor house at Kinghorn was frustratingly close...

Above: *King Alexander III takes his fatal tumble over the cliffs at Kinghorn.*

Right: *The monument to Alexander III by the Firth of Forth where his body was discovered.*

It was 18th March, 1286 and King Alexander III had been meeting with his council at Edinburgh Castle. The king had remained there with his lords, and as they ate and drank into the evening, his mind wandered to thoughts of his queen of six months, Yolande de Dreux, who was alone at Kinghorn. He had lost his first wife, Margaret, the daughter of King Henry III of England, 10 years ago, and now he could not bear to be parted from Yolande. A wise and strong king, Alexander had ruled Scotland for 37 of his 45 years, but this night, perhaps due to the drink, he made an error of judgement. Against the protests of his company, the king decided that he would return home to be with her. The storm which had been brewing throughout the day now threatened his safety, yet he set out on the twenty-mile journey which involved a long, hard ride either side of a turbulent crossing of the River Forth. When his party reached Queensferry, on the south shore of the river, the ferry master warned them not to go any further, but still the king would not be persuaded. They managed the river crossing, but faced a dangerous cliff-top route in darkness to complete the journey. There were no witnesses to his last hours on that hazardous, coast road, but King Alexander III of Scotland never made it to Kinghorn. His body was found at the foot of those cliffs the next morning.

In some ways, despite the drama of this incident, the death of a king does not seem so unusual. What makes the death of Alexander exceptional is that it unleashed on his hitherto peaceful kingdom such devastation that almost led to the annihilation of Scotland and her people in a manner unseen anywhere in medieval Christendom.

In retrospect, we can analyse history and find that in any period of time, wars and revolutions occur due to a complicated set of circumstances, like the fusion of harmless substances combining to make a dangerous explosive; and, like explosives, they need a detonator, a spark to ignite them, leading us to ask the question; *"what if that initial spark had not happened?"*. Scotland in the late 13th century is no exception and one may ask: What if Alexander had not made his reckless journey from Edinburgh Castle to Kinghorn on that tempestuous night in 1286? If he had been patient and travelled the next day, Scotland would not have lost an extremely able king, and his continued existence would have prevented the cataclysm about to befall his kingdom. As it was, King Alexander's death broke forever the Celtic dynasty begun by King Kenneth MacAlpin in the 9th century and which had provided Scotland with a continuous line of kings.

Right: Detail of a 15th Century manuscript showing the coronation of King Alexander III.

Above: William Hole's frieze of figures from Scottish history, in the Scottish National Portrait Gallery. This section shows monarchs from Kenneth MacAlpin to Alexander III.

England covets Scotland

It was the fate of most Scottish Kings to die young so leaving their heirs, as children, to pick up the pieces. Alexander III inherited his kingdom in 1249, when, at the age of eight, he was inaugurated as King of Scots upon the Stone of Destiny at Scone. Two years later, a marriage was arranged between himself and Princess Margaret, the daughter of King Henry III of England, an act which secured a long period of peace between the two countries. This occasion was made significant by Henry's attempts to make Alexander pay him homage as overlord of the Kingdom of Scotland. The young King of Scots refused, showing a great sense of responsibility uncommon in child-monarchs. Scotland may well have enjoyed peace for a while longer, but here was an indication of impending trouble.

The origins of English claims over Scotland can be traced back to an earlier time, notably after 1066 when William, Duke of Normandy began his invasion of England. His conquest did not extend to Scotland and William recognised that he held a claim only to the English throne. Nevertheless, he saw a potential threat from the then Scots king, Malcolm III, who was regularly raiding into northern England. Added to that was Malcolm's marriage to Margaret Atheling, the future Saint and sister of the rightful Saxon heir to England's throne, providing a reason for William's incursion into Scotland in 1072. It did not amount to much as Malcolm did not wish to fight William who could have easily defeated the Scots. What Malcolm did, however, was something that his successors would curse him for. He submitted to the English king, becoming William's 'man', and in order to guarantee good behaviour, Malcolm was required to send Duncan, his eldest son, to the English Court. It is not certain exactly what Malcolm was conceding to William, but successive English kings came up with their own interpretation.

For a number of years, other Scottish princes were sent into this pampered captivity south of the border, making friends at the English Court and learning valuable military skills. After a while the royal 'hostages' returned home and were considerably better off, in material wealth, as a result. Early in the 12th century Malcolm's youngest son, the future King David I of Scotland, married Matilda of Huntingdon. As a wealthy heiress, she brought him vast estates in England, making the King of Scots a wealthy English landowner. This could be seen as influential to Scotland, but it meant that the Scots king had to pay homage to the English king for lands held in England. However, future English kings soon began to twist the meaning of this act of fealty as being an acknowledgement of their superiority over the Scottish kingdom. This arrangement did not work the other way, as English kings did not own land in Scotland. By the time of Alexander III's reign, the Scottish Royal House had held lands in England for more than one hundred and fifty years.

Above: *King David I, son of King Malcolm III and St. Margaret, with his grandson Malcolm IV. David's marriage to Matilda of Huntingdon brought vast English estates to the Scottish Crown.*

Left: *King Malcolm III greets his future queen, Margaret, exiled from England by William the Conqueror.*

There was a notable incident concerning English claims over Scotland in 1174. The then King of Scots, William the Lion, ancestor of Alexander III, was captured at Alnwick in Northumberland by King Henry II of England. To buy his freedom, William was forced into accepting Henry as lord superior of Scotland by signing The Treaty of Falaise. However, in 1189 this was revoked by Henry's son Richard the Lionheart who, while fundraising for the Crusades, sold these rights back to the Scots for 10,000 merks. It appears that Scotland's sovereignty was an expendable bargaining tool for nobles on both sides of the border.

Above: *Conwy Castle today: a reminder of Edward's subjugation of Wales.*

Right: *The site of her grave is unknown, but this recent monument to Gwenllian, daughter of the last Prince of Wales, is at Sempringham in Lincolnshire, where she was imprisoned until her death.*

ER COF AM
In Memory Of
GWENLLIAN,
MERCH LLYWELYN EIN LLYW OLAF,
Daughter of the last Prince of Wales,
GANED YN ABERGWYNGREGYN 12. 6. 1282.
Born at
BU FARW YN SEMPRINGHAM 7. 6. 1337
Died at
WEDI BOD YN GARCHAROR YMA AM 54 MLYNEDD.
Having been held prisoner here for 54 years.

King Henry III may not have pursued any aspirations towards Scotland, but by the time of his death in 1272, he had managed to instil the principal firmly into the mind of his son, England's next king. Edward I initially showed little sign of outward ambition towards Scotland although, once again, at his own coronation he attempted to gain submission from Alexander. As with the earlier occasion involving Henry III, Alexander refused the English king, stating:

> *"I become your man for the lands which I hold of you in the kingdom of England for which I owe homage to you, reserving my kingdom... nobody but God himself has the right to the homage of my realm of Scotland, and I hold it of nobody but God".*

But annexation of the Celtic nations within Edward's reach soon became an obsession for him. Edward was also Duke of Gascony, over which he was constantly in dispute with the king of France. If Edward could strengthen his hand on his side of the English Channel, he believed he would be a force to reckon

with. At the time of Edward's ascension to the throne, Alexander, his brother-in-law, was ruling a peaceful and prosperous Scotland; Wales was still an independent principality and England was relatively at ease with itself. But Edward was not happy with the situation as it was and soon began nurturing his vision. He would consume his neighbouring countries, incorporating them into his own kingdom in a way which did not involve asking their permission. All he needed was the opportunity.

Edward's conquest of Wales was completed in 1282 when a long war with the principality was ended by the death of the last true Prince of Wales, Llywelyn ap Gruffudd. It is thought that Llywelyn's daughter, Gwenllian, born the same year, was imprisoned at Sempringham Abbey in Lincolnshire, far away from any rescue attempt, and died there 54 years later. Edward gave Wales to his eldest son, the future king Edward II, who was born at Caernarvon in 1284. Edward now secretly turned his sights to the north and waited for an opportunity which, on 18th March 1286, with the death of Alexander, finally presented itself.

Above: Dominating the shore at Largs, this monument commemorates King Alexander III's victory over the Norwegian fleet in 1263. The battle precipitated the end of Norway's hold over the Western Isles.

Right: Berwick from across the River Tweed. Today's quiet English border town was once Scotland's most prolific sea port.

One nation, many cultures

What was it like to live in Scotland in the years leading up to the death of king Alexander? Geographically, the definition of her borders was not too dissimilar from those of today. The most significant event in Alexander's reign was his triumph in bringing the Hebrides and the Isle of Man into the kingdom of Scotland. They had for long been held by the Kingdom of Norway but, in 1263, the Scots defeated a large Norwegian force led by King Haakon at the Battle of Largs. These islands were ceded by Norway in the The Treaty of Perth in 1266, although the Northern Isles of Shetland and Orkney continued to remain outside the Scottish Kingdom until the 15th century. Scotland's border with England had been disputed territory for hundreds of years.

Both sides of the border would suffer terribly in the years to come as it became the rope in a tug-of-war contest between the two countries. The most vulnerable point was the town of Berwick, situated on the east coast just north of the River Tweed. Today it is a quiet English border town but, in the 13th century,

it was Scotland's most prolific seaport with an affluent populace benefitting from strong trade links with countries on the European seaboard. Much of the east coast was colonised by merchants from Germany, France and the Low Countries. Exports to these countries in timber, wool, hides, and fish was flourishing, with Berwick at the hub of trading activity. Tragically, at the time of Alexander's death, Berwick's days of prosperity were numbered. It was to suffer the worst atrocity of all in an unforgiving war and never again would it achieve such eminence.

But what of Scotland's people; who were they? Seven hundred years ago Scotland's population numbered 500,000 people compared with about 5 million in England, a similar ratio to that of today. Now, most of the population of Scotland inhabits the industrial central belt, but centuries ago it was more evenly spread throughout the country. There were more people in the countryside than in the towns and cities. The Highlands were not deserted as they are at present, but speckled with small communities inhabiting almost every glen.

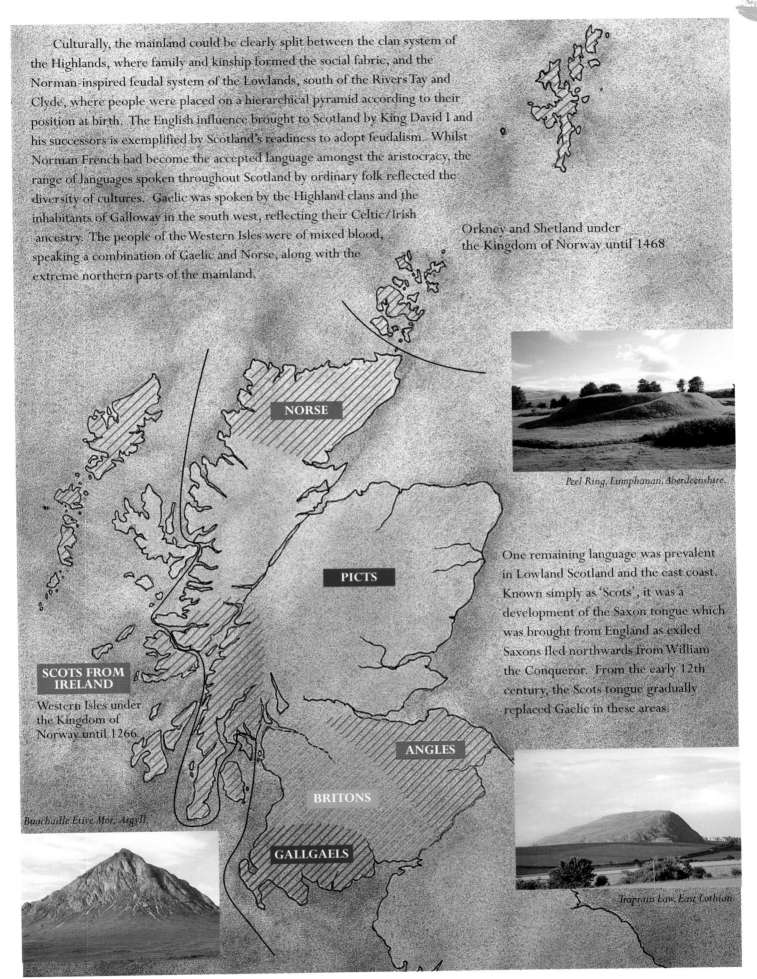

Culturally, the mainland could be clearly split between the clan system of the Highlands, where family and kinship formed the social fabric, and the Norman-inspired feudal system of the Lowlands, south of the Rivers Tay and Clyde, where people were placed on a hierarchical pyramid according to their position at birth. The English influence brought to Scotland by King David I and his successors is exemplified by Scotland's readiness to adopt feudalism. Whilst Norman French had become the accepted language amongst the aristocracy, the range of languages spoken throughout Scotland by ordinary folk reflected the diversity of cultures. Gaelic was spoken by the Highland clans and the inhabitants of Galloway in the south west, reflecting their Celtic/Irish ancestry. The people of the Western Isles were of mixed blood, speaking a combination of Gaelic and Norse, along with the extreme northern parts of the mainland.

Orkney and Shetland under the Kingdom of Norway until 1468

Peel Ring, Lumphanan, Aberdeenshire.

NORSE

PICTS

SCOTS FROM IRELAND

Western Isles under the Kingdom of Norway until 1266.

One remaining language was prevalent in Lowland Scotland and the east coast. Known simply as 'Scots', it was a development of the Saxon tongue which was brought from England as exiled Saxons fled northwards from William the Conqueror. From the early 12th century, the Scots tongue gradually replaced Gaelic in these areas.

ANGLES

BRITONS

Buachaille Etive Mòr, Argyll.

GALLGAELS

Traprain Law, East Lothian.

Behind much of this culture and prosperity, the Church was playing a major rôle, not just spiritually, but in terms of wealth and infrastructure. The church in Scotland had grown on the world stage since Saint Margaret had introduced the Roman Catholic Church to replace the old Celtic Church. By the late 12th century, the Pope recognised Scotland's Church as a 'special daughter' of Rome. This was to help underline the strength of the Church whose independence was also under threat from the Church in England. Scotland had no Archbishops and it was argued from England that the church there should be controlled from the nearest archbishopric which just happened to be at York. So as far as the Church in Scotland was concerned, with its own survival to consider, those fighting for Scotland were defending not just national freedom but religious freedom as well.

Above: Once much of Scotland was covered with ancient woodland, like these birch trees on the edge of Rannoch Moor, Inverness-shire.

Above: Melrose Abbey, the richest of those built by David I along Scotland's border with England.

Despite Scotland's advancement in the civilized world, much of its land was untamed. Little did the Scots know then just how much the land would prove itself as their greatest asset in the war-ravaged years to come. When at war with an enemy who could provide 10 men for every one of theirs, making the land fight for them and using its resources was vital in planning battle strategies. Today intensive cultivation, particularly in the Lowlands, belies the fact that once there were vast expanses of natural forest into which men could disappear for months. The mountains in the West Highlands provided a wilderness which would shelter and protect thousands of refugees fleeing the devastation, of which the Lowlands was to take the brunt.

Transport by river, sea and loch was the most effective way of getting around, although a network of highways criss-crossed their way over the land from north to south. These connected all the Royal Burghs and their castles, helping to ease communications. However, in the years before effective land-drainage, marsh lands were abundant and flooding was commonplace, making land transport very unreliable. Waterlogged land did, however, work to the advantage of the Scots, who knew their country well. In the years to come, they would adapt their warfare to the elements using agility and lightfootedness against the cumbersome strength of their southern neighbour.

Who would rule Scotland?

As Scotland mourned the passing of Alexander III in 1286 she began to assess her predicament, and the outlook was bleak. Despite the recent blossoming of wealth and opportunity, the kingdom was ill-prepared for any period of instability. Scotland was vulnerable and unpractised in war even though, in theory, a mechanism was in place for defending the realm. But, as in all feudal kingdoms of the age, this depended on the presence of a monarch to give leadership and direction. The death of the king had created an insoluble dilemma. Although no-one at this stage was threatening war, Scotland was severely exposed and internal divisions were rife. One might expect Edward I of England, given this opportunity, to declare his hand at once, taking Scotland by surprise. But he would bide his time and observe movements north of the border. The succession to the throne was yet to be decided and Edward knew it would all take time. He was a king skilled in manipulating the law to his own ends and he would only resort to the military option if all else failed.

Although King Alexander died with no immediate heir, his first marriage to Margaret of England, Edward's sister, had provided three children. The two boys had died as children, but the girl married the King of Norway. Their daughter, Margaret, was, at the time of Alexander's death, only three years old and far away in a distant land. A more inappropriate ruler for Scotland could not be imagined but 'the Maid of Norway', as she became known, was next in line for the Scottish throne.

It was at this time that the aristocracy in Scotland became restless. Alexander had led a sound government in which the Church had provided an over-arching influence, but now that the king was gone, the Church alone could not hold the nation together and different factions began to side with several powerful families. Enter the main players in the years to come: the families of Bruce, Balliol and Comyn. If The Maid had not existed, then all these families held a claim to the throne through their close ties with the royal house. In the 12th century, when David I had returned from England in possession of his estates in Huntingdon and Northampton, he also brought with him wealthy Norman nobles, offering them estates in his new kingdom. This was the beginning of his feudal obsession and soon, more Norman nobles were invited north - a peaceful invasion, unlike the English one of 1066. These Normans did not replace their Celtic equivalents, but married into their families, proliferating their way through David's descendants.

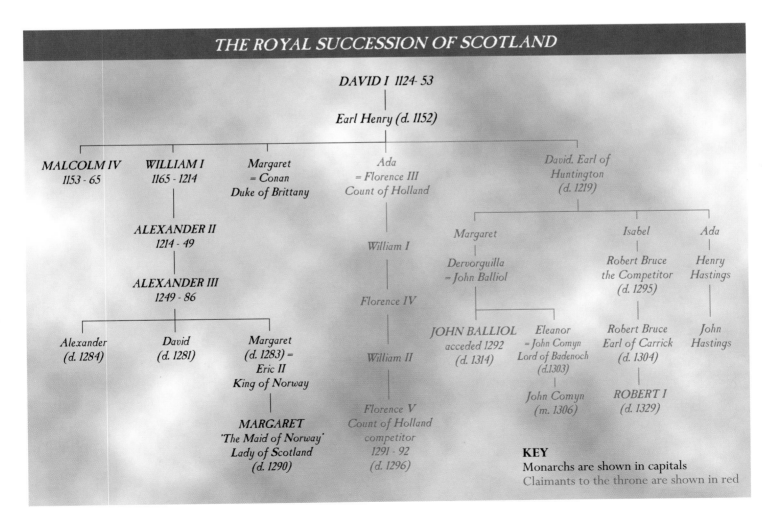

THE ROYAL SUCCESSION OF SCOTLAND

DAVID I 1124-53

Earl Henry (d. 1152)

MALCOLM IV 1153-65 — WILLIAM I 1165-1214 — Margaret = Conan Duke of Brittany — Ada = Florence III Count of Holland — David, Earl of Huntington (d. 1219)

ALEXANDER II 1214-49

ALEXANDER III 1249-86

William I

Margaret Dervorguilla = John Balliol — Isabel Robert Bruce the Competitor (d. 1295) — Ada Henry Hastings

Alexander (d. 1284) — David (d. 1281) — Margaret (d. 1283) = Eric II King of Norway

Florence IV

JOHN BALLIOL acceded 1292 (d. 1314) — Eleanor = John Comyn Lord of Badenoch (d.1303) — Robert Bruce Earl of Carrick (d. 1304) — John Hastings

William II

MARGARET 'The Maid of Norway' Lady of Scotland (d. 1290)

Florence V Count of Holland competitor 1291-92 (d. 1296)

John Comyn (m. 1306) — ROBERT I (d. 1329)

KEY
Monarchs are shown in capitals
Claimants to the throne are shown in red

Bruce, Lord of Annandale   **John Balliol**   **Comyn, Earl of Buchan**

Above: Coats of arms belonging to three of the most powerful
families in Scotland at the end of the thirteenth century.

The Bruce, Balliol and Comyn families had agreed in 1284 that if King Alexander died without issue, following his marriage to Yolande, then they would accept the succession of the Maid of Norway. However, the stark reality of the situation as it stood was that Scotland needed a firm hand to rule it, or it would descend into civil war, and they began doubting whether their allegiance to the Maid had been a good idea. Ambitious eyes began to look towards the throne whilst each rival family watched to see if anyone would dare to make a move. In April 1286, the situation was defused somewhat. One month after the king's death, the prelates of the Church and the nobles gathered at a parliament at Scone to swear allegiance to the absent child-queen, and pledge their support in protecting the interests of her kingdom. A regency comprising six Guardians was appointed to maintain some level of continuity. The Guardians included two bishops, two earls and two barons. It appears though that the main concern of this Guardianship was not the well-being of the land or people of Scotland, but of protecting the interests of the aristocracy.

It was agreed that those with the strongest claims to the throne, other than the Maid of Norway, should not be included amongst these Guardians. They were John Balliol and Robert Bruce, Lord of Annandale, grandfather of the future king. The latter, now an old man, had in 1238 been made heir presumptive during the reign of Alexander II. This position lasted only three years, until the king succeeded in producing an heir, the future Alexander III. Having been so near the throne once already, Bruce now realised the opportunity before him. To include Bruce and Balliol as Guardians was problematical due to their own self interests, so it was decided that they should be given an equal representation by those sympathetic to their cause. Of the Guardians, three were to represent Scotland north of the River Forth, namely William Fraser, Bishop of St. Andrews, the Earl of Fife and the Earl of Buchan. The other three were responsible for Scotland south of the Forth and they were Robert Wishart, the Bishop of Glasgow, John Comyn of Badenoch, and James, High Steward of Scotland.

Left: The Great Seal of Scotland as used by the Guardians in 1286. There is no image of a monarch, just the royal arms on one side and Saint Andrew, the patron saint, on the other.

Above: There is no trace today of Dumfries castle, but Dervorguilla's thirteenth century footbridge over the River Nith survives.

It was at this parliament that the decision was taken to inform King Edward of the situation in Scotland. This was intended primarily as an act of international diplomacy from one country to another, rather than an invitation for Edward to become involved. The English king was away in Gascony, and when the Scottish envoys arrived, they were politely received but little interest was shown in their cause. Perhaps Edward was preoccupied with his dukedom in which he was to remain for the next three years. He wished them well and the envoys returned home.

While the envoys were contributing to international relations, the situation in Scotland had deteriorated. The Guardians were trying their best to defuse a revolt in the south west. Geographically, this was always going to be a contentious area as Bruce and Balliol lands bordered each other. Bruce had come out in open revolt, taking Balliol's castles at Dumfries and Wigtown, and Buittle Castle in Galloway, which was Balliol's lordship. Bruce of Annandale and his son the Earl of Carrick entered into *The Turnberry Band* with their supporters, James the Steward, one of the guardians, MacDonald, Lord of the Isles and the earls of March and Menteith. This band, settled at Turnberry Castle, seat of the Earl of Carrick, was intended as an agreement of mutual support. It also appears that Bruce of Annandale was actually looking to England for help. He had once been a companion at arms with Edward I on crusade in the Holy Land. Bruce's strike in the south west was a signal to the English king that he, Bruce, could assume control of Scotland with Edward's backing. Now that the envoys had returned home with England's endorsement of the status quo, Bruce was at a loss as to what to do. He could not call upon enough men to take hold of the whole country, and he could not be certain of Edward's support. It is worth mentioning that at this time Robert Bruce, the future king, was only twelve years old and could not have been party to his grandfather's attempted coup.

The actions of the Bruce family at this time demonstrated the predicament facing many noble families in Scotland throughout the years to come. Where a strong feudal system existed across neighbouring countries, and the earls and barons had interests of property and family ties in both, they often looked to each other for support, regardless of national borders. The notion of loyalty to the nation was a grey area and was a concept which could easily be compromised. A nobleman in Scotland could be instinctively more loyal to a nobleman in England, to whom he might be related, than he would be to a fellow countryman lower down the social scale or of equal rank if he posed a threat to him. For example: the Bruce family owned estates in England as well as Scotland and they also had strong connections with the English royal court. So Bruce of Annandale thought it was reasonable to look to a foreign king, with whom he was friendly, to the detriment of Balliol, compatriot though he may have been. The principle of nationhood and unity amongst the people of a nation whatever their rank would prove to be a long, arduous lesson for the aristocracy and one which, ironically, the ordinary folk were to teach them.

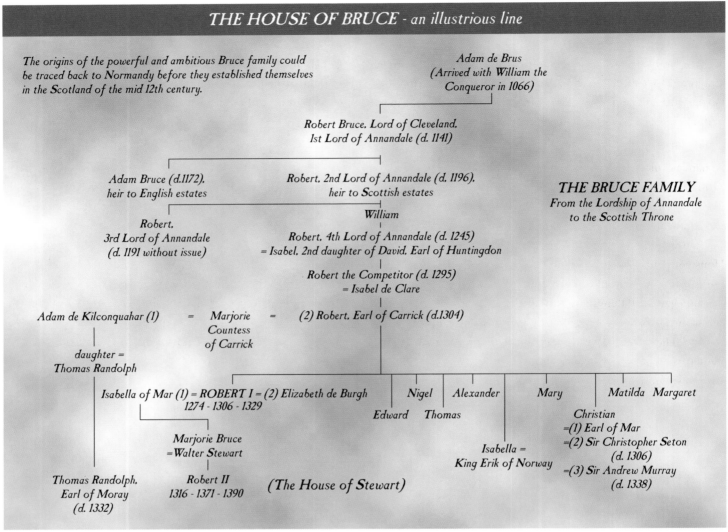

THE HOUSE OF BRUCE - *an illustrious line*

The origins of the powerful and ambitious Bruce family could be traced back to Normandy before they established themselves in the Scotland of the mid 12th century.

Adam de Brus
(Arrived with William the
Conqueror in 1066)

Robert Bruce, Lord of Cleveland,
1st Lord of Annandale (d. 1141)

THE BRUCE FAMILY
*From the Lordship of Annandale
to the Scottish Throne*

Adam Bruce (d.1172),
heir to English estates

Robert, 2nd Lord of Annandale (d. 1196),
heir to Scottish estates

Robert,
3rd Lord of Annandale
(d. 1191 without issue)

William

Robert, 4th Lord of Annandale (d. 1245)
= Isabel, 2nd daughter of David, Earl of Huntingdon

Robert the Competitor (d. 1295)
= Isabel de Clare

Adam de Kilconquahar (1)   =   Marjorie   =   (2) Robert, Earl of Carrick (d.1304)
Countess
of Carrick

daughter =
Thomas Randolph

Isabella of Mar (1) = ROBERT I = (2) Elizabeth de Burgh
1274 - 1306 - 1329

Nigel   Alexander   Mary   Matilda   Margaret

Edward   Thomas

Isabella =
King Erik of Norway

Christian
=(1) Earl of Mar
=(2) Sir Christopher Seton
(d. 1306)
=(3) Sir Andrew Murray
(d. 1338)

Marjorie Bruce
=Walter Stewart

Thomas Randolph,
Earl of Moray
(d. 1332)

Robert II
1316 - 1371 - 1390

(The House of Stewart)

THE ROYAL
BURGH OF ANNAN

The Bruce name originated from Brus, known today as Brix, near Cherbourg in Normandy. They were desended from the Viking Earl of Orkney who came to this region of northern France after it was granted to the Vikings in the 10th century. Its name was derived from the Viking settlers - Norman meaning 'northmen' and the Viking Chieftain, Rollo, became the first Duke of Normandy. Adam de Brus was the first of his name to rise to prominence when, in 1066, he formed part of William the Conqueror's invasion force. After the initial success of the Normans, Adam played a significant rôle in 'the harrying of the north', an aggressive policy which devastated the land and extinguished the smouldering flames of Anglo-Saxon rebellion in Yorkshire and northern England.

To honour Adam's participation in the Norman Conquest, he was given estates and manors across the county of Yorkshire, which he passed on to his son, the first in a long line of Roberts. This Robert Bruce became one of the most powerful men in northern England when he was made Lord of Cleveland. It was

Left: The town of Annan was at the heart of the Bruces' Annandale territory.

then that the House of Bruce crossed paths with King David I who was feudal overlord of the Bruce's English estates. When David became King of Scots in 1124, Robert was amongst those granted lands there. He was created Lord of Annandale, which amounted to 200,000 acres of rich land along the south-west border with England. From this point, Scotland was the destiny of the House of Bruce, and their stories were interminably linked.

For the following century, the second and third Lords of Annandale played a major part in the development of feudal Scotland. Then, in 1209, events took a dramatic turn. The fourth Lord married Isabel, daughter of David, Earl of Huntingdon. David was the younger brother of King William the Lion, thus the Bruce name was drawn into the royal family tree. That the House of Bruce was growing in influence goes without saying, but future events would catapult them even further than they had anticipated. If things had turned out differently, then perhaps the name of Bruce would have disappeared into the mists of history. They were, after all, just one name on a branch of the family tree which might never have risen to prominence, had Alexander III not taken his fatal tumble later that century.

The product of Isabel and the fourth Robert Bruce's union was the fifth Robert and it was he who became heir presumptive in 1238. In later years he was to be known as "The Competitor" for his campaign to ascend the Scottish throne. He spent many years crusading in the Holy Land alongside his companion at arms, Edward I of England.

The sixth Robert was The Competitor's son and father of the future king. This sixth Robert did not inherit his father's stamina, and neither did he contribute greatly to the cause of his family's House. But his marriage was significant, not only because it produced a king, but also because it linked the Norman-bred Bruce family with the great Earldom of Carrick in the southwest, an ancient, almost independent kingdom. When Robert Bruce married Marjorie, Countess of Carrick, he also inherited this earldom as part of her dowry. The House of Carrick was descended directly from a Celtic Prince, Fergus, Lord of Galloway who had virtually ruled it as his own country. From this point onwards, the Bruce dynasty now had Celtic as well as royal blood in its veins.

***Right:** Lochmaben was the seat of the Annandale Lordship. The Bruce Arms there displays its heritage.*

***Above:** The rich farming lands of Annandale lay open to the English border and were vulnerable to invasion.*

The marriage of Robert and Marjorie was by no means arranged, as was usual in the schemes of great families. In fact the story surrounding their introduction indicates that this was a love match. Robert Bruce, aged 24, had joined a Crusade in the Holy Land, in accordance with most young nobles of his standing. It was a glorious opportunity to fight for God, and all men like Bruce left their shores with a sense of hope and optimism. Their souls would be the better for having fought the infidels, and their coffers full of riches plundered from the towns and cities which they 'liberated'. However, these brave crusaders often returned home disappointed and, in 1272, Robert Bruce arrived back in Scotland grief-stricken and dejected. His close friend, Adam de Kilconquhar, had been killed in Palestine and now he must take the news to Adam's widow. They had not been married long when Adam left her side to travel abroad, but she was with child and still young, so Robert would not find his task easy. The young woman, however, was grateful for Robert's benevolence and they developed an affinity for each other, sharing together their mutual loss. Their meeting was prophetic to say the least as the widow of Adam de Kilconquhar was none other than Marjorie of Carrick.

Marjorie was safely delivered of her child and within weeks, Robert Bruce became her second husband and the new Earl of Carrick. Their blissfully happy marriage was certainly prolific, producing ten healthy children of which their famous son, Robert, was the first, born two years later on the 11th July, 1274. All of Robert's brothers and sisters played a significant part in their country's future and most of them, including the women, suffered dreadfully at the hands of the English because they were the family of Robert the Bruce.

This new generation of Bruces was cast in a different mould. They were no longer products of a purely Ango-Norman aristocracy, as the Celtic inheritance brought to them by their mother was more than skin-deep. Part of their upbringing in the southwest would have involved schooling in local traditions and language, so they were not isolated. The future king was trilingual, knowing Gaelic from his mother's household, Norman French from his father, and also the Scots language from the communities around his grandfather's Annandale estate. It is understood that the success of Robert the Bruce's leadership in the years to come was partly due to his understanding of the cultural differences in his kingdom, and his use of that knowledge to bridge the divides and unite his people against a common enemy.

Adolescence saw young Robert spending more time in England learning the skills of knightly combat. He became a renowned champion in international tournaments and this, in turn, won him the favour of Edward I. Little did Edward know how effectively Robert Bruce would turn his training against the English king's self-acclaimed superiority over the Scots in the years to come.

The fertile Carrick countryside with the island of Ailsa Craig in the backgound. This part of southwest Scotland was the possession of Marjorie, Countess of Carrick, and where the future king probably spent much of his childhood.

King Edward's hand of friendship

However, in September 1286 in the aftermath of King Alexander's death, the young future king was only 12 years old, and had all his adventures ahead of him. In the short term, at least, the aspirations of the Bruce family were to be short-lived, with no help outwith those who had pledged their support in the Turnberry Band. The rebellion was dispelled and all was quiet in the southwest.

Scotland's queen remained in Norway and the Guardians continued to rule in her absence. A decision would have to be made as to the young queen's future and at what point she should make the journey to her new kingdom. She was only 3 years old and it was not realistic to expect her to be on the first ship out of Bergen. In fact, apart from the death of two of the six Guardians, the Earls of Buchan and Fife, the situation remained unchanged for another 3 years. Then, in 1289, King Edward returned to England from Gascony and the four surviving Guardians prepared the ground for discussions with him as to the future of the queen 'over the water'. Edward was the great-uncle of The Maid and his judgement of the situation would be welcomed. The English king quickly got down to business, sending out invitations to Scotland and Norway to meet in England. So in October of that year Norwegian ambassadors met in Salisbury with an English delegation and a representation from the Scottish regency, namely, Wishart and Fraser, the two bishops, Comyn of Badenoch and Robert Bruce, the Competitor.

Left: Shetland's connections with Norway are shown by this stained glass window in Lerwick Town Hall, which depicts The Maid of Norway.

This cordial meeting resulted in the Treaty of Salisbury, the signing of which confirmed that the Maid of Norway should be received into her kingdom by the same time in the following year, 1290. With the potential for many ambitious hands to grasp the new queen on her arrival, the most important issue was to safeguard her marriage and, to this end, it was agreed in the Treaty that her betrothal should only be by consent of the kings of Norway and England, her father and great uncle respectively. There was no indication here of Edward's slowly hatching plans for Scotland but, now that they had dispensed this initial act of diplomacy, he began to declare his hand more openly. With the benefit of hindsight we can see that it was simply a matter of time before Edward acted but, in 1289, his next move was a complete surprise to all concerned. Suddenly, without ceremony, he revealed a Papal Bull giving consent for the marriage of The Maid of Norway to Edward of Caernarvon, his son. This was clearly a first attempt to bind Scotland legally to his own kingdom. There had been no prior consultation with the Guardians who, nevertheless, reluctantly accepted the idea despite the potential threat to Scotland's independence. It was better for The Maid that her betrothal be arranged before she set foot in Scotland, given that it would placate the power-hungry nobles and deter a looming civil war which posed, by far, a bigger threat than England.

Above: *Edward of Caernarvon being created Prince of Wales by his father.*

Left & above: Looking towards the River Tweed and the English border from the village of Birgham. A plaque in the village commemorates the Treaty.

In July of 1290 the details of this marriage were negotiated by commissioners from all sides at Birgham, a small Berwickshire villiage. Set on rising ground on the Scottish side of the River Tweed, this unlikely place became the scene for The Treaty of Birgham which made sure, as far as possible, that Scotland's interests were protected. The future king and queen, as man and wife, would each rule their respective kingdoms separately and, more importantly, Scotland would retain its own parliament:

"The kingdom of Scotland shall remain separate and divided from the kingdom of England by its right boundaries and marches as has hitherto in the past been observed, and that it shall be free in itself and without subjection"

Despite the emphasis on Scotland's separateness, while the Treaty was still being hammered out, Edward signalled his contempt for the proceedings at Birgham with an attack on the Isle of Man. Man had only recently become part of the Scottish kingdom and the implications of its seizure by Edward were dire. However, the English king showed no signs of aggression towards the Scottish mainland, and the Guardians did not retaliate in any way. Their concern seems to have been with the diplomatic manœuvres securing the future of Scotland, on paper at least. To an extent, they were also naively seeing what they wanted to in the peaceful outcome of negotiations at Birgham, while Edward flexed his military muscles on the Isle of Man.

In August 1290, before the Maid of Norway even set sail for Scotland, Edward attempted to squeeze his influence on the Scots through any crack he could find, although he had agreed to the principles laid out in the Treaty of Birgham. Now that he was about to become father-in-law to the Queen of Scots, he would appoint Antony Bek, Bishop of Durham, to act as lieutenant in Scotland for The Maid and her husband, the future king of England. The Guardians were agreeable for the time being and were simply concerned to keep all sides at bay.

So everything was prepared for Queen Margaret, The Maid of Norway's eagerly awaited entrance to her kingdom. Seldom can any monarch have been so oblivious to all the scheming and manipulation surrounding their position. At six years old, The Maid was certainly unaware of what awaited her once she reached Scotland's shores. As she set out on the long journey from Bergen, delegations from England and Scotland awaited her arrival at Orkney. The great and the good began to gather at Scone for her enthronement and the whole country looked forward as the years of uncertainty were about to end.

On September 26, 1290 the little Maid's ship docked at Orkney. But the joy of her arrival soon turned to sadness as it was realised that all was not well. Terribly weakened by the rough journey across the North Sea, the Maid succumbed to the elements and gave the last breath of her short life. Years of planning now lay in ruin as everything had depended on Queen Margaret succeeding to the throne. It is true that, at her age and as a girl, she would have simply served as a figurehead, but as undisputed queen, all those beneath her would have fallen into line, each carrying out their pre-ordained duties. The Maid's death had brought an ancient royal line to a close and the prospects for Scotland could not be more bleak. There were now many who would step forward to claim the empty throne and the stage was set for an unprecedented confrontation as great families were poised on the brink of civil war.

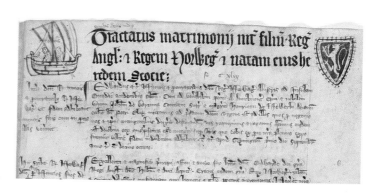

Right: The Treaty of Birgham.

The Great Cause

Despite the immediate dilemma, government in Scotland did not break down and the Guardians remained in control. The first move was made by Bishop Fraser of St. Andrews who, anticipating trouble, wrote to King Edward in October 1290, imploring him to assist the Scots and to intervene before events got out of hand. Fraser also asked Edward to send an armed force to the border should any clashes break out between rival factions. He was not exaggerating as already the ageing Bruce of Annandale had raised a small army and made his way to Perth. John Balliol was styling himself 'heir to Scotland', and a further 11 claimants were jostling for position as Scotland's next king.

All these events must have seemed providential to King Edward, as matters were effortlessly falling into place for him. However, something now happened which was, indirectly, to have a profound effect on Edward's behaviour towards the Scots. In November 1290, Edward and his court progressed north to Scotland in response to Bishop Fraser's letter. They reached Harby near Lincon when his queen, Eleanor of Castille became ill and died. Edward was bitterly grief-stricken as they had loved each other deeply throughout 35 years of their arranged marriage, a remarkable achievement in any age. Her kindness had certainly brought to Edward a calming influence, the absence of which at this time unleashed a side of his character unseen before. For a while, Edward suspended his Scottish affairs, but his attitude towards Scotland merely hardened. As Eleanor was laid to rest, he declared openly his intentions to suppress Scotland

Left: Statues of Edward I and Queen Eleanor at Lincoln Cathedral.

as he had done Wales. The Scots were now at their most vulnerable and, despite Edward's declarations, the Guardians had little choice but to involve the English king.

In May 1291, Edward set out north once again. The task in hand was to prepare for his part in the adjudication of The Great Cause, as the competition for Scotland's throne later became known. The stage was Norham Castle situated, once again, on the River Tweed, but this time on the English side of the border 9 miles downstream from Birgham. This imposing fortress was the property of the Bishop of Durham, and kept an intimidating eye across the river into Scotland. For 15 miles of its length the

The ruin of Norham Castle stands guard above the River Tweed.

*Norham Castle seen from Upsettlington,
on the Scottish side of the River Tweed.*

Tweed formed a natural borderline between England and Scotland, and bore witness not only to the aggression of war, but to countless negotiations as the two sides bargained for peace on either side of its banks. Today the gentle and tranquil landscape around the Tweed belies its ancient use as a military no-man's-land. It provided a rallying point for invading armies of both countries, and many locations on that river were to provide a setting during the Wars of Independence.

Edward had invited all the Scottish claimants to Norham in preparation for The Great Cause. What Edward had planned for this occasion was not to the benefit of the competitors, but to himself. Soon he would have the most powerful men in Scotland before him on his own territory and he would not leave Norham without their acceptance of him, Edward, as feudal overlord of Scotland. He claimed his rights by carefully selecting the documents of his ancestors who had succeeded in extracting concessions from Scottish kings in the past, no matter how meaningless these claims now were.

After the various Scottish contingents arrived, Edward proclaimed that he was only prepared to sit in judgement over the Scottish throne if the Scots would recognise him as lord superior. He put it to them cleverly in the form of a negative question, which asked: *"Can you produce any evidence to show that I am not the rightful suzerain?"* The Scots were given three weeks to respond and by then Edward's armed host, initially invited by Bishop Fraser to prevent any outbreaks of violence in Scotland, would be at his shoulder. They could be put to better use against the whole of Scotland, instead of saving the Scots from civil war.

In the light of Edward's acceptance of the Treaty of Birgham, the Scots knew they had the law on their side. There does, however, appear to be a split in the response to Edward between the claimants to the crown who were eager to satisfy him, and the Scots as a whole who were less willing to compromise the freedom of their country. Towards the end of May, the Guardians had prepared a letter representing 'The Community of the Realm of Scotland' in which they stated that:

"they have no knowledge of your right, nor did they ever see it claimed and used by you or your ancestors...they have no power to reply to your claim without a lord to whom the demand ought to be addressed."

The point they were making was that in the circumstances, only a King of Scots could agree to or reject Edward's claims and since no one in the realm of Scotland was of the rank of king, they could not possibly respond. By June 1291 however, the claimants were choosing expediency over and above these principles and duly submitted to Edward saying:

"We, by our own free will, without any kind of constraint....do desire, concede and grant that we should receive justice before him, as lord superior of the realm."

This choice had not been an easy one for the claimants who saw themselves in an impossible position. They knew the military capabilities of Edward's armed host should the Scots go against his will; the Scots themselves were unpracticed in war and too disunited to face a common enemy. Their submission to Edward was not total and they did obtain concessions, but one cannot overemphasise the seriousness of the situation. The greatest prize for Edward was the possession of Scotland and all its castles for the duration of the forthcoming competition, all without a blow struck. These possessions would then be handed back to the new king, whoever he might be. The claimants were resigned to Edward becoming a royal referee, preferring to trust his neutrality rather than doubt his committment to their cause and it was not long before the whole Scottish contingent fell into line. The English king would never let them forget that which they had given away at Norham on June 4th 1291. One week later on June 13th, the Guardians and nobles of Scotland swore fealty to Edward in a ceremony on Scottish soil, in the village of Upsettlington across the River Tweed from Norham. Edward's first act was to reappoint the Scottish Guardians, under his own authority and not that of the Scots. The original four Guardians were joined by an Englishman, Brian FitzAlan of Bedale.

Edward then rewarded himself and his good work by leading a procession into Scotland towards Stirling and Perth. He returned south through Fife and down the east coast to Berwick on Tweed and it was here in August that Edward opened the case to decide the next King of Scots. The Great Cause would be decided on Scottish ground, which was a small concession to the Scots! But this was no trivial occasion and Edward took it very seriously. Fourteen would-be kings submitted claims to the court which comprised no less than 104 auditors. The make-up of these auditors tells us much about the bias facing the competition ahead: 40 were nominated by Bruce the Competitor; 40 by John Balliol and the remaining 24 by Edward himself. It was clear that the competition would focus on the claims of the two main rivals and it was true that many of the claimants had only tentative links to the throne. Nevertheless, there were in fact at least four legitimate claims; of Bruce and Balliol we are aware, but there were two others, namely John Hastings, Lord of Abergavenny and Florence V, Count of Holland. Like Bruce and Balliol, both of these men were direct descendants of King David I, although they were not as powerful or influential in Scotland as the former two. Once all the claimants had presented their cases, the proceedings were formally underway, and the court adjourned until June the following year. Some of the claimants went in search of vital evidence substantiating their claims, and Edward was keen to return to England. However, he had to show patience throughout the whole process and his scrupulous attention to detail was essential for a conquest already made without one blow struck.

The remains of Berwick Castle, where the competition to find the next King of Scots was held.

Route of Edward I from Berwick - 1291

Perth · St. Andrews · Stirling · Dunfermline · Linlithgow · Edinburgh · Haddington · Coldingham · Berwick upon Tweed · Thirlestane · Roxburgh

- - - - Journey Out
- - - - Journey Back

Bruce versus Balliol

The court did not meet again until October of the following year, 1292, and its priority seems to have been with the four main claims of The Great Cause. Bruce, Balliol, and Hastings were all descendants of David, Earl of Huntingdon, the youngest brother of King William the Lion. However, arguments arose as to who was most eligible for the throne. The Earl had begotten three daughters: John Balliol was the grandson of Margaret, the eldest; Robert Bruce was the son of Isabel, the second; and John Hastings was the grandson of Ada, the third. Under the usual laws of primogeniture, the right of succession belongs to the eldest son. On this basis Balliol, being of the oldest branch, was clearly the winner; however, Robert Bruce was a generation older and had already been heir presumptive 54 years previously, before King Alexander II of Scotland had produced any heirs.

Primogeniture was only one factor in selecting a king when all the claimants were so far removed from the original line. The most important issue should have been the competence and abilities of the candidate in question. However, as we are by now aware, the priority of Edward was that the new King of Scots should be anything but capable of ruling his own country and, since the English king in effect had the casting vote over the final decision, it seemed a foregone conclusion that Balliol would

be chosen. If Robert Bruce had thought that his friend and former companion at arms, King Edward, was sympathetic to his cause then he was a bad judge of character. Bruce's pedigree was his problem and Edward knew him well enough to know that once he was given the reins of power, The Competitor's pride would not stand for Edward's superiority. Robert Bruce was old and knew his own mind too well for Edward to manipulate it for his own ends. Alas for the House of Bruce, Robert, the fifth Lord of Annandale, was perceived as over-qualified, too patriotic and not flexible enough for Edward's grand plan.

John Balliol was the opposite extreme to Bruce. At 43 he was nearly half The Competitor's age, lacked his experience in war and leadership and was, naturally, the perfect choice for Edward. Like the Bruces, the Balliol family were Norman in origin and had substantial interests in English property. Whereas the Bruces had a greater pride in their Scottish inheritance, Balliol was more sympathetically English. Significantly, he was married to the daughter of a powerful English commander, John de Warenne, Earl of Surrey, who would play a leading rôle in the years ahead. The court not only found his claim more legitimate than that of Bruce, but saw Balliol's sympathies as being in the right place.

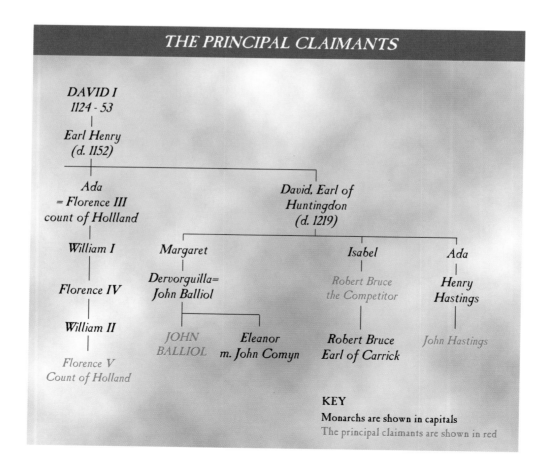

THE PRINCIPAL CLAIMANTS

DAVID I
1124 - 53

Earl Henry
(d. 1152)

Ada
= Florence III
count of Hollland

David, Earl of
Huntingdon
(d. 1219)

William I

Margaret

Isabel

Ada

Florence IV

Dervorguilla=
John Balliol

Robert Bruce
the Competitor

Henry
Hastings

William II

JOHN
BALLIOL

Eleanor
m. John Comyn

Robert Bruce
Earl of Carrick

John Hastings

Florence V
Count of Holland

KEY
Monarchs are shown in capitals
The principal claimants are shown in red

Left: John Balliol and his
consort, Isabel de Warenne,
as illustrated on the Seton
Armorial.

Of the two other main claims, that of John Hastings was dismissed due to his descent from the youngest and therefore least significant daughter of David of Huntingdon. Hastings had also argued that the land of Scotland should be shared between himself, Bruce and Balliol, a suggestion which hardly endeared him to the judges. The claim of the enigmatic Florence, Count of Holland, was on the basis of his descent from Ada, the older sister of the Earl of Huntingdon. Florence tried to persuade the court that the descendants of Ada should be granted the rights of succession over those of her younger brother, which would have disqualified the other claimants altogether. His evidence was tentative and as the custom of primogeniture was that *"a woman should not have the kingdom so long as there was a brother or nephew who could have the kingdom by right"*, the Count's claims were dismissed.

By the beginning of November, the court had unofficially decided in favour of Balliol. The more distant claims had yet to be dealt with, but Bruce and his contingent were given the verdict privately. One can imagine the disappointment of Robert Bruce of Annandale. Ever since 1238, when the throne had so nearly been within his grasp, he had waited patiently for an opportunity and this had been his last chance. Despite his disappointment,

Bruce very quickly drew a line under the whole episode. The next day, November 7, 1292, he passed on his claim to his son Robert Bruce, Earl of Carrick. In order that their claim be recorded, The Bruces produced a document which had a special significance for the future king,

> *"we have granted to our well-beloved son Robert Bruce, earl of Carrick and his heirs, the whole right and claim that we had...to sue for the realm of Scotland"*

It is thought that Bruces acted swiftly to maintain continuity, so that if Bruce the Competitor died, his claim would live on. However, no sooner had this document been sealed, than the Competitor's son passed on the earldom to his son, the future king. Marjorie of Carrick had died a few months previously, and the Earl was not of the same steel as his father, or for that matter, as his son.

Robert Bruce, the new Earl of Carrick, had keenly observed all that had gone on around him. Now a young man of eighteen, he would not forget the injustice done to his family and from now on, he alone would carry the torch for their cause. The young earl was starting out on the long road to his destiny.

THIS STATION STANDS ON THE SITE OF THE GREAT HALL OF BERWICK CASTLE. HERE ON THE 17ᵀᴴ NOVEMBER 1292, THE CLAIM OF ROBERT BRUCE TO THE CROWN OF SCOTLAND WAS DECLINED AND THE DECISION IN FAVOUR OF JOHN BALIOL WAS GIVEN BY KING EDWARD I BEFORE THE FULL PARLIAMENT OF ENGLAND AND A LARGE GATHERING OF THE NOBILITY AND POPULACE OF BOTH ENGLAND AND SCOTLAND

Above: *This plaque above the steps on Berwick railway station commemorates the events of 1292.*

A new king for Scotland

Thus it was that, on November 17, 1292, The Great Cause came to an end and after all had assembled in the Great Hall of Berwick Castle, the announcement in favour of John Balliol was made. Two days later the promises made by King Edward at Norham were upheld and all Scottish Castles were formally handed over to Balliol. The Guardians, their usefulness now effectively over, stood down and to emphasise to all Scots that Balliol was only a vassal king, Edward made sure that Balliol swore fealty to him before his enthronement. The people of Scotland were not to assume that the inauguration of this king was as important as those of his predecessors. On 30 November 1292, St. Andrew's Day, John Balliol was installed on the Stone of Destiny at Scone. However, the glittering ceremony was only a symbol of Balliol's kingship. The real reins of power were about to be taken up by Edward himself and he quickly began exploiting Balliol's position.

The first sign of the new Scots king's vulnerability came within a matter of days following his inauguration. In December 1292, the freedom of Scots law from the English legal system was called into question. An insignificant case in the court of the former Guardians had tried Roger Bartholomew, a burgess of Berwick who, as executor for a dead man's property, was accused of withholding money from his widow amongst other crimes. He had been found guilty but, now that the Guardians

were dismissed and the Scottish king virtually powerless, Bartholomew saw an opportunity to take his case to a higher authority. He appealed to King Edward who, whilst in Berwick heard him in person. Within two weeks Edward had overturned the Scottish court's decision. Balliol and his closest advisors had predicted that Edward would assert his power in this way and the outcome came as no surprise to them. They responded immediately by lodging a petition asking Edward to keep his promises made in the Treaty of Birgham which had protected Scots laws and customs. Edward's response was brisk: Any promises made to the Guardians whilst Scotland had no king, a period known as the interregnum, were *"for the time being"* and now declared null and void. The declarations were not worth the parchment they were written on.

The Scots could now expect no concessions from Edward. His word was the law and King John could do nothing without the approval of the English King. In hindsight, we can see this situation as predictable: Balliol had publically paid homage to Edward on two occasions and the Guardians and competitors had conceded too much ground before and during the Great Cause. The situation would prove to be unsustainable and could only break down, as for one king to be subordinate to another was a contradiction in terms and could not last for long.

It would be unfair to claim that King John Balliol was a completely ineffectual monarch and, although he has been lambasted throughout the centuries, more recent historians have recognised his impossible situation. There is evidence, however, that he was able to carry out the less controversial duties of a king, such as maintaining law and order. It is also thanks to Balliol that today we have some documentary evidence from the time of The Great Cause to prove the course of events, for it was he who made sure that valuable papers in English hands were returned to the Scottish chamberlain.

A further two years of legal humiliation persisted for the Scottish king. Most notable was his requirement to attend Edward's court in London to hear an appeal by a Scottish noble, John Macduff, who had seized lands in Fife held by Balliol. Despite the powers that Balliol had submitted, this was a case whch his court could rightly have dealt with in Scotland. But the puppet king's nerve was beginning to fail and he now trembled at the end of Edward's string. He was summoned to London to appear in front of an English judiciary to answer for his decision and was practically treated as a criminal himself. Needless to say, the English court reversed the decision in favour of Macduff. King John was threatened with the confiscation of his three chief castles of Edinburgh, Roxburgh and Berwick, until he redressed his contempt of court.

We can presume from Edward's behavior that he was going to provoke Balliol until he snapped. The English king wanted to create anarchy in Scotland which Edward himself could put down, but he wanted Balliol's weakness to be the cause. King John was becoming increasingly unpopular in his own land where he was perceived as an English puppet. Edward would soon be presented with his opportunity, but not before being humiliated himself, in a way similar to that endured by Balliol, from an unexpected quarter.

The Auld Alliance

"If that you will France win, then with Scotland first begin"

It was May 1294 and Philip the Fair, King of France, had been keenly observing all that had gone on between the two countries across the Channel. Scotland and France already had an informal alliance going back to 1173, and Philip was looking for ways to make life difficult for the King of England. Edward was Duke of Aquitaine and, as such, was vassal to the French king for the dukedom. Philip decided to give Edward a taste of his own medicine by calling him to the French court to account for acts of piracy by English ships towards French ships in the waters off the west coast of France. Naturally, Edward refused to respond to such a ridiculous demand, whereupon Philip immediately confiscated his lands. Nothing was more likely to make Edward's hackles rise than being put in his place by another, even if they were of equal rank. His response was swift and he renounced his homage to the French king and prepared for war. The contrast between the behaviour of King Edward and King John Balliol over the demands of their respective overlords could not be more stark.

Now that Edward had declared war on the French, he expected the subjugated Scots and Welsh to fall into line behind him, as overlord, and provide military service to help the English fight their war. This was, after all, what Edward had intended all along. He had ordered his own feudal host in England to be assembled at Portsmouth by the beginning of September and called upon the Welsh to join them there. Balliol had also received his call to arms, but now that Edward was preoccupied, both Wales and Scotland had a surprise in store for him. It was ten years since Edward had conquered the Welsh and, confident that they would show loyalty, he sent weapons directly to them before they left Wales. Ignoring his orders, they promptly rose in revolt against him. When we consider the carefully planned legal takeover of Scotland, it seems incredible that Edward could be so nâive as to give the Welsh such an opportunity. But it emphasises Edward's shortcomings: like a child bored with a new toy, he put Wales to one side in favour of his next adventure. But he had ignored the potential of its people to rise up again. He would show many examples of this behaviour in the years to come.

Above: The seal of King John Balliol.

Edward did not pursue his French campaign, but instead turned around to deal with the Welsh revolt, which took until May 1295. Meanwhile, the Scots had taken heart from the Welsh and soon resistance was stirring towards Edward's ambitions and Balliol's incompetence. The nobles and the church had been watching Balliol's performance very closely and were not prepared to see him give in any further to Edward's demands, least of all to put at risk Scotland's relationship with France. In July, the Scots arranged a parliament at Stirling which removed most power from Balliol and gave it to a group of newly elected Guardians known as the 'Council of Twelve'. This consisted of four earls, four barons and four bishops, and they had 2 principal aims: the first was to prepare the country for an almost inevitable war with England; the second was to gain international support by sending a diplomatic mission to Paris. On 23 October 1295 these commissioners, led by the veteran diplomat William Fraser, Bishop of St. Andrews, had secured a treaty with King Philip renewing The Auld Alliance. It guaranteed mutual support between France and Scotland for as long as England was at war with either country. The treaty was ratified by King John in February 1296, and sealed by the Council of Twelve.

Conspicuous by their absence from all this were the Bruces. The old Competitor had died in May of the previous year and his son and grandson seemed more concerned with family affairs than with those of Scotland. Robert Bruce senior had travelled to Norway to marry off his eldest daughter, Isobella, to King Erik of Norway and, upon his return in the autumn of 1295, took over his father's inheritance. Interestingly, Bruce was given governership of Carlisle by King Edward, clearly in order to keep the family on his side and against Balliol. Scotland's future king, the new Earl of Carrick, had married Isabella, daughter of Donald, Earl of Mar. He held substantial lands in the north east secured by a major castle at Kildrummy. Sadly, their marriage was short lived as, in 1296, Isabella died giving birth to a daughter, who Robert named after his mother, Marjorie. So the future king found himself a widower at 21 with an infant daughter, who in her own time would provide the link between house of Bruce and the longest running royal house ever to reign on these islands – the Stewarts.

Left: The Auld Alliance between Scotland and France was originally agreed by King William the Lion in 1165. It was renewed in 1295 by King John Balliol.

The remains of Wark Castle, above the Tweed, give few clues today about its part in the conflict.

By the beginning of March 1296, the days of precarious peace between England and Scotland were numbered. The Scots treaty with France was seen by Edward as the declaration of war for which he had been waiting and he zealously wasted no time in obliging. He had already made preparations for a Scottish invasion by ordering his forces to gather at Newcastle. Now he and his army advanced on Berwick upon Tweed. The Scots, meanwhile, were not idle in their preparations to defend the border, but they certainly underestimated the might of the English army. King John sent out summons to all the Scots nobles to raise their levies and join him in defence of the realm. The Bruce family now faced a watershed. Neither the Earl of Carrick nor his father had sworn allegiance to Balliol, whom they considered to be a usurper. The choice for them was to either fight with others for the survival of Scotland, or side with the English to overthrow Balliol. King Edward had promised the Bruces that if the uprising was put down, they would inherit the throne. The choice was simple and they, along with the supporters of their cause, prepared to join Edward.

Striking the first blow

Ironically, it was not the affairs of state which sparked the conflict, but a romance between a Scots girl and an Englishman; one Robert de Ros, Lord of Wark. Wark was on the English side of the river Tweed and, in his desire to be with his beloved, de

Ros had sided with the Scots and plotted to hand the castle over to them. News of the plot reached Edward in Newcastle who immediately sent a small force north to relieve the castle. But de Ros was ready and fell upon the English before they reached Wark. So the fight had begun and, to the delight of Edward, by the Scots themselves.

Edward mobilised his whole army and marched up to Wark, taking the castle with no trouble. It was 25 March and Easter celebrations called a halt to his progress. But he set up camp in Wark while planning his next move. As the English army was poised to invade the south east of Scotland, the Scots abandoned the border there and prepared an assault on northwest England. Edward led his army unchallenged over the border towards Berwick on Tweed where he waited outside its simple earth and timber palisade defences. The Scots, under the Earl of Buchan and John Comyn, laid waste the English countryside, burning villages en route to Carlisle. With the absence of siege engines which were necessary to breach the walls of the ancient city and its castle, Carlisle remained unassailable, thanks also to the stern defence by its governer Robert Bruce and his son. The Scots abandoned Carlisle and headed east ravaging Northumberland as far as Corbridge. We cannot be sure how much devastation occured, as the accuracy of accounts is clouded by the reams of propaganda from contemporary English chroniclers.

Left: The 15th century St. Alban's Chronicle depicts the siege of Berwick, which led to the infamous massacre of the entire town.

The Scots were wasting their efforts, and this futile offensive on northern England served no purpose. Edward's eye was on the north and nothing would distract him. Initially, Berwick held firm against the English siege. An attempt by English ships to attack the town from the sea ended in disaster as they ran aground and were set alight by Berwick's defenders. This delighted the town's folk who, from the supposed safety of the town, mistakenly began to provoke the English. At this Edward's patience snapped and he ordered the full might of his armoured chivalry to bear down on the town's defences and destroy all within. The pathetic timber palisade gave way with little effort, and what followed was the worst atrocity ever committed by the English army, and a shameful event in English history. We cannot be certain how many lost their lives on April 4 1296, but it is understood that somewhere between 10 – 20,000 men, women and children were remorselessly cut down. The destruction was indiscriminate as even the foreign merchants caught up in the conflict were not spared. The most notable of these were the Flemish merchants who perished while defending their quarters in the Red Hall. The whole town was razed to the ground whilst only the castle was spared, its Scottish garrison commanded by Sir William Douglas was forced to surrender. Douglas himself was sent to London in chains.

To Edward, this pointless waste of life served a useful purpose. It was not carried out as punishment for an act of defiance by the people of Berwick, but an example to the rest of Scotland that if they dared to stand against him then this was what they could expect. Berwick was to become a new English town from where Edward could administer Scotland. During this time, the exact whereabouts of John Balliol were not known, but no sooner had the carnage of Berwick ended than a messenger arrived from Arbroath with a letter from Balliol renouncing his oath of allegiance to Edward, an act which hardly concerned the English king. Now the puppet master could seek out Scotland's puppet king and finally cut the strings.

It was not until April 23, two weeks after the dreadful slaughter at Berwick that Edward sent his cavalry under the Earl of Surrey, further north into Scotland. Dunbar Castle, an important stronghold on the Firth of Forth, was the next target. The Earl of Dunbar and March had supported Edward, but his wife had remained loyal and had helped a Scots force overthrow the castle's English garrison. The Earl of Surrey now came to retrieve it back from the Scots, and while he laid siege, the main host of the Scottish army came hot foot from the borders.

The scene was set for the first of many battles to come as, on April 27, the Earl of Buchan, commanding the Scots, prepared his cavalry on the Lammermuir hills above Dunbar. The English broke off their siege and began to advance on the Scottish position. The lie of the land was such that the English cavalry had to descend into a valley and cross the Spott Burn beneath the Lammermuirs, before they could ascend the hills. As they disappeared from view, the Scots thought that they were making a retreat. In an undisciplined surge, the Scottish cavalry charged down the hill expecting to scatter the fleeing English, but to their horror, Surrey had formed his armoured horse into an impenetrable wall on to which the Scots fell. Complete carnage ensued as the disciplined ranks of the English cut through the ill-prepared rabble that was the so-called feudal host of Scotland. The Scots infantry stood no chance and many of the nobles were taken hostage. What did survive of the army turned and fled back whence it had come.

What Scotland had witnessed that day was the hopeless inability of those in command of the feudal host to defend their country responsibly. They understood the basic principles of war but, without military experience, they could not compete with a nation which had a two hundred year passion for pitched battles inherited from William the Conqueror. Scotland's defensive capability had been crushed and her army effectively dispersed.

The remains of Dunbar Castle which once stood impressively on a chain of rocks.

Route of Edward I from Berwick - 1296

Elgin · Banff · Fyvie · Kildrummy · Lumphanan · Aberdeen · Brechin · Forfar · Montrose · Clunie · Dundee · Arbroath · Perth · St. Andrews · Stirling · Dunfermline · Dunbar · Linlithgow · Haddington · Edinburgh · Berwick upon Tweed · Lauder · Roxburgh · Jedburgh · Castleton

- - - - - Journey Out
- - - - - Journey Back

Edward's triumphant march

At first John Balliol did nothing and retreated north with his supporters. Edward left Berwick with his entire armed host and began what amounted to a victory parade through Scotland. Not one sword was raised against him as he accepted the surrender of one town and castle after another. He headed south through Lauder towards the castles at Roxburgh and Jedburgh whose garrisons yielded without a siege. Then moving north again he reached Edinburgh on June 6, waiting there only one week before its mighty castle succumbed. A week after that he arrived at Stirling, its castle proudly defending the gateway to the north. However, on this occasion, Edward found its ramparts unmanned as all had fled before him. The march north of the English host was surprisingly calm; there was no harrying, burning or pillaging; their objective was to intimidate the Scots by their very presence and besides, no one opposed them! Continuing ever northwards, Edward reached Perth on midsummer's day, and it was to here that, finally, John Bailliol sent a message of his own surrender. With the Scots army destroyed at Dunbar and his credibility as a king non-existent, Balliol had no other option.

As the English army continued its journey through the north east John Balliol came before Edward. On July 8 at Stracathro church near Brechin, he was subjected to a humiliating abdication ceremony. He was forced to renounce the treaty with France and resign the kingdom. He was physically stripped of his tabard on which were embroidered the Royal arms of Scotland, an act which forever gave him the nickname *'Toom Tabard'*, meaning empty coat. By this time Edward had been joined by both Bruce of Annandale and his son. They were only too pleased to see Balliol ridiculed and deprived of his title, but if they were expecting any sympathy for their own cause from Edward, they were to be sadly disappointed. They may have helped Edward put down King John's rebellion, but Edward never intended to replace Balliol with Bruce. He turned on the Bruces asking them rhetorically *"Have we nothing else to do but win kingdoms for you?"*. Scotland was effectively no longer a kingdom but a northern region of England. Balliol was sent south to the Tower of London where he remained for three years before being allowed to retire to his ancestral home in Picardy. With Edward becoming more confident by the day, he continued north with a greater pace, finally turning south at Elgin.

Above: John Balliol after his forced abdication, with torn surcoat and broken crown and sceptre.

Above: In 1996, the Stone of Scone was reunited with the Honours of Scotland, the Scottish Crown Jewels, and was placed on display in the Crown Room at Edinburgh Castle.

It was the end of July and as he returned to Perth, Edward began the process of removing all symbols of Scottish sovereignty: the Scottish regalia, St. Margaret's Holy Rood and the royal records were removed, together with the alleged Stone of Destiny. To lose these treasures was tragic enough for Scotland, but along with the royal records went a large part of Scotland's history before 1296.

All but the Stone disappeared without trace. and since its official return to Scotland in 1996 after an absence of 700 years, there has been much speculation about its authenticity. It is certainly the stone that Edward plundered all those years ago, but equally certain to be a fake. The Stone of Destiny, on which Scotland's kings were inaugurated for centuries, did not originate from Scotland. It is thought to have been brought from Ireland to Iona by St. Columba in the 6th century and, from earlier descriptions, it was a richly decorated basalt stone. Abbot Henry of Scone, knowing that Edward was on his way to remove the Stone, quarried a chunk of local sandstone, and exchanged it for the genuine Stone, which was hidden away. It is recorded that Edward's soldiers returned to the Abbey at a later date in search of their lost treasure once Edward realised he had been fooled.

With the whole of Scotland on its knees, Edward arrived back at Berwick on August 1 to make preparations for his first official parliament as overlord of Scotland. On August 28, amid the stench of rotting corpses left in the streets after the slaughter, all the freeholders of Scotland, noble and common, assembled in Berwick to swear fealty to King Edward. No less than 1,500 men put their names to The Ragman Roll, the lengthy document on which they formally submitted to Edward.

"I will be faithful and loyal and will bear fealty and loyalty to King Edward, king of England and his heirs..."

Those who did not sign, and there were many, were immediately outlawed and disinherited. Consequently all who had the most to lose, the Bruces amongst them, signed without hesitation. In the years to come all but a few of these names reneged on their oath to Edward, claiming that an oath made under duress was not binding. It all made the Ragman Roll a rather absurd waste of time, giving the origin of the word *'rigmarole'*.

Edward did not return to England for another month. He made Berwick the new capital of Scotland and appointed English administrators to oversee its transition to English rule. The Earl of Surrey was made viceroy, Sir William Ormesby became chief justice and Sir Hugh Cressingham was given the position of treasurer, thereby becoming the most hated man in Scotland. Across the land, every church and castle was staffed with English clergy and garrisons, making life insufferable for the majority of Scots. Edward's rule permeated the whole country and no one was left in any doubt as to who was in charge.

Edward left Scotland on September 29 to turn his attentions on France. Before he went he is said to have remarked to his new viceroy that: *"He who rids himself of shit does a good job"*. Thus he departed, signalling his hatred for Scotland and believing his conquest to be complete. But he was wrong.

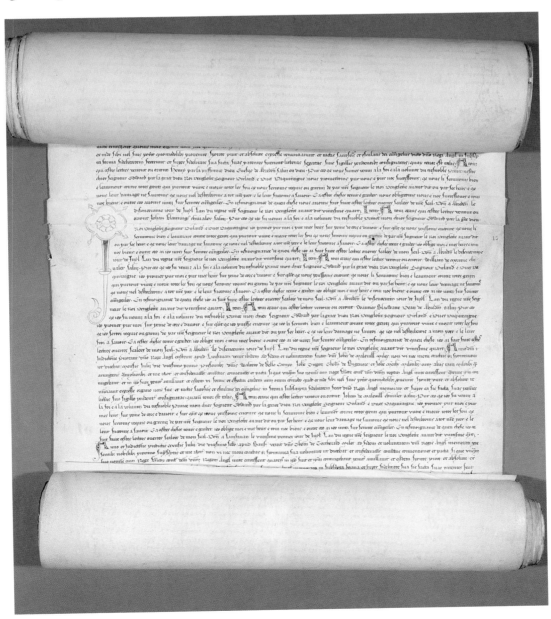

Left: *The Ragman Roll to which 1500 freeholders put their names, thus formally submitting to King Edward.*

Part 2. 1296 – 1305
FIGHTING FOR A LOST CAUSE

"William Wallace raised his head"

The ease with which King Edward of England had absorbed Scotland into his kingdom deceived him and belied the nature of the country he thought he had subjugated. In winning over the feudal hierarchy, Edward believed he had done everything necessary to subdue the whole land. So sudden and efficient had his conquest been that he had met no serious opposition from the nobles, and assumed that everyone beneath them would fall into line.

Right: *The monument to William Wallace at Elderslie, near Paisley, the place of his birth.*
Inset: *Detail from the monument.*

But resistance was growing and Edward could not expect his enforced peace to last long. The fuse of national anger had been lit and, early in May 1297, Scotland exploded into action. It was clear that most who had put their names to the Ragman Roll had not expected the easily won occupation to last and were just biding their time. Many who had lost their possessions and been outlawed by Ormesby, the new English Justice, had nothing to lose by fighting back; all they needed was the means to rise up and a leader to show them the way.

It was now that Scotland's saviour, a man today of almost immortal status, made his entrance into the history books. He was not of noble birth but came from a small family of landed gentry in Ayrshire and Renfrewshire, in the south west. He was the second son of the Laird of Elderslie, and his name was William Wallace. Born around 1270, he had received a good education from his uncle, a priest at Dunipace near Stirling and, as a younger son with no land to inherit, might well have gone into the priesthood had his country been at peace. But William's uncle gave him more than an education; he instilled in him an enduring love for the ancient freedom of his country with the words: *"My son I tell you truthfully, no gift is like liberty, then never live in slavery."*

Patriotism ran through the veins of his family, although their origins were not Scottish. The name Wallace meant 'Welshman' or 'Celt', and the ancestors of William came from the Welsh Marches 150 years before when many great noble families like the Bruces arrived in Scotland with King David I. The first known Wallace was William's great-grandfather, Sir Richard Wallace, who was granted land near Kilmarnock. Indeed, 'Richard's Town' was named after him and is better known today as Riccarton. Richard's grandson was Sir Malcolm Wallace, William's father, who married Margaret Crawford, the daughter of the Sheriff of Ayr. As a middle-ranking family, they held a responsible position in society, and therefore came face to face with English aggression on the ground.

Above: The parish church, Lanark, near Wallace's home at the end of High Street.
Below: The ruins of St. Kentigern's church, Lanark, where Wallace probably married Marion Braidfute.

The Wallaces already had cause to resent the English occupation, for Sir Malcolm had been killed during an encounter with English soldiers in 1291 before Edward's invasion. There had been a heavy English presence before and during the Great Cause, as castles were handed back and forth during negotiations, and the Laird of Elderslie had clashed with a small English force at the foot of Loudoun Hill in Ayrshire. In the fight, Sir Malcolm was killed by an English knight, Sir John Fenwick. William's brother, also called Malcolm, had become the new Laird and, as a minor land owner, he had been expected to sign the Ragman Roll. It hardly seems surprising that the name of Malcolm Wallace was absent from the document and so the Laird of Elderslie and his whole family were outlawed.

William could not stand by and watch his country being trampled by a ruthless invader and, since his father's death, he had been involved in a number of minor reprisals, usually provoked by English soldiers spoiling for a fight. At six feet, seven inches tall, he stood head and shoulders above the crowd and was perceived as a challenge. He had gained a formidable reputation with the use of a five foot broad sword and, as all such weapons were forbidden to the Scots, the English authorities were on the lookout for him. During this time, William had disappeared into the depths of Ettrick Forest. Very little of the original forest exists today but, at the end of the 13th century, it was a great expanse of woodland, covering much of the central lowlands. So far he had evaded capture and, during the winter of 1296-97, the 26 year old Wallace quickly became an inspiration for others, and he gathered the dispossessed around him.

Like the incident at Wark castle, where a love affair between its governor and a local girl was responsible for provoking King Edward's invasion, it was a love story that incited the next stage of this bloody war. At about this time, William had met Marion Braidfute, a young woman born into a respectable Lanarkshire family. We cannot be certain, but it is thought by some that he had married her before becoming an outcast; whatever their relationship, he was in love with Marion and paid many visits to her house in the town of Lanark under cover of darkness. Eventually, rumours about William and Marion reached the ear of the English-appointed Sheriff of Lanark, William de Heselrig, and he ordered that her house be watched closely until the culprit showed himself. One night, William managed to gain entrance to the house secretly, but in the early hours of the morning he was spotted while making his escape. A desperate chase through the streets of Lanark followed as William, with no weapons, tried to give Heselrig the slip. The pursuit led him back into Marion's house and, as he slipped out through the back door, Marion tried to hold off Heselrig, whose soldiers were now hammering at the front.

Whether or not William realised what would become of Marion for helping him escape we cannot know. His later behaviour proves that he was not one for endangering the lives of women or children, but here he acted instinctively for his own survival, perhaps thinking that with chivalry prevailing, Heselrig would do no harm to Marion. Whatever went through his mind as he ran from Lanark that morning in May 1297, William did not know that would never see Marion alive again. Heselrig, enraged at the escape of William Wallace, outnumbered and unarmed as this outlaw was, ordered that Marion be put to the sword and her house burned to the ground. When word reached him of Marion's cruel murder, a transformation occurred in Wallace. Gone was the youthful, dashing adventurer; in his place a hard and calculating man with a single purpose, who would never sway from his objective: to rid Scotland of its tyranny.

His vengeance on Heselrig was uncompromising and ruthless. On the very night following Marion's death, Wallace approached Lanark with a small band of disciplined men. They quietly entered the Sheriff's lodgings searching every room and dispatching every man they could find, until they came across Heselrig himself. Waking him from his sleep, Wallace then plunged a dagger into his heart. Before the night was out, every Englishman in Lanark was dead and the town belonged to Wallace. The first blow for Scotland had been struck. In the words of the 14th century historian John of Fordun, William Wallace had *"raised his head"*.

Right: William Wallace is avenged on Heselrig, the English-appointed sheriff of Lanark.

Resistance gathers momentum

By his actions in Lanark, William Wallace had inspired the nation to revolt. That he had so easily overcome an English-occupied town brought about the realisation that the English occupation was not, after all, invulnerable to attack. The audacity of Wallace had given others the encouragement to join the fight and he began to rally hundreds to his cause. Of those who joined him, some were from a similar background to Wallace, such as Adam Wallace, his cousin, and Edward Little, his nephew. Also with him from these early days was a man without whom the story of Wallace and his deeds would not have travelled down the centuries to inspire us today. During his education, Wallace had made friends with John Blair, a Benedictine monk. After hearing of Wallace's adventures, Blair decided to seek out his old companion and take up arms at his side. He became Wallace's personal chaplain and his biographer but, sadly, the original Latin document has been lost. We know it existed, because a much later storyteller, Blind Harry the minstrel, used it to construct his epic poem *'Wallace'* in around 1478.

As faithful friends gathered at his shoulder, Wallace began planning his next move. Throughout May 1297 he amassed a formidable fighting force, with no less than 1,000 horsemen from the southwest of Scotland, as well as those on foot. Compared with the full armoured cavalry of England, this force was hardly significant, but as an efficient, hit-and-run strike team, it was deadly. Wallace would wage a guerrilla-style war on the enemy, not from cowardice, but because until enough brave men came together in one place to face the enemy on the field of battle, this was his only means of progress.

His success at Lanark had alerted the English but had not seriously threatened their grip on power. However, with his next move, Wallace aimed to do just that. Before May was out, he mobilised his troops and headed north towards Perth. His target was William de Ormesby, the English Chief Justice who had perceived Scone, the most symbolic place of Scotland's sovereignty, to be the ideal place to dispense English justice. Before Wallace reached Perth, he was joined by Sir William Douglas - he who had been forced to surrender Berwick Castle shortly after the town's sacking. Douglas had, somehow, been released from his chains in the Tower of London and had made it back home. Fiercely patriotic, he was a Scottish nobleman with a strong mind and ruthless disposition. It was with good reason that he was known as *'le Hardi'* and, smarting from his imprisonment, he wanted revenge. The presence of Douglas gave Wallace vital legitimacy, as it was the first occasion that noble and commoner had come together in a common cause.

Together, Wallace and Douglas stealthily advanced on Scone, but the English had got wind of their approach and what troops there were had disappeared into the forests and hills around Scone. Disappointingly for the Scots, Ormesby had also made his escape but, more importantly, he had been given a fright, and in a panic had left valuable booty, most of which had been plundered from the Scots. Although not a victory, the Scots had forced a retreat of the most important Englishman in Scotland. Now King Edward would begin to sit up and take note.

Not only Edward was stirred by this act of bravado. Now that Douglas was involved, other Scots of noble rank began to take an interest and it was largely thanks to the Church that certain Scottish magnates became actively involved in the rebellion. Robert Wishart, the Bishop of Glasgow, had for a long time maintained a peaceful protest against English rule since it had crushed the independence of the Scottish Church. The Scottish clergy were in a unique position of influence without being beholden to the English regime due to land ownership. Wishart openly declared his support for the uprising and persuaded James Stewart, the High Steward of Scotland to join him. These two men had been amongst the original guardians of 1286 when King Alexander had died, and therefore were veterans of the political situation. It is interesting to note that all those participants in the initial uprising, like Wallace, came from the south west of Scotland: James Stewart as Lord of Renfrew was Wallace's overlord; William Douglas held lands and a mighty castle in a town named after his family just south of Lanark and, of course, Wishart himself was Bishop of Glasgow. But one other important figure, also from the south west, now emerged; a young Scottish nobleman of 22 who had been inspired by the exploits of Wallace and was ready to join the fight. His name was Robert Bruce, Earl of Carrick.

Above: *The site of Douglas Castle, where the young Robert Bruce first decided to fight alongside his countrymen.*

Left: *Paisley Abbey, a fifteenth century rebuild, but originally a place of worship for Wallace. Its support for him caused its destruction by the English in 1307.*

Upon the outbreak of war, both Robert Bruce and his father had fought for King Edward to overthrow John Balliol. As far as the Bruces were concerned, they were not traitors to Scotland's cause, but rather loyal to their own and, until he had come of age, the young Earl of Carrick would undoubtedly have put family before country. However, for the first time in his life Bruce was about to become his own man.

Bruce had been at Carlisle, alongside his father, defending the city against the Scots invasion into England in the previous year. King Edward now called upon the Bruces to gather their forces, advance into Scotland and punish William Douglas for his part in the rebellion. Young Bruce left Carlisle alone and went to his father's Annandale lands to raise men and arms for an attack on Douglas's castle. But Robert Bruce had no intention of assailing the stronghold and when he arrived there he addressed the men around him with the following words: *"No man holds his flesh and blood in hatred and I am no exception. I must join my own people and the nation in which I was born"*. The men of

Annandale were his father's vassals, and as Robert Bruce senior was still King Edward's man, they were beholden to him. Some stayed with young Bruce, but most returned to Annandale without a blow struck against Douglas Castle. Bruce relieved the castle, which was being defended by Douglas's wife and his eldest son, 12 year old James Douglas. The boy hero-worshipped Robert Bruce from that day onwards, and became his greatest friend.

Although Bruce had acted decisively in siding with his fellow countryman, this was by no means a *fait accompli* for him. At the time, it may have seemed like an irreversible step, but over the next few years Bruce would submit to Edward on several occasions. He thought in his early days that compromising with the English and using politics would eventually secure Scotland's independence but, in fact, the only way to succeed was to fall on one side or the other, and Bruce was to learn this the hard way. Wallace would teach every Scot that they must fight the English completely if they wanted to be free.

Following his assault on Scone, Wallace returned to the southwest via Glasgow. Anthony Bek, the Bishop of Durham, had taken up residence in the Bishop's palace there, having replaced Bishop Wishart. Bek had seen to it that the see of Glasgow was now accountable to the see of Durham and Wishart's fears that the Church would no longer be independent were now a reality. Wallace entered the city with the intention of ousting Bek but, as with Ormesby at Scone, he had received warning and fled in advance. With a fearless determination growing by the day Wallace now headed for Ayr with a very specific target in mind: the English garrison at the Barns of Ayr.

Shortly before this move, Wallace's uncle, Sir Reginald Crawford, the displaced Sheriff of Ayr, had been invited with others to the Barns, a vast building on the edge of the town, to discuss terms with an English judge called Arnulf. As each man entered, a noose was thrown around his neck and they were hoisted into the rafters. It is thought that more than 300 men, noble and common, died in this way and, once the bodies were removed, the Barn was used as a barracks for the new English garrison. Arnulf himself became the new Sheriff and resided at the Castle of Ayr which was itself too small to house his troops, hence the need for additional accommodation. Wallace, burning with anger at the treachery of his uncle's death, saw Ayr and Arnulf as an obvious target. He knew the town well and the garrison was in an unprotected building.

In the still of the night, Wallace and his men approached the Barn and, setting fire to brushwood around the building they waited, swords in hand, for fleeing soldiers. As the fire took hold panic-stricken Englishmen began pouring from the doors and windows. All who did not succumb to the flames died by the sword. With his garrison obliterated, Arnulf was left exposed and his castle defenceless. It fell to Wallace with no trouble and he promptly hanged Arnulf from its walls.

Wallace pursued his objective relentlessly. His motivation was more than revenge; it was the principal of liberty which he would resolutely fight for until his dying day.

Left: William Wallace leads an attack on the English barracks at the Barns of Ayr.

Above: The Barnweil Tower, near Tarbolton, commemorates Wallace's attack on the Barns of Ayr.

Andrew Murray – the forgotten hero

As William Wallace inspired southern and central Scotland to rise up, another remarkable young man was also achieving great things further north. He is seldom given the recognition he deserves for his contribution to the fight for freedom, but Andrew Murray stands alongside Wallace as one of the first great leaders of this long and arduous war. Murray was the son of a northern baron, Sir Andrew Murray, Lord of Petty near Inverness, and their family had inevitably suffered in the aftermath of the invasion. Their position as one of the most influential families in the north was compounded by the fact that Sir Andrew had been Scottish Chief Justice (Justiciar of Scotia) for the whole of Scotland north of the Forth before the new English regime toppled him.

Sir Andrew and his son had fought in the Scottish army which had suffered the pathetic rout at the Battle of Dunbar in the previous year. Both survived, but were captured and sent to English prisons. Because of the importance of his position, Sir Andrew was sent to the Tower of London, but his son was not considered to be worthy of such a prestigious gaol and imprisoned much closer to home in Chester Castle. Here he remained until his dramatic escape some time during the winter of 1296-97. It is uncertain how he made it out of Chester, but it is known that he had returned to his home territory in the northeast by the spring of 1297.

In May, as Wallace was taking the town of Lanark, Andrew Murray gathered as many men as would follow him from Inverness. They headed down Loch Ness to Urquhart Castle which they took with little effort and, within 3 months, all other main castles in the north - Elgin, Inverness and Banff - were in Murray's hands. He had at his back a proud army of men equal to that of Wallace. What a formidable national army they would make if they could only join forces!

Left: *The ruins of Elgin Cathedral.*

Below: *The present castle at Inverness stands on the site of that taken by Andrew Murray in 1297.*

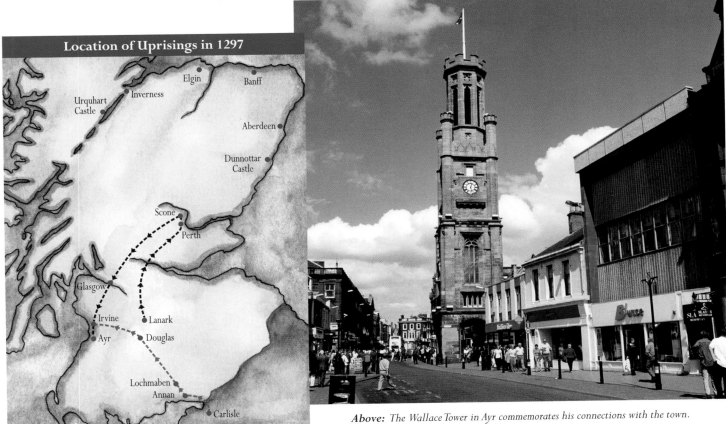

Location of Uprisings in 1297

--- Route taken by Robert Bruce
● Locations of the first uprisings of 1297
--- Possible route taken by William Wallace

Above: The Wallace Tower in Ayr commemorates his connections with the town.

While Murray gathered strength in the north, Wallace had joined Robert Bruce, William Douglas, Bishop Wishart and many others at Irvine on the Ayrshire coast. They had gathered to discuss tactics, but it appears that a rift was created between Bruce and Balliol supporters. To complicate things further, Wallace himself was fighting in the name of King John Balliol who, despite being removed by Edward, was still the incumbent monarch, and had irreversibly been enthroned on the Stone of Destiny. However Bruce insisted that, since Balliol had been forced to abdicate, he was hardly relevant as an effective king. Wallace had no time for these political arguments and wanted action. He left them to it and headed north once again towards Perth and Fife.

Throughout this summer of renewed Scottish pride, the English may have been consistently humiliated but they were not going to take it lying down: as far as they were concerned this was now *their* country. Edward, while still away in France, was kept informed of events in Scotland and, on June 4 1297, he ordered an army to be raised by Robert Clifford and Henry Percy, Earl of Northumberland. Their lands were the furthest north in England and they could act quickly to put down this uprising. They marched over the border, through the Bruce lands, making their way to the gathering of Scots nobles at Irvine. Before June was out, Percy and Clifford reached Ayr, just south of Irvine, where they waited.

Aware of the English presence, the Scots were at a loss over what to do. Wallace had left them, taking all his men north. They had only infantry to match the far greater English cavalry led by Percy and Clifford, and it would be foolish for them to throw themselves at defeat when Scotland had gained so much ground already. They decided to play for time and negotiate with the English commanders. There followed one of the most lengthy surrenders in history, known as the infamous 'Capitulation of Irvine'. For one month the terms of this surrender were spun out as the Scots agreed to accept Edward's peace, although Bruce did not. The peace terms did not extend to Wallace who was merely considered a base-born brigand, unworthy of forgiveness; not that Wallace would have accepted them in any case. However, this period of inertia proved invaluable to him as he was able to continue his campaign unchallenged.

On the face of it, this surrender by the Scots nobles appears faint-hearted, but we should not accuse them of cowardice. They had not given in to bribes of land and title, but only to the promise of King Edward's peace if they did not rise up against him. They were realists taking the opportunity to delay the conflict until they could match the English in the field man for man, even though that scenario was virtually impossible. Nevertheless the whole situation was deplored by one Scots knight, Sir Richard de Lundie, to the extent that he renounced his allegiance to the Scots crown and joined the English army.

Above: Dunnottar Castle, Kincardineshire, which Wallace besieged and overcame.

The capitulation of the nobles by the end of July meant that Wallace and Murray were, separately, in charge of national resistance. Despite the continuing English presence in Scotland, their capacity to rule effectively was diminishing by the day. The Scots began disposing of English appointees, who had either fled or met with a violent death, replacing them with their own men once castles and towns had been won back. On July 24, a desperate Hugh Cressingham, the English Treasurer, wrote to Edward from Northumberland requesting money, since *"Not one of the sheriffs, bailiffs or officials.....can at this time raise a penny....on account of a multitude of different perils which daily and continually threaten them."*

During the summer, Wallace waged his war in the West Highlands, which had by now also become involved in the conflict. Several Scots earls of the north - Buchan, Atholl and Menteith - had declared their support for King Edward and, along with a large army of Irish mercenaries under one MacFadyen, had raided into the lands of those clans in Argyll who had remained loyal to the Scottish cause. Highland chiefs always fought their own battles, but knowing his reputation for success, Duncan of Lorne and Sir Neil Campbell had requested

the assistance of Wallace. Together, they inflicted a heavy defeat on MacFadyen in the Pass of Brander and, with the disturbances in the west over for the time being, Wallace led his army east out of the Highlands. On hearing of his approach, thousands of English soldiers fled in front of him, making for the safety of Dunnottar Castle. But this mighty stronghold, perched high aloft the treacherous east coast cliffs, was not completely impervious to attack, as Wallace demonstrated. He had one driving principle: when faced with an enemy, do not spare him or he will return to kill you. This principle Wallace carried out to devastating effect as he ordered the death of every Englishman inside, not even sparing those who sought sanctuary in the castle's church.

From Dunnottar Wallace moved north to Aberdeen, there attacking English supply ships, and then continued inland towards the River Spey where he finally joined up with Andrew Murray. We can only imagine their first meeting, at which they must have found an affinity with each other: two like-minded young men, each with a talent for leadership and one driving ambition.... to rid Scotland of English tyranny.

Stirling Bridge – the humiliation of England

Together, William Wallace and Andrew Murray mobilised their troops and at the end of July 1297 turned south. Almost all of Scotland north of the River Forth was now back in Scots hands, but it was effectively ungoverned. However, it was now that a new aspect of Wallace's character emerged, as he began to demonstrate a talent, not just for leading an army, but for governing the people. They returned to Aberdeen where Wallace saw to it that a new administrative regime would control the north while he and Murray were in the south. If those who were born to it would not take the reins of power, then he would. Continuing the journey, their destination was Dundee Castle which was still under English occupation and now about to be besieged by the Scots.

Throughout August the siege of Dundee continued but, as it did, the English began to gather their strength and march north. Following the Capitulation of Irvine, the army of Henry Percy and Robert Clifford had moved east to meet up with the Earl of Surrey and Hugh Cressingham, who had been instructed by King Edward to head north and relieve the castles of Stirling and Dundee. Inevitably this would lead to the long awaited clash with Wallace and Murray, unless they fled in front of the English army, which by now seemed highly unlikely. For the English army, this campaign was simply a matter of routine which would result in one of three alternatives for the enemy; to watch them flee ahead of their arrival; to accept their surrender before a blow is struck; or to crush them under foot. The Norman feudal host had done this many times before and had rarely failed.

As Warenne progressed north, scouts arrived at Dundee bringing news to Wallace and Murray that an English army was on its way to Stirling. Unlike the nobles at Irvine, these two young commanders did not hesitate and, leaving the siege in the capable hands of one Alexander Scrymgeour, they too made their way to Stirling with an urgent pace. In military terms, Stirling was the single most important location in the whole of Scotland, sitting right at the heart of the country with the Highlands to the north and the Lowlands to the south. The town was situated to the south of the River Forth whose course traversed much of the width of Scotland, virtually splitting the country in two. The castle, in its hilltop position, guarded the only crossing point of the river along its entire length - Stirling Bridge.

The Scots army were the first to arrive on the scene early in September. To the north of the river the land rose dramatically up to the Abbey Craig, a crag named after the monastery of Cambuskenneth at its foot, and beyond to the more gently rising Ochil Hills. On this high ground Wallace and Murray set up camp to wait for their first sight of the enemy. On September 9, Warenne's army arrived at Stirling, and it must have been an extremely daunting sight for the Scots as they observed the endless array of proud chivalry, glinting armour and fluttering banners. The English host had somewhere approaching 60,000 men, mainly infantry, but including over 1000 of their terrifying armoured cavalry, as well as newly recruited Welsh longbowmen. Between them Wallace and Murray had a meagre 10,000 men armed with spears, with a handful of cavalry belonging to the only nobles who had decided to join them. James Stewart and the Earl of Lennox had joined up with the army without firmly committing themselves or their men to any battle. The Scots feudal host had bad memories of the defeat of Dunbar by the same English commander, and they saw all this ending the same way. Many of them were also bound over to keep the peace by their concessions at Irvine.

Right: How Scotland and England were viewed in the thirteenth century is shown in this map completed by Matthew Paris in 1250. The importance given to the strategic position of Stirling bridge, in the centre of Scotland, can clearly be seen.

As the English set up camp on the southern bank of the river, the two Scots commanders continued to watch and wait. They had chosen their battle site and were well protected in their present position. They may have been heavily outnumbered, but they were all there by choice, to fight for their very existence. Many in the Scottish ranks had suffered enough under English rule and they would now rather die than endure it any longer. By contrast, the English had their traditional feudal host, whose foot soldiers were recruited from the estates of English commanders. They were fighting because they had to, not because they knew what they were fighting for.

The next day, Stewart and Lennox rode over the bridge to speak with Warenne. It appears that they wished to negotiate the terms of a Scots surrender before yet another disastrous defeat, but their efforts did not sway Wallace and Murray who held their ground. Warenne could not believe that the Scots did not wish to surrender, so he later sent two Dominican friars across the bridge to urge them to give in and also to ascertain their situation. Wallace sent them back with a response which left the English in no doubt: *"Tell your people that we have not come here to gain peace, but are prepared for battle, to avenge and deliver our country. Let them come up when they like, and they will find us ready to meet them even to their beards".*

Wallace knew the English would not be able to resist this challenge. He and Murray wanted the English to come to *them*, knowing that once they began to cross the bridge they would be vulnerable and, once across, the heavy cavalry would find it difficult to hold their own on the soft, marshy ground either side of the causeway which ran right up to the Scots positions. Despite the temptation, Warenne still did not order his men across the bridge but instead called a council of war. The English had been unnerved, not just by the behaviour of the Scots, but by bad information brought back to them by the two friars. They had grossly over-estimated the size of the Scots army, calculating it to be nearer 40,000 strong. At this point, Sir Richard de Lundie, the Scots knight who had deserted to the English at Irvine intervened with an idea. He knew the territory around Stirling extremely well and suggested that he himself could lead 500 of the English cavalry around to the west and cross the river by a ford, visible at low tide, situated upstream at a place called Kildean. They could then attack the Scots from behind. Alas for Lundie, the English did not trust this newly-recruited Scot enough to heed his advice. He was immediately shouted down by Cressingham, who insisted that all this delay was costing the treasury too much and that they should proceed across the bridge forthwith. Had they not defeated the Scots at Dunbar, an army led by greater men than Wallace, a common criminal?

Above: *Looking east from the Kildean cattle market towards Stirling Castle on the right and Abbey Craig on the left. The River Forth could have been crossed here by the English, avoiding the narrow bridge at Stirling itself.*

Right: The River Forth meanders across the landscape, as can be seen from the top of Abbey Craig. From here, Wallace had a perfect view of Stirling Castle and the movements of the English army to the south.

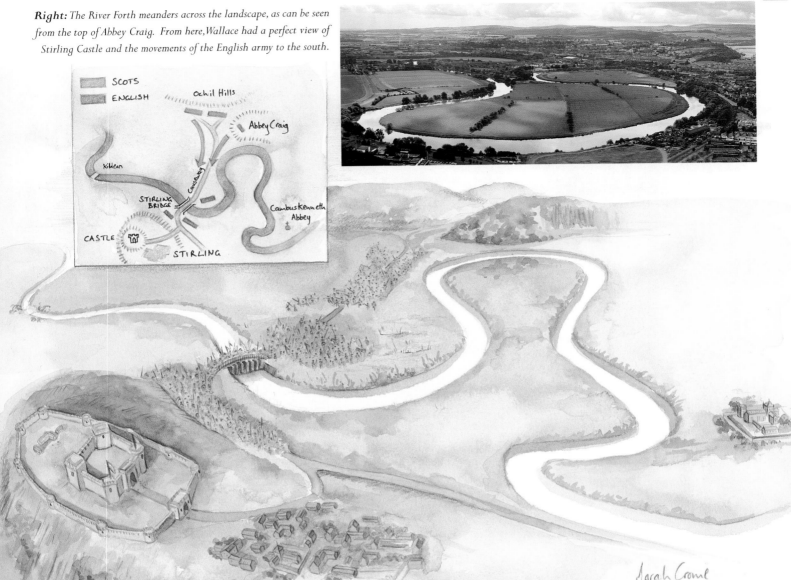

Above: The Scots engage the English across the bridge at Stirling. Most of England's army is trapped on the south side of the bridge, unable to fight.

Warenne needed no more persuading and he ordered that the next day, September 11, the vanguard led by Cressingham would make its way across the bridge. On the other side of the river the two leaders prepared their men for battle which, for them, could not come soon enough.

As first light dawned, Wallace climbed the Abbey Craig to survey the scene, whilst Murray and the army waited lower down on the slopes of the Ochil Hills. He watched as the English began to march slowly, two abreast, over the bridge. After a fair number had managed to cross, Wallace could surely not have believed his eyes as they appeared to be turning around and heading back across the bridge. Later it was learned that Warenne had overslept and had not himself given the order for them to cross, so his men all had to return. There then followed the customary knighting of young hopefuls, and inspecting of troops before Warenne finally gave the order.

Once again, the vanguard started out on its cumbersome journey across the bridge, and the Scots made ready. Wallace watched and counted as the English began to gather around the causeway to the north of the bridge. When enough of the English army had crossed over for the Scots to handle, he would give the signal for the Scots to charge down the slopes. His timing had to be perfect, allowing for the long run from the hills to the bridge head. One cannot speak highly enough of the discipline Wallace and Murray must have instilled in the Scots. The temptation to break ranks and charge the English must have been unbearable for many there. Then, at approximately 11 o'clock, over two hours of waiting was over. About 5000 English, mainly infantry, now swarmed around the causeway waiting for orders and they could not have expected what was to happen next. With one loud blow on his horn, Wallace ordered the Scots advance and with that, they hurled themselves towards the enemy, using the hill for momentum. Wallace himself followed on after them.

The strategy was for the main army to make a frontal assault on the disorientated English, while a smaller force went around behind them to seal off the north end of the bridge, trapping the English on the north side, and preventing any more coming across from the south. This the Scots succeeded in doing before their enemy could gather their wits, and what followed was a systematic slaughter as the heavily-burdened English, unused to close hand-to-hand fighting, were beaten down into the mud and bog on the banks of the River Forth. Those on horseback, Cressingham amongst them, did not stand a chance, as the Scots cruelly slashed at the horses bellies to bring down their riders. Foot-soldiers frantic to escape the mêlée tried swimming the Forth, but were drowned by the weight of their armour.

As all this happened, Warenne stood helplessly across on the other side of the river. He was hamstrung, unable to assist in any way. He had sent the longbowmen over in the vanguard, so they could not shoot their arrows across the river, and the tide was now up so the ford at Kildean was no longer accessible. The veteran English soldier could only watch as his army was annihilated. He soon realised that the day was lost and, fleeing the scene, he did not stop until he reached Berwick, riding his own warhorse to death in the process. Now leaderless, the rest of the English army also began to depart. The Scots soon realised that Warenne's banner had disappeared and that they had been victorious. Searching through the dead, they came across the obese body of Cressingham and, in an extraordinary act of disrespect to the dead, they flayed the body of this most hated man in Scotland, making souvenirs out of his skin.

Above: William Hole's depiction of the battle of Stirling Bridge, on a mural in the Scottish National Portrait Gallery.

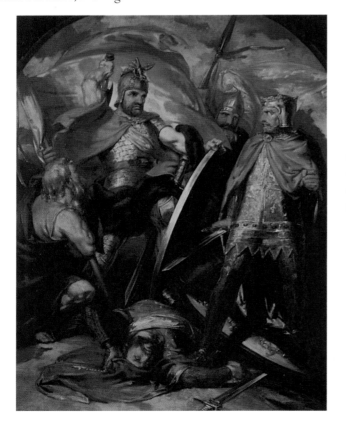

Left: Wallace defending the realm of Scotland against King Edward at the Battle of Stirling Bridge, his shield placed upon the body of Cressingham.

Above: The 220ft high National Wallace Monument stands on top of the Abbey Craig, and was begun in 1861 and completed in 1869. It is seen here from the ramparts of Stirling Castle, overlooked by a statue of Wallace's successor, Robert the Bruce.

Right: This bronze statue of Wallace stands high on a corner of the Wallace Monument overlooking the battle scene.

Although Stirling Castle was still under English occupation, it did not take long for it to fall. With the English army having fled, the garrison could not get the supplies it needed to maintain its hold there and it surrendered.

The Scots were jubilant. For the first time in over 200 years, the superior, professional army of Norman England had been outwitted and defeated by a common army of poorly equipped, ordinary folk led by two men, untrained in the art of warfare. If they thought this a miracle, then their joy was soon turned to sorrow, as they realised that although the Scots fatalities were low, their brilliant young commander Andrew Murray had been grievously wounded. Wallace was grief-stricken as he had found in Murray a great comrade in arms, and now he would have to continue as he had begun - alone.

The Guardian of Scotland

Having sustained serious injuries at Stirling Bridge, Andrew Murray was clinging on to life. With their triumph at the battle, he and William Wallace were now effectively the masters in Scotland. No one could dispute the fact that it had been a great victory - an English defeat in the open field through a pitched battle which every great lord in Scotland had tried to avoid. The English were not invincible after all, and Wallace, never taken very seriously as a guerrilla leader, was looked upon in a different light. With Murray alive but incapacitated, Wallace took it upon himself to take up the reins of power in the name of Scotland's absent king, John Balliol. His aim was to see Scotland return to some semblance of normality before England licked its wounds and returned north. Time stands still for those at war, while the rest of the world continues to trade, and Scotland's prosperity had inevitably suffered over the previous year.

Over the next few weeks, Wallace made efforts to re-establish international trade. One of the few surviving documents from this time proves that Wallace was engaged in such governmental activities. On October 11, one month after victory at Stirling, he sent a letter from the East Lothian burgh of Haddington to Lübeck, Germany, in his and Murray's name proclaiming that:

> *"Andrew de Moray and William Wallace, leaders of the army of the kingdom of Scotland, and the community of that kingdom, to.....the mayors and citizens of Lübeck and Hamburg, greeting.....we request that it be made known among your merchants that they can have safe access to all the ports of Scotland, as the kingdom, God be thanked, has been recovered by war from the power of the English. Farewell."*

This letter, originally discovered in 1829 amongst Lübeck's archives, disappeared during the World War II, but was found in Russia's archives in the 1970s. Returned to Lübeck in 1990, it has since been displayed at the National Museum of Scotland.

Throughout the autumn of 1297 Wallace also began to make preparations for the English backlash which would most likely begin in the following spring. The campaigning season was now over for that year, as armies rarely marched in the winter; besides which, the only English commander capable of taking on Wallace now was King Edward himself and he had not yet returned from the Continent. In Scotland Wallace was the only man, besides a king, who could unite the country in a common cause. He was by now adored by ordinary Scots and respected by those above himself, although nobles could scarcely countenance the prospect of taking orders from this landless laird's son.

Wallace had his mind set on another task: invasion into northern England. With winter approaching, many in Scotland would suffer starvation if depleted food stocks were not replenished. Invading armies lived off the land if they could and the Scottish countryside had lost more than its share of crops and livestock. By invading England, Wallace would not only take back what had been stolen, but would prove that Scotland was just as capable of attacking others as of defending itself. However, Wallace led his army over the border into Northumberland without Murray, and any discipline they had managed to engender into their men at Stirling Bridge was not adhered to here. There followed a particularly brutal and vindictive harrying of northern England, as Wallace seemed unable to control his army.

Left: The letter from Wallace and Murray to the merchants of Lübeck and Hamburg.

Fortunately for the Northumbrians, most of them had sufficient warning of the approaching Scots and had made for the safety of Newcastle. With no one left to assail, Wallace led his army west into Cumbria, burning deserted villages as they came upon them. They passed through Hexham, where Wallace was at least able to save the monks of the priory, giving them his own protection from the destructive obsessions of his men. Raiding as far west as Cockermouth, looting and destroying as they went, the Scots then turned north to Carlisle, its castle no longer defended by Robert Bruce's father who had been dismissed due to his son's behaviour. Nevertheless this stronghold was stoutly defended by the Bishop of Carlisle, and with deteriorating weather, Wallace decided not to waste valuable time besieging its walls.

It was now well into November and the Scots returned to Northumberland, making a fresh assault on the now returning population. Thousands of innocent English men, women and children died as the Scots pressed on with their attack to Newcastle. By now, snow began to impede their progress and, as blizzards developed, Wallace decided there was nothing more to gain and they turned north. It appears from this whole episode that Wallace did not command the full respect of those he led, whilst in England at least, and perhaps this was an early indication of his weakness: that he was not the feudal superior of his army, and that they were not obliged to follow every order.

By the time they had crossed the border in early December, Andrew Murray had already lost his fight for life. For the past two months, Wallace and Murray had acted as unofficial leaders of the Scots, without the apparent authority of any of the former Guardians or nobles of Scotland. Now these men recognised the strengths of this commoner and took an unprecedented step in Scottish history. In a ceremony held at Selkirk Abbey towards the end of 1297, William Wallace was knighted, most likely by Robert Bruce, and took on the official mantle of the Guardian of Scotland. Records of the time show his title as: '*William Wallace, Guardian of the kingdom of Scotland and commander of its army, in the name of the famous prince the lord John, by God's grace illustrious king of Scotland, by consent of the community of that kingdom.*' This was not some ethereal title and, at a time when position at birth meant everything, this ordinary man was regent of his country with all the power that it brought. However, Wallace was not a king and he would keep his position for as long as he made no mistakes. Critical eyes watched him carefully.

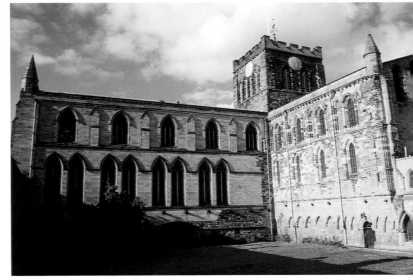

Above: Hexham Abbey, Northumberland, was attacked by Wallace's unruly army.

Left: The site of Selkirk Abbey. A plaque commemorates the place where William Wallace was knighted and proclaimed Guardian of Scotland.

At the beginning of 1298, Wallace was making his own appointments, the most notable of which was the choice of William Lamberton as the Bishop of St. Andrews. Prior to this, Lamberton had been chancellor of Glasgow Cathedral, so this was a significant promotion for him. He was a fierce patriot and known to have taken up the sword himself at times so, for Wallace, he was just the man to make sure that the all-important Church kept its full weight behind the fight for independence. Wallace also rewarded his friends for their support, and a charter issued in March confirmed Alexander Scrymgeour, he who had held the siege of Dundee, to be constable of that city.

Scotland had now enjoyed a few months of normality, but that was soon to be shattered with the news that Edward had now returned from his campaigning in Flanders. Over the next two months he would systematically move his seat of government to York which was to become the capital of England for the next six years - a suitable place to plan his subjugation of Scotland.

Above: St. Andrews, the ecclesiastical centre of Scotland in medieval times, seen from the cathedral ruins.

Right: As Guardian, Sir William Wallace used Balliol's seal, showing that he represented the king.

Falkirk – England's Revenge

King Edward found a new lease of life following his inconclusive campaign in Flanders. Scotland was an easy target and he was very businesslike in his approach to its conquest. What distinguished this most able king from his nobles was his thoroughness in preparation for war. He took nothing for granted and could never be accused of complacency, so when it came to planning his military offensives, he considered every eventuality.

Throughout the spring of 1298, Edward began to raise his army. Despite the fervour of anti-Scottish feeling throughout England since Wallace's ferocious invasion of the northern counties, most of Edward's 12,000 infantry were in fact Welsh recruits. In addition, Edward had also amassed an impressive 2,500 heavy cavalry. To feed his army, the English king would not depend on the land for sustenance. Instead, he made Carlisle a base for supplies and ordered ships with food and wine to sail up the east coast. During this time Edward held parliaments at York, to which he had summoned certain Scottish nobles, and it is to Wallace's credit that none of them made an appearance.

Scotland's Guardian had also been making preparations for the arrival of Edward's army. In an unprecedented development, Wallace had created his own system for recruiting men which dispensed with the traditional feudal methods. The whole of Scotland was split into military districts and all men between the age of sixteen and sixty were simply conscripted into the army. As an extreme measure, Wallace ordered that gallows be set up in all towns across the country to punish those who did not comply with orders. In one situation, Wallace himself supervised several hangings in Aberdeen as an example to others. Although he had no military training, the theory by which Wallace structured the Scottish army reflects his classical education: to create an effective chain of command, he drew his inspiration from ancient Rome, making *quaternions* (a fifth man) command every 4 men, *decurions* command every 9 men, *centurions* command every 99 men, all the way up to *chiliarchs* commanding 999 men. Inevitably, all this led to resentment from the nobles who were effectively prevented from raising their own vassals as the new regime went straight over their heads.

Route of English army - June/July 1298

Falkirk ✕✕
Leith
Linlithgow
Kirkliston
Lauder
Roxburgh
Edward's supply ships
Alnwick
Newcastle
Carlisle (supply base)
York

✕✕ Site of Battle

Above: Scorched earth: a lone English soldier looks out across a burnt and barren landscape. The invading army expected to feed off the land, so the Lothians were laid waste by the fleeing population.

With expectations that the English army would march in June, Wallace initiated a scorched earth operation throughout southeast Scotland. It was predicted that Edward would take the route up through Berwickshire so this county along with Lothian were evacuated and the people were sent north to safety. Every town was destroyed and the land was burnt to a cinder. Edward could not expect his troops to live solely off their own supplies.

As this went on the morale of England was being raised by more vigorous propaganda against Scotland, but particularly Wallace. In one instance, he was portrayed as *"...an ogre of unspeakable depravity who skinned his prisoners alive, burned babies and forced the nuns to dance naked for him."* The King of England would bring him to his knees and crush Scotland in the process. It is an interesting fact that at no time did Edward attempt to negotiate with Wallace, an act which would have been beneath his dignity.

Scotland's Guardian was a base-born man who may have proven his worth against the pride of England but he was not to be served with offers of peace, only by the hangman's noose. By contrast, in future years Robert Bruce would be readily accepted back into Edward's peace and forgiven for being misguided.

On June 25 1298, the English set out from York on their journey north. They must have been surprised at the extent of devastation as they marched through the Borders towards Edinburgh. There was no sign of Wallace or his army who had fallen back towards central Scotland, primarily to hold the English ahead of the River Forth crossing, but also to allow Edward's army to tire and sicken through a land devoid of food and shelter. Their supply ships had failed to materialise at Berwick or Leith due to bad weather or acts of piracy and, for two weeks, Edward's army suffered near-starvation, as they scoured the land for what precious little nourishment they could find.

Dirleton Castle (left) and Hailes Castle (below) were both attacked by the Bishop of Durham while the English army waited for supplies to arrive by sea, prior to the Battle of Falkirk.

Then, as the army camped at Kirkliston just west of Edinburgh, one ship eventually made it through. However, to Edward's dismay, it carried practically no food, but several hundred barrels of wine! Deciding that giving his troops this was better than nothing, the wine was distributed amongst the army with dire consequences. Alcohol and the stomachs of ravenous men is a lethal combination and before long fighting broke out between some Welsh and English soldiers. Edward seemed to be losing control of his army, whose morale was now so low that he considered abandoning the campaign.

However, fortunes can suddenly change and for Edward, on July 21, good fortune smiled upon him. Anthony Bek, the Bishop of Durham, had accompanied Edward as one of his cavalry commanders and had been sent on a mission to bring down the Lothian castles of Dirleton, Hailes and Tantallon. They were known to be occupied by Scots, and Edward had ordered their destruction. At first, Bek's men had trouble sustaining a siege due to their continuing hunger, but then one of the ships carrying food docked at Dunbar and they were able to press on their attack with renewed vigour. All three castles yielded, were burned to the ground and Bek returned to the main army. He arrived to see Edward in high spirits: more supply ships had made it through to Leith and the entire Scots army had been spotted east of Falkirk. Within one day the desperate situation had reversed itself and there was at once a clamour for action. Edward ordered an immediate advance towards the enemy although it was too late in the day for any action. They reached Linlithgow by dusk where the army camped down for the night. Everyone had to be prepared for battle by sunrise and so all men were required to sleep in their armour, or next to their horses.

All looked promising for Edward the next day, but in the still of the night those near to the king were awakened by cries of agony. Whilst Edward had been sleeping, his war horse had grown nervous and trampled him, breaking several of his ribs. Writhing with pain but determined to lead his army, the king was lifted into his saddle the next morning as if nothing had happened. At first light the army broke camp and headed towards Falkirk. As the sun lit up the countryside ahead of them, there was immediate excitement as a glint of armour appeared on a ridge in the distance. It was a small patrol of Scots horse which made a quick retreat, but the English had sniffed their quarry. Keen that things be done properly, Edward ordered a halt to celebrate Mass and then they advanced.

Battle was joined at Falkirk on July 22, 1298, though the exact location is not certain. All tangible evidence has been lost due to land development over the centuries, and the landscape is not as distinctive as that around Stirling to make contemporary written evidence unequivocal. The most likely site seems to have been just south of Falkirk and, when the English approached, they saw Wallace deploying his troops on a rising slope with a wood, known as Callendar Wood, directly behind him. Why the victor of Stirling Bridge should have chosen to face the English in this location is a mystery. We would not have expected a guerrilla leader to turn and fight the English with very little natural protection. The main reason for this was probably that Wallace had intended to attack Edward as his starving army retreated, an event which very nearly happened. He must have been taken by surprise at the sudden English advance towards them at Falkirk. Wallace did not wish to fight a pitched battle with Edward, but what would it have meant for the Guardian of Scotland if he had turned and fled?

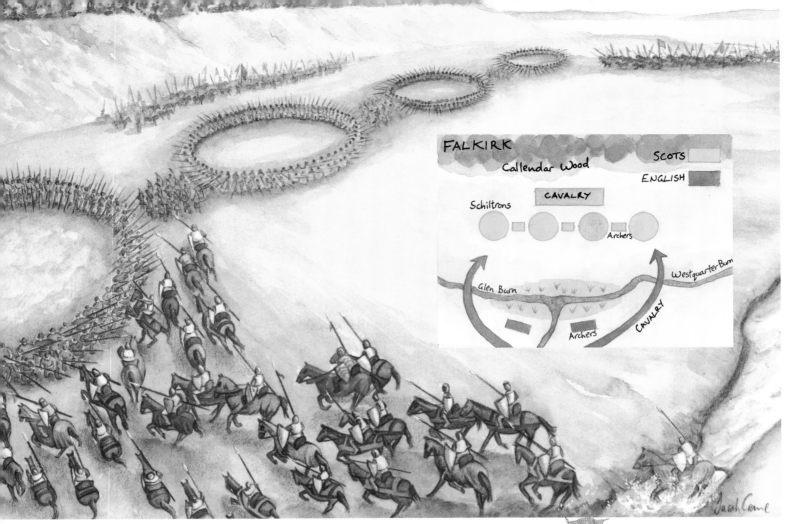

Falkirk

SCOTS

ENGLISH

Callendar Wood

CAVALRY

Schiltrons

Archers

Glen Burn

Westquarter Burn

Archers

CAVALRY

Despite his drive to recruit more men, Wallace still had considerably fewer than the English. Many of them came from the west, notably Galloway and the Hebrides. Throughout the spring he had developed his own battle formation known as the *schiltron* and at Falkirk he put this into practice. In appearance it could be described as a giant hedgehog - a circular formation of about 2,000 men each with 12—foot long spears pointing outwards, and around each of these formations was a ring of stakes, roped tightly together. These rings must have been reminiscent of arenas in which wrestling and dancing took place when people gathered in their villages, for Wallace is said to have remarked to his men that *"I have brought you to the ring, now dance if you can"*. He drew up four of these schiltrons between which he placed his archers, armed only with short bows, under Sir John Stewart. As usual, the support of the nobles had been patchy, but to the rear of the schiltrons was John Comyn with 1,000 light cavalry. The fundamental difference between tactics at Falkirk and Stirling Bridge was that the Scots took a defensive, not an offensive, position.

Edward ordered the vanguard under the Earls of Lincoln and Hereford to advance and as battle commenced it became clear why Wallace had chosen his ground. As the 600—strong armoured horse thundered towards the Scots, they found themselves pulling up sharply. Had the English checked out the

Above: The English begin their relentless attack on the Scots' schiltrons at Falkirk, but the battle was not won until the deadly longbow shattered the circular formations.

Left: The Bishop of Durham leads one of the cavalry charges at the Battle of Falkirk.

terrain, they would have discovered the Westquarter Burn, opening out into a loch directly in front them before the land began to slope upwards towards the Scots. These obstacles served in slowing down the cavalry, but did not stop them altogether. The vanguard soon gathered its wits and veered off to the left, splashing across the burn to reach the Scots right flank. The defenders held firm as the terrifying English horse hurled themselves towards the spears, throwing lances and axes into the schiltrons. As this attack continued, a second cavalry division under Bishop Anthony Bek approached, crossing the opposite side of the burn and attacking the Scots left flank. At this attack from two directions, John Comyn and the Scots light horse panicked and fled into the woods behind them.

Whatever Wallace had intended for his own limited cavalry was now lost to him. The English very quickly cut through the Scots bowmen who did not stand a chance, being unprotected between the schiltrons. However effective the English horse proved to be, it was not they who decided the outcome of the battle: it was Edward's deadliest weapon - the longbow. The Welsh now began dropping their famous arrows by the thousand on the disintegrating schiltrons and, as gaps began to show in the circular formations, the English infantry charged in to finish off the slaughter. Wallace himself managed to escape through the woods as did some others, but many good men fell. Of the noblemen, Sir John Stewart, MacDuff of Fife and Sir John Graham gave their lives, the latter giving his name to Grahamston in Falkirk itself.

The whereabouts of some nobles, particularly Robert Bruce, is uncertain. Blind Harry's poem has him fighting for the English and later returning to Wallace for forgiveness. However, none of the contemporary English accounts show Bruce to have been present at all on either side, and he seems too important to ignore if he had been there. We know him to have been fighting for Scotland in the southwest at about the time of the battle, but his part in Falkirk, if any, remains a mystery.

So what of Wallace, and where did his failure at Falkirk leave him now?

The gravestone of Sir John Stewart (above) and the tomb of Sir John Graham (left) in Falkirk parish churchyard. Both were buried here following the disastrous Battle of Falkirk.

The Fight Continues

The English might have won the Battle of Falkirk, but their summer invasion of 1298 was a failure. Edward had not been able to continue his march further north due to his exhausted army which got no further than Stirling even though, ironically, there was no proud Scots army to defend its river crossing. After several days rest in the ancient town, Edward ordered the retreat and the long march south began. He marched his men down through the southwest, to find all of Ayrshire deserted and laid waste by Robert Bruce, who himself had disappeared into the hills. It seems very unlikely in these circumstances that Bruce could have fought on the English side at Falkirk, only to burn the land in front of them immediately afterwards. As Edward prepared to leave Scotland he attacked Lochmaben Castle, stronghold of the Bruces, no doubt to teach the young Earl of Carrick a lesson. When the army reached Carlisle at the beginning of September they discovered it had been raided of its supplies, hence continuing the shortage of food for the army. However, Edward promised to gather his strength once again, and finish next year what he had started.

Scotland had won a reprieve thanks to the seasons of the year. If military campaigns continued regardless of bad weather, then England's grip on Scotland would have been relentless. Edward had won the battle but he had not yet won the war. Scotland's situation, though, could not be more dire. They had held off the English, but at what cost to the land and the people? Southern Scotland was devastated and all but a few had suffered some personal loss at the Battle of Falkirk. If Scotland's leaders had learned one thing it was that they would never face England in the field again unless they were certain of victory; and they did not do so for another 16 years. For Sir William Wallace, there was only one course of action: to resign the Guardianship, which he seems to have done voluntarily. His position had depended on complete success, and failure at Falkirk had ended his period at the top. He knew now that he could never depend on the support of Scotland's hereditary leaders, though he never sought revenge on those who had let him down in battle. He had achieved far more in the time before being honoured with knighthood, and he was eager to return to the guerrilla warfare at which he excelled and where he relied on no one but the men at his back.

Left: The ruins of Lochmaben Castle, the main Bruce family seat in Annandale.

Route of English army after Falkirk 1298

Throughout the late summer of 1298 all was not lost in Scotland and in fact only East Lothian continued to remain in English hands. The effective failure of Edward's campaign that year brought about a renewed confidence amongst Scotland's leaders, as they realised that victory in a pitched battle was not the only means of winning a war. Wallace officially stood down as Guardian and two men were elected in his place. They represented the two most powerful families in Scotland and as joint Guardians they would in theory unite the whole country. But Robert Bruce and John Comyn could not bear the sight of each other, Comyn being John Balliol's nephew and a hot-headed character. Nevertheless, both Guardians acted in the name of the abdicated king, as Wallace had done, and for a while the partnership was successful.

When Edward returned to England, he decided to put an end to John Balliol's three-year captivity in the Tower of London. He released him into the Pope's custody, which meant he could exile him and be rid of him forever without resorting to regicide. Balliol saw out the rest of his days in the family's ancestral home near Cambrai in Picardy.

At this time Scotland decided to turn its attention to international diplomacy, with the objective of persuading other countries to apply pressure on Edward to stop his campaign. Wallace's friend Bishop Lamberton had persuaded the young patriot to take on a new rôle for his country and lead a mission to France and Rome. Before beginning this Wallace continued to wage his own war, harrying the English in the Lowlands where he could, and stopping much needed supplies getting through to castle garrisons. The new Guardians also decided that an attack on the English-occupied Lowlands was timely.

However, the Bruce/Comyn relationship was barely holding together. They had joined forces with other earls and barons in an attempt to assail Roxburgh Castle, an attack which ended in failure. In disarray, they retreated to Peebles, there holding a council which degenerated from bickering into a violent outburst. An English spy had slipped into this meeting and documented what followed. It appears that the bitterness felt by some nobles over being sidelined under Wallace's Guardianship had been festering below the surface. Sir David Graham had demanded that, as Sir William Wallace was leaving the country without the permission of the Guardians, his land and goods should be forfeit. Sir Malcolm Wallace was amongst Robert Bruce's following and insisted that no one had the right to take his younger brother's possessions. According to the spy *"the two knights gave the lie to each other and drew their daggers…And since Sir David Graham was of Sir John Comyn's following, it was reported to Comyn that a fight had broken out. Comyn leapt at Bruce and seized him by the throat."*

It seemed that the two Guardians would never get on and, from 1299 onwards, William Lamberton was made chief Guardian to stand between them. The Bishop of St. Andrews wasted no time in asserting his new authority and made sure that all aggression was directed positively. He suggested that Bruce return to the southwest and attempt to take Lochmaben and Annan castles back from the English, while Comyn should return north to deal with a rebellious kinsman. Alexander Comyn, the Earl of Buchan's brother, had joined forces with one Lachlan MacRuarie and was invading Argyll. It was a civil disturbance which Lamberton knew they could well do without, and John Comyn's departure north to deal with it would keep him away from Bruce. A division of troops under Sir John de Soule s was despatched north to besiege Stirling castle, still in English hands. Lamberton himself remained in the south with Sir Ingram de Umfraville whom he appointed as Sheriff of Roxburgh, and Sir Robert Keith who was created Warden of Ettrick Forest. Together they guarded the main routes from the border.

Left: The ruins of the Cross Kirk in Peebles, one of the few remaining buildings there from the time of the War.

*Left: The siege of Caerlaverock
Castlle by the English in 1300.*

The Scots were soon alerted to the news that Edward was on his way to relieve the siege of Stirling. Lamberton mobilised his men in the Forest and sent word to the other Guardians to gather at Tor Wood, south of Stirling. In fact, Edward was having his own problems in northeast England, as many vassals refused to serve in his Scottish campaigns. The threat of an English army never materialised and the Scots successfully starved out the English garrison at Stirling Castle.

An uneasy peace

In the summer of 1299, while Lamberton kept the restless lords of Scotland busy, Wallace set sail for France. The details of his mission are lacking, but we know he had reached Paris with five other knights before the thirteenth century was out. The French king, Philip IV, had agreed a truce with England in the previous year allowing Edward to concentrate on his Scottish assault without the threat of French retaliation. If Wallace could persuade Philip to honour the terms of the Auld Alliance, Edward's own borders would not be so secure. Wallace spent a year in France, during which time he served in Philip's army fighting in English-occupied Guienne. He appeared to achieve some success with the French king who, in November, attempted to instigate a truce between England and Scotland. Edward, however, refused to co-operate.

Throughout 1300 relations between the Guardians remained difficult. John Comyn suddenly declared that he could no longer serve alongside Bishop Lamberton. Despite this, it was not Comyn who stood down, but Robert Bruce. Much of Bruce's career was marked by dramatic developments in his personality and at about this time, he seems to have become disheartened

with his country's predicament, and more concerned with events in his own territory. Bruce was replaced by Sir Ingram de Umfraville, a Comyn sympathiser, and returned to his earldom of Carrick. The Comyns were attempting to gain the support of the men of Galloway, an independent people who cared little for the national cause and were more inclined to wage war on Bruce's Carrick lands to the north. Bruce felt he would soon be needed there.

The English king had succeeded in raising his army for a Scottish campaign in the summer of 1300. But Edward did not command the full respect of his nobles and their support was on condition that they were required for no longer than two months. In June they assembled at Carlisle for an invasion of the southwest and marched towards Caerlaverock, supported by a fleet of ships in the Solway. They took the castle with ease and continued towards Kirkcudbright, where Edward was met by John Comyn and the Earl of Buchan. They attempted to negotiate with Edward in a deal that would guarantee their support if John Balliol was restored to the throne and all English lands withdrawn from Scots were returned to them. Edward would not hear of such terms and sent them away. He continued his march unhindered until he reached the River Cree where the Comyns and their forces stood in an attempt to hold the crossing. However, there was no battle. One sight of the advancing English caused panic amongst the Scots, as it had at Falkirk under the same commander, and they turned and fled into the marshes. The English infantry pursued them, capturing Sir Robert Keith and others in the process. They were all sent to English prisons.

Above: The ruins of Caerlaverock Castle on the flooded marshes of the Solway Firth.

Yet despite his show of strength, Edward's campaign failed yet again. By the end of August, he had returned to Caerlaverock having lost the support of his barons. They had promised him only two months and now they began to break away from Edward's host. The English king returned home and, by October 1300, had agreed to a seven-month truce with the Scots, under more pressure from King Philip of France.

Meanwhile Wallace was making an impression at the French Court and, continuing his journey on the Continent, he reached Rome carrying with him a recommendation from Philip to his representatives at the Vatican: *"Philip, by the grace of God, King of the French, to my agents, appointed to the Roman Court. We command you to request the supreme Pontiff to hold our loved William the Waleis, of Scotland, knight, recommended to his favour, in those things which with him he has to despatch."* If the Pope could condemn England's behaviour and her attempts to take over Scotland's Church which was, after all, a 'special daughter' of Rome, then Edward could not ignore it. However, before Wallace had even left Scotland in the previous year, the Pope had already sent an edict to Edward stating that: *"the realm of Scotland belongs to the Roman church and it is not lawful for you to dominate it by force and to subjugate it to your rule".* It made it clear that at no time in history had Scotland come under English sovereignty, a fact persistently ignored by Edward. In order to prove the Pope wrong, he would work tirelessly on his legal justifications for coveting Scotland.

At the turn of 1301, the Scots decided that the idea of joint Guardianship was no longer workable, so the three acting Guardians, Bishop Lamberton, John Comyn and Ingram de Umfraville stood down and were once again replaced by one man, namely John de Soules. He was a rare commodity, having no family allegiances on either side of the power struggle, and having fought consistently for the Scots cause. As this was going on, Edward was sorting out his own problems in England. He had managed to assemble his nobles and held a parliament at Lincoln cathedral, one result of which was a letter to the Pope which stated that Edward's war with Scotland was a domestic affair and therefore no concern of the Holy Church of Rome.

By the end of May 1301 the truce was over and Scotland braced itself for a fresh assault. The new Guardian, de Soules, began to organise the resistance when the Scots learned that Edward was planning a double attack. Throughout the summer, two vast armies gathered at Berwick and Carlisle in readiness for Edward's sixth invasion.

Edward's relentless grip

The King of England's campaign of 1301 began in July. As the previous year's assault on the southwest had failed, Edward would now try a different approach. This area, where most of the Scots power had accumulated, was still the main target but the principal tactic would be a pincer movement. The army based at Carlisle would be led by the Prince of Wales towards Dumfries, while the army at Berwick would make its way along the Tweed and up towards central Scotland, with Edward at its head. There he would hold the Highlands and Lowlands apart and move south to trap the Scots between himself and his son's southern army. Although the plan demonstrated Edward's flair for strategy, it was less than effective in reality. The Scots, under de Soules, had watched both armies closely. Whilst remaining out of sight in Dumfriesshire, they had succeeded in terrorising the English flanks without making a direct challenge to either army. If Edward had not achieved his main objective of crushing the Scots army, his campaign of 1301 was certainly more successful than the previous year. They had succeeded in bringing down specific targets, such as Bothwell and Turnberry castles. The latter had been held by Robert Bruce, as it was the seat of his earldom, but he eventually abandoned it to the Prince of Wales' forces.

Most significantly, the English invasion had survived long enough for them to spend the winter months occupying Scotland. Edward and his son retreated to the royal manor at Linlithgow where the English king began building a castle. While thus engaged, he received envoys from Philip of France who successfully persuaded him to adopt yet another truce, to run throughout 1302. This time, Edward was better placed to accept it as he was in a position of strength, and he could use the extra time to consolidate his grip on the Scots without engaging in aggressive warfare. Then, on February 16 1302, an unexpected prize came Edward's way: the submission of Robert Bruce.

Ever since he had resigned the Guardianship, Bruce had become discontented with the national cause. Now further events contributed to his desertion to the English side and they involved John Balliol. The Scots had almost been too successful at fighting their own corner at the Vatican. Wallace had already left Rome, but subsequent envoys had managed to destroy the claims over Scotland made by Edward in his letter following the Lincoln Parliament. Not only that, but they had won the release of Balliol from papal custody. Bruce feared that his position would weaken if Balliol returned home with a French army, an event which had already been rumoured. He now found himself in the same situation as his father and grandfather had been in before him. He knew the Scots could not defeat Edward in these circumstances and the survival of his family's claims became a priority.

Above: *Linlithgow Palace stands on the site of the earlier castle built by King Edward I in the early fourteenth century.*

Right: *'The Belfry' arrives at the siege of Bothwell by the English in 1301.*

Another motivation for Bruce's conversion was marriage to his second wife, Elizabeth de Burgh. As daughter of the Earl of Ulster, an ally of Edward, she was close to the English Court and the wedding may even have taken place at Linlithgow in the spring, where Edward was residing. Although the marriage had approval from all sides, it was not simply a marriage of convenience, as the couple's devotion to each other in the years ahead proved.

Throughout 1302, fortune continued to favour Edward, due mainly to international events. The support for Scotland achieved by numerous diplomatic successes over the years, was now all but reversed. In July, King Philip's army had been humiliated at Courtrai in Flanders, in a situation similar to that at Stirling Bridge. An inferior Flemish army of infantry had utterly destroyed a proud host of French armoured horse, and Philip would not recover his military or diplomatic strength for some time to come. The Pope, who was in disagreement with Philip, was now reluctant to support Scotland which was an ally of France. What the Scots feared most was that with France militarily hamstrung, they would call a truce between themselves and England, allowing Edward to turn his complete fire on Scotland with no threat from across the Channel. The Scots moved quickly sending an impressive delegation to Paris in attempts persuade Philip not to treat with Edward. By this time, Wallace had returned to Scotland and with boundless energy continued his own guerrilla war as if he had never left.

Wallace was not alone in his fight and despite Edward's heavy presence in the Lowlands throughout the winter, other Scots were also active. The six-month truce was over in November 1302 and Edward ordered the gathering of a new army from England which would march north in May 1303. But before that, Edward sent out a small force into the Lowlands to assess the capabilities of Scots' resistance, and where it was likely to be strongest. They could not have received a more direct answer when, on February 23, they were attacked by a large detachment

Above: *Robert the Bruce is shown on the Seton Armorial with his second wife, Elizabeth de Burgh.*

of Scots cavalry. The Scots, led by John Comyn and Simon Fraser of Oliver Castle surprised the English at Roslin, 7 miles south of Edinburgh. Many were killed and the English commander Sir John Segrave was captured. However, events at Roslin were not a great success for Scots, and their captive was eventually rescued. Nevertheless they hailed it as a victory in the hope of raising morale before Edward's next campaign.

By the beginning of May, all of King Edward's preparations for the swift and final annihilation of Scottish resistance were in place. Once again, he went to extraordinary lengths to cater for every eventuality. A remarkable feat was the delivery of three prefabricated pontoon bridges, built in Kings Lynn and floated up the east coast into the Firth of Forth. These would enable the English Army to cross the River Forth, downstream of Stirling, straight into Fife. Also brought by sea were Edward's elaborate siege engines, to be used against all strongholds that did not submit, for he did not intend to waste time starving out Scottish garrisons. His army marched from Newcastle on May 5 and headed towards Roxburgh.

Left: *Edward I built his pontoon bridge at Kings Lynn and shipped it up to the River Forth. Here, part of Kings Lynn docks has been embellished as a film location.*

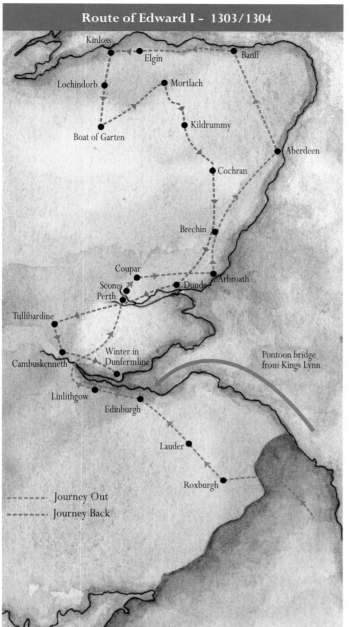

Route of Edward I – 1303/1304

Kinloss
Elgin
Banff
Lochindorb
Mortlach
Boat of Garten
Kildrummy
Aberdeen
Cochran
Brechin
Coupar
Scone
Dundee
Arbroath
Perth
Tullibardine
Winter in Dunfermline
Pontoon bridge from Kings Lynn
Cambuskenneth
Linlithgow
Edinburgh
Lauder
Roxburgh

- - - Journey Out
- - - Journey Back

What followed was almost a repeat of England's victory march of 1296, just after the sack of Berwick. They had not travelled far when Edward received the news he had been waiting for. Philip of France had finally decided to make peace with Edward, in a deal which renounced the French alliance with Scotland. The agreement gave Edward the lands in Aquitaine for which he had been fighting, and also the betrothal of Philip's eight-year old daughter, Isabella, to the Prince of Wales. Frustratingly for the Scots, they were left out of the agreement, which killed forever the chances of John Balliol returning to his throne. Edward continued his self-righteous parade to the north as the army advanced through Roxburgh and on towards Linlithgow, crossing the Forth east of Scots-held Stirling. For four months the English pressed on with their intimidating march, through Aberdeen, reaching Kinloss Abbey on the shores of the Moray Firth on September 14.

Edward turned south taking an inland route to Kildrummy, then towards Brechin, where he had accepted the surrender of Balliol seven years previously, and onwards to Dunfermline where he finally called a halt to his journey. It was November, and he decided, once again, to spend the winter in Scotland. While all this was going on, the Scots nobles had received a communication from their envoys in France. It urged them to consider making peace with Edward, stating that: *"If the King of England agrees to a truce, you should likewise agree…"* It assured the Scots at home that the French king would do everything in his power to create peace for Scotland. Whatever the nobles thought of this, they saw it as their cue to surrender and, in February 1304, many did just that.

Right: *At Kinloss Abbey, Edward I finally turned south after his march through Scotland. The Abbey ruins stand today amongst more recent graves of naval and air force personnel.*

Scotland subdued

There was one person throughout all this who would never submit on any condition - William Wallace. He had remained active in Ettrick Forest, harrying where he could, but he alone was becoming a thorn in the side of those Scots who had given in. As long as he continued his personal fight with the English, the Scots could not be at peace with Edward, who would only accept the unconditional surrender of this base-born criminal. In fact, a condition of the surrender for all Scots nobles was that *"No words of peace are to be held out to William Wallace in any circumstances."* Edward held some of them personally responsible for Wallace's deliverance in order to test their loyalty. It must be added that all who did surrender were not bribed with land or title, but were simply promised Edward's protection and the right to retain their possessions.

Throughout all of this, Robert Bruce played along with Edward's plans. He continued the pretence of actively supporting the King, though he never took up arms against his countrymen, instead stalling and playing for time when he could. It was most likely Bruce's influence on Edward that led to his relative leniency when accepting the surrender of the Scottish nobles who had, after all, already submitted to him on the Ragman Roll and then turned against him. However, it was clear that Bruce was not happy with the situation, or his own deceptive behaviour and since his desertion from the national cause, two incidents had occurred which altered his outlook: firstly, the situation in France meant that John Balliol was never likely to return to Scotland and was therefore no longer a threat to the Bruce family name; secondly, with the death of his father in April 1304, Bruce was now closer to the Scottish crown than he had ever been before. King Edward watched his every move.

The Scottish surrender was not absolute. Bishop Lamberton, who was in France with the envoys, refused to accept the line that peace should be made with Edward. To this end, he sent letters to Wallace encouraging further resistance, even providing funds to aid him. Others were inspired to do likewise, and the Scottish garrison at Stirling castle, led by Sir William Oliphant, refused to surrender. As the most important fortress in Scotland, Edward was determined to get the Scots out of it. He was even delighted at the prospect of demonstrating his siege weapons. In preparation for the siege of Stirling, Edward ordered that all church roofs in Dunblane and Perth be stripped of their lead, which would be put to use during the bombardment of the castle.

The siege of Stirling marked a turning point in Edward's behaviour towards the Scots. Since the sack of Berwick, he had shown remarkable patience and a controlled sense of purpose with each yearly invasion. But now with final victory in sight he smelt blood once again and, in true Plantagenet style, began a particularly cruel and vindictive campaign against all those who opposed him. Before the siege got under way Edward demonstrated his contempt for chivalry. Oliphant had requested communication with the Guardian of Scotland, Sir John de Soules. It was the Guardian who should decide whether the castle held out or surrendered to the enemy and Edward denied Oliphant this privilege. A surrender was no good to Edward and, in the event, this Oliphant stood his ground while, for three months, Stirling castle was virtually demolished around him and his brave garrison. It was starvation which caused them to raise the white flag on 20 July but, in a savage climax to the siege, Edward refused to accept. He had not yet tried out his latest weapon - the Warwolf, perhaps a large trebuchet – and for one whole day he battered what was left of Stirling Castle.

Below: *Siege engines like this mangonel were used against the walls of Stirling Castle.*

Top: *The church at Stobo near Peebles was standing at the time when Bishop Lamberton had a manor house near the site.*

Left: *In 1304, this letter was sent by King Edward to Robert Bruce, who was outwardly supporting the English.*

Fifty Scottish defenders, including Oliphant, were brought before Edward. It was only due to the pleading of certain English commanders in admiration of the Scots effort that the king did not execute them on the spot, deciding instead to send them all to English prisons. Never again was he to be so forgiving.

Throughout the summer, as the siege of Stirling raged on, Robert Bruce continued reassessing his position. Edward's change of behaviour and his frenzied enjoyment of destruction caused the Earl of Carrick to gradually realise that this king had no right to treat Scotland or her people in this way. He also knew that, for the moment, he alone did not have the support to effectively overturn Edward. However, one month before the siege had ended, Bruce made a secret band with Bishop Lamberton. When the time was right, Bruce would claim his throne and both men would help and confide in each other to that end. To go on appearing to support Edward may have been

unprincipled, but why should the future King of Scots not be as shrewd as his English counterpart?

As Bruce made plans, Edward went about finalising his conquest of Scotland. His task, as he saw it, was nearly complete and there only remained the new administration to be set up. In February 1305 a new constitution for Scotland was arranged at Westminster. All the nobles had submitted, no castles were left in Scottish hands, the ordinary folk had been pacified and the kingdom of Scotland no longer existed, but still Edward was not happy. One man carried on the fight, and as long as William Wallace was alive, so was the torch of freedom and the potential for the people to rise up once again.

Wallace would never surrender, nor would he hide. His fate was sealed and he would be hunted down relentlessly to the very end.

The birth of a legend

Despite pressure on the nobility of Scotland to betray Wallace and hand him over to Edward, those charged with the responsibility for his capture made little effort to do so. It was an indication, as in 1296, that their submission was not whole-hearted or permanent. In fact for some it was simply a question of time before the opprtunity arose once again to throw off the English yoke. Bruce and Lamberton were already preparing themselves for this and it may have been that Wallace, in his closeness to the Bishop, was party to the pact between the two men.

Long after the surrender of nobles, Wallace remained active in and around central Scotland. His final known clash with the English came in September of 1304 when, at Bridge of Earn, he and his last remaining supporters attacked a division of cavalry who were pursuing him. The Scottish patriot remained at large until August 3, 1305, when he was betrayed by Jack Short, a servant in the pay of Sir John Menteith. Wallace had been seen in the Glasgow area and Menteith, as Sheriff of Dumbarton, ordered Short to seek him out and join his company. The arrest was made during the night at Robroyston, a farmstead to the north of Glasgow, whereupon Wallace was taken before Menteith. This Scotsman had sworn fealty to Edward, like many another and did what no other Scot was prepared to do - hand Wallace over to the English authorities. To this day the name of Menteith has been remembered for this infamous act.

Above: *Wallace's Well, Robroyston, Dunbartonshire, close to the site where Sir William Wallace was captured.*

Left: *Dumbarton Castle. Wallace is thought to have been held here before his humiliating journey to London.*

*Top: The nineteenth century painting
'The Trial of Sir William Wallace at Westminster'.*

***Above:** An eighteenth century transcript of the charges against Wallace.*

Following his capture Wallace was immediately sent to the English border. There had been no time for any rescue attempt, as Menteith had carried out his orders efficiently and by stealth. Wallace was handed over to Aymer de Valence, the Earl of Pembroke, just north of Carlisle and from there he was taken south by Sir John Segrave. Now his ordeal began and Edward had special plans for the treatment of this chief of brigands that would spare him no dignity. Strapped to a horse for two and a half weeks he suffered a humiliating journey to London. His captors paraded him through the entire length of England and as they went, the word went ahead that Wallace, the barbarous savage of the north, was on his way to face Edward's justice. He arrived in London on August 22, to an ecstatic population who were baying for blood. He was not taken to the Tower of London, but imprisoned in a simple house in Fenchurch Street.

We can only hope that the strength of character which Wallace had demonstrated throughout his life saw him through his ordeal. But however bravely he faced his predicament, he could not have been aware of how quickly his fate was approaching. The very next morning, he was taken in procession on a grand horse to Westminster Hall were he faced an immediate show trial without defence. The bizarre events continued as he was shackled and forced to wear a laurel wreath around his head, this apparently in response to his claims that one day he would be crowned at Westminster. Edward himself was not present, but he had carefully planned the proceedings. Wallace stood proudly as a list of his crimes was read out in front of him and the thronging Hall. Only when the last accusation of treason against Edward was read out did Wallace speak up. To all the other 'crimes' he admitted, although they had been carried out during a period of war throughout which both countries had been guilty of atrocities, but he vehemently denied the charge of treason. Never at any time in his life had he sworn allegiance to an English king, unlike many others in Scotland, and so could not be guilty of treason. Wallace had fought in the name of his own king and country, therefore it was not possible for him to be a traitor to England. Nevertheless, treason was the main charge of which Wallace was found guilty.

Above: *The execution of Sir William Wallace at Smithfield.*

Right: *The memorial plaque to Wallace on the wall of St. Bartholomew's Hospital, London, near where he was executed.*

No time was spent deliberating the evidence and the punishment was to be carried out at once. The details of his immediate execution were carefully read out to him. For treason, he was to be drawn behind a horse for four miles from Westminster to the Tower of London and on to the Elms at Smithfield. There, for the robberies, murders and felonies he had committed, he would be hanged, cut down while still alive, disembowelled and decapitated. For the crimes against God and the church, his heart, liver and lungs would be cast into the fire and to serve as a reminder of the fate that would meet all such traitors, his head would be set upon London Bridge. The four quarters of his body would be hung on gibbets at Newcastle, Berwick, Stirling and Perth.

Resigned to his fate, Wallace met his end with great fortitude. As the inscription beneath his statue in Aberdeen states, he was:

> "ARRAIGNED AS A TRAITOR TO THE ENGLISH KING, AMID MOCKERY AND INDIGNITY, WHICH, CONSCIOUS OF HIS INTEGRITY, HE BORE WITH DIGNIFIED COMPOSURE. ON THE 23RD AUGUST, 1305, THIS GREAT HERO WAS LED TO SMITHFIELD, AND WAS THERE PUT TO DEATH SOLELY FOR HIS LOVE OF LIBERTY, HIS EFFECTUAL RESISTANCE OF AGGRESSION AND HIS FIDELITY TO HIS NATIVE LAND."

Cut down in his prime, Wallace had worked selflessly towards ending English tyranny and one can only hope that he did not die thinking that all was lost and all his work had been in vain. There was so much more he could have achieved in life, but by some strange paradox, he in fact achieved more in death. Wallace was Edward's last obstacle to a subdued Scotland, but by making a martyr of him, Edward reversed all his own achievements. No one in Scotland had expected Wallace to be treated in this way and Edward's actions simply served to make sure that his example would never be forgotten.

The statue of Sir William Wallace in Aberdeen, erected in 1888.

Part 3. 1305 – 1314
TURNING THE TIDE

"Great was the task."

The barbaric execution of Wallace took many by surprise in Scotland. Not only did it happen suddenly but, for some, Edward had gone too far. He had thought to cow all those minded to follow Wallace's road, but that had already been done by the time of Wallace's arrest. It might have been wiser to imprison Wallace than to end his life so vindictively, for he would have been out of the way; instead, Sir William Wallace became an immortal legend to the Scots people.

Left: *The statue of Robert Bruce at Lochmaben, the ancestral seat of the Bruces in Scotland.*

By the end of August, all had gone Edward's way and steps were taken to set up a new system of government for Scotland, which was proclaimed at a Westminster parliament on September 15th 1305.

All seemed quiet north of the border, but events were stirring. Robert Bruce was becoming restless and he felt ready to follow the way prepared by Wallace, whatever fate it would lead to. He was aware of his past shortcomings, and had also been angered by the injustice of Wallace's treatment. Bruce himself had sworn fealty to Edward, had revoked it, yet had been forgiven. Whatever the risks to his own life on the path ahead, he could do no less than follow Wallace's example. But he was sure that this time things would have to be different, or Scotland would forever suffer the same perpetual cycle of

rebellion followed by subjection. He had hoped to bide his time until Edward lived no more, but in view of the present circumstances, even though Edward still had some life left in him, it was now or never.

Earlier in that year Bruce had participated in Edward's constitutional plans for the *land*, not the kingdom, of Scotland. He also maintained his band with Bishop Lamberton as they both waited for an opportunity, possibly after Edward's death, to move for independence. It is an interesting fact that upon his arrest, Wallace was found with correspondence from Bruce. We do not know the details of this, but had they planned to act together, what a spectacle it would have made. It is a tragedy that the death of Wallace was necessary for Bruce to finally make his move.

Robert Bruce and John Comyn were both to be included in the new administration for Scotland along with eight other noblemen and clergy. They had been summoned to attend the parliament at Westminster in September 1305, following the execution of Wallace. Bruce was conspicuously absent from these proceedings, perhaps deliberately keeping a low profile and signalling his displeasure at the previous month's events. Whatever Bruce's reasons, Edward knew he could not trust the Earl of Carrick and probably enlisted the support of Bruce's rivals to spy out his every move. However, Bruce and Lamberton continued moving things forward and approaches were made to John Comyn. Comyn, as the closest relative of John Balliol, was Bruce's main rival to the throne, and any action by Bruce needed the agreement of Comyn. Bruce is often unfairly accused of having only fought for a crown, whereas Wallace fought for a principal, but it must be recognised that Bruce was not acting purely out of personal ambition. He was driven by the knowledge that only a king could unite the people and lead Scotland to a lasting freedom: all other alternatives had been tried and failed.

As winter approached, the news came that Edward's condition was deteriorating badly, and it was thought that he did not have much longer to live. At this, Bruce put his proposals to Comyn in the form of a dramatic ultimatum. It stated that if Robert Bruce took the crown, John Comyn would get all the Bruce lands; or, if he preferred, Comyn should take the crown

and Bruce would be given the Comyn lands. It was a simple exchange of possessions for title. Bishop Lamberton and his clerics drew up the documents, and asked Comyn to make the decision. Comyn was too tempted by the prospects of receiving the rich Bruce estates of the southwest to be concerned with the responsibilities of becoming king, so he chose the latter option. They put their trust in each other and signed two documents, each taking a copy and hoping the other had too much to lose by thoughts of betrayal.

Unfortunately, events turned around rather quickly and Edward found new life, putting Bruce and Comyn's agreement at risk. The man most likely to weaken in these circumstances was John Comyn, Bruce's position being highly vulnerable as his name was on the document in Comyn's posession which proved his ambitions to become king. Meanwhile, Bruce continued to act on behalf of the English regime in Scotland, making regular journeys to London. Early in the following year, 1306, Bruce was making one such visit and while in his lodgings at night a messenger arrived from the Earl of Gloucester. The messenger said very little but gave Bruce a shilling, pointing to the head of Edward, and a pair of spurs, indicating that he should make a rapid departure. The warning could not have been more clear: Bruce had been betrayed and his arrest for treason was imminent. But for the timely consideration of Gloucester, Bruce would have suffered the same fate as Wallace. Edward showed no mercy now.

Below: *A messenger from the Earl of Gloucester brings a warning to Robert Bruce.*

Right: *Robert Bruce stabs John Comyn at the altar of Greyfriars church in Dumfries.*

Below: *This plaque in Castle Street, Dumfries, marks the site of Greyfriars church.*

HERE STOOD THE MONASTERY OF THE GREY FRIARS WHERE ON THURSDAY 10TH FEBRUARY 1306 ROBERT THE BRUCE AIDED BY SIR ROGER KIRKPATRICK SLEW THE RED COMYN AND OPENED THE FINAL STAGE OF THE WAR FOR SCOTTISH INDEPENDENCE WHICH ENDED VICTORIOUSLY ON THE FIELD OF BANNOCKBURN 1314
"I MAK SICCAR"
ERECTED BY THE CITIZENS OF DUMFRIES & THE SALTIRE SOCIETY.

To stay ahead of Edward and to seek out Comyn, Bruce returned home at such an urgent pace that he reached his castle at Lochmaben within five days. As chance would have it, he passed a servant of Comyn on the road to London, coming the other way. He was bearing the precious document that would seal Bruce's fate. Having dispatched the poor servant Bruce took his merchandise to confront Comyn. Clearly, that traitor had informed Edward of Bruce's intentions, but had not yet supplied the evidence. Bruce arrived at Lochmaben, where most of his family were staying. Having discovered the whereabouts of Comyn, Bruce, supported by some friends and family, made straight for him at Dumfries. With Comyn residing at his castle of Dalswinton, Bruce arranged to meet him in the town, at the church of Greyfriars. Comyn must have been surprised to see Bruce, but he may not have suspected that his double-cross had been discovered. The meeting was at first cordial and the two men decided that, for the sake of privacy from their respective parties, they would talk in front of the altar. We cannot be certain of what passed between them but once alone, Bruce must surely have challenged Comyn over breaking their agreement and his subsequent betrayal to Edward. John Comyn, who could be as equally hot-tempered as Bruce, would not have taken kindly to any insults or accusations and, before long, a bitter exchange of words developed into violent confrontation. Forgetting where they were, both men drew their daggers, but Bruce struck the first blow, felling Comyn there on the altar steps. At that, the supporters of both men rushed in, Comyn's uncle attacking Bruce who, in turn, was defended by his brother in law, Sir Christopher Seton. The Bruce party eventually got away, but Comyn had been left dying and Bruce was too shocked to be certain if he had killed him. To make sure, some of his party led by Roger Kirkpatrick returned to Greyfriars to finish the deed. To this very day, the motto of the Kirkpatrick family has been *"I mak siccar"* - 'I make sure'.

The implications of Bruce's actions that day were dire, and he knew it. He has often been accused of plotting the murder of John Comyn. Murder in any circumstances is wrong, but Bruce was a deeply religious man and would not have lured anyone into a church with the intention of killing them. Whatever his reasons, he could be certain that his life from this day forward would never be the same again. By his actions on February 10, 1306 Bruce, with the crime of sacrilegious murder around his neck, would be worthy of nothing less than excommunication but, worse than that, he would be at the mercy of Edward's wrath. There was no turning back now and Bruce had to act quickly.

A new king for Scotland

Within the hour of Comyn's death, Bruce did not delay in striking the first blow. It was vital that he acted decisively before word of his deed spread. He and his supporters made straight for the castle at Dumfries. Fortunately the English garrison had not expected a revolt by Bruce of all people, and were quickly overcome.

Nevertheless, things were off to a bad start for Scotland's king in waiting, and his prospects did not look good. England would throw its weight against him; with Comyn dead, half of Scotland would be against him and the whole of Christendom would curse him. However, all was not lost. With communications to Rome being as slow as they were, an excommunication could take weeks to implement. In this matter, endorsement of Bruce's cause from the Church of Scotland was crucial. Its spiritual, logistical and financial support would form the backbone of his campaign, and without it he was lost. With this in the forefront of his mind, Bruce headed north to seek out the Bishop of Glasgow, Robert Wishart. The old Bishop heard his confession and gladly gave Bruce his blessing.

At this time Bishop Lamberton was in Berwick playing a superficial part in Edward's Scottish council, and unaware of events on the other side of Scotland. Despite their secret band, Bruce could hardly go there to receive absolution for his sins, but he was certain that the Primate of Scotland's Church would give his whole-hearted support. Bruce sent word to him that he was about to take the kingdom and that the Bishop should be present at the inauguration at Scone. The preparations for this would take time and before then Bruce had plenty to occupy his mind. As word began to spread of his uprising, supporters came from all over the southwest to join the fight. The people of Scotland were not as war-sick as Bruce might have thought. From the immediate outset, his movements went unchallenged and there was no co-ordinated attempt by English commanders to go on the attack. They had presumed that the days of rebellion were now over. Taking advantage of this situation, Bruce sought to gain the upper hand by taking as many castles as possible around the western seaboard approaches to southern Scotland. Whoever held the strongholds at Ayr, Inverkip, Rothesay and Dunaverty on Kintyre controlled the main route for supplies up the Firth of Clyde. The latter castle had a dazzling view on each side towards the Scottish and Irish mainlands, enabling a close guard to be kept on ships leaving Ireland. All these castles were taken in the run up to Bruce's enthronement: Rothesay, by a daring attack from the sea by Robert Boyd, a veteran warrior who fought alongside Wallace and became a loyal supporter of Bruce. Interestingly, they failed to take Dumbarton Castle with Menteith, the betrayer of Wallace, securely inside and remaining loyal to Edward.

All this activity meant that Bruce was partly secure and at least in control of some of his new kingdom. Before making the journey to Scone, he stayed in Glasgow in preparation for his inaguration. Bishop Wishart had kept the suitable robes and banners safely to hand for the day that he had only dreamt would dawn. As Bruce made his way to Scone, his party was approached by a young squire, a messenger from Lamberton with word that the Bishop would steal away from Berwick if opportunity permitted. Having delivered his message, the young man immediately pledged his personal allegiance to Bruce: he was none other than James Douglas. As a boy, nine years before, Douglas had watched from the battlements of Douglas Castle as Robert Bruce turned from supporting the English to, in his words at the time, *"join my own people and the nation in which I was born"*. James and his family had been led to safety by Bruce, and Douglas hoped that one day he would fight at his side. His father was William Douglas, the great patriot who had, with Wallace, chased away the English Justiciar from Scone. He had since perished in the Tower of London and the Douglas inheritace had been given to Sir Robert Clifford. The young James had an axe to grind and would fight tirelessly alongside his king until vengence was served.

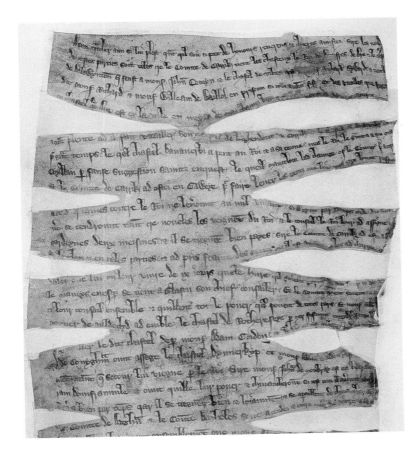

Left: *This report tells of Robert Bruce's activities immediately after John Comyn's murder. It was damaged by fire in the 18th century.*

Left: Robert the Bruce is crowned by Isabel of Buchan at Scone.

Above: The second seal of King Robert I.

On Lady Day, March 25, 1306, and with as much ceremony as the Church and his supporters could put together, the 32-year old Robert Bruce, Earl of Carrick, was created Robert I, King of Scots. It was exactly ten years to the day since Edward's first invasion of Scotland, when he attacked Wark Castle and moved on to wreak havoc in Berwick. It was also six weeks after Comyn's death at the altar of Greyfriars church, and still no word from Rome of King Robert's anticipated excommunication. The inauguration took place at the traditional location, in Scone Abbey upon the Moot Hill. Although Edward had looted the Abbey, he could never have removed the meaning of the place to all Scots. Since the days of Kenneth MacAlpin 450 years before, it had always been the ancient seat of the Kings of Scots. Despite the supposed Stone of Destiny being held at Westminster, legend has it that Henry, the Abbot of Scone had hidden the real stone from Edward and brought it out for Robert's enthronement.

Of all those present at Scone on that day, all had put their lives at risk for supporting Bruce and his cause, and most would suffer direly for their loyalty to him. Lamberton had come secretly from Berwick, and Wishart was at the forefront of the proceedings. The new king was not short of support amongst the nobles and of the earls of Scotland, Lennox, Atholl and Menteith, although not the infamous Sir John were all present.

The most notable absentee was Duncan, Earl of Fife. It was his ancient right to place the crown on the king's head, but he was only a boy and presently held in England. As all symbols of Scottish monarchy had been removed, there was no crown either, so here was a poor start for the new king. But all was not lost. A circlet of gold, which today allegedly forms the base of the Scottish crown - the oldest in the British regalia - was quickly fashioned. So who would place it upon Robert's brow? Word of the inauguration had reached Isabel, Countess of Buchan. As sister of the young Earl of Fife she could have an important rôle to play, but she faced a dilemma; as wife of the Earl of Buchan, a Comyn, she would have to defy him to take part. Her sense of patriotism took over and, leaving her husband's side, she took his fastest horse and arrived at Scone to place the new crown upon the head of her hero-king.

The festivities for Scotland's new monarch continued for some time. Another ceremony took place two days later when, on Palm Sunday, Bishop Lamberton celebrated High Mass for King Robert and, as if to underline the support of the Church, he was crowned yet again at this religious ceremony. For two hundred years Bishops had taken part in these inaugurations and they sought to maintain as many traditions as possible so that the king's position could not be reversed. It was now a simple fact that Robert Bruce was unquestionably King of Scots.

King in name only

Robert I may have been Scotland's king, but he did not yet rule his new kingdom and he had much to achieve before those he wished to rule could respect him as their leader. His country was a divided nation and, by killing John Comyn, the king himself had made the situation worse. Half the nobles would not pay homage to him and amongst the ordinary people were many who could not trust a man who had previously sworn fealty to the king of England. To them blind ambition and self-interest had been his motivation for taking the crown. Robert was the first King of Scots who would have to earn the loyalty of his subjects.

The events of the spring of 1306 inevitably caused shock and alarm beyond the borders of Scotland. Sure enough, the message of excommunication arrived from Rome, making Robert's life all but forfeit. It also took effect on family, friends and those who helped him or gave him shelter. He would no longer receive the protection of Holy Church and his title of king was proclaimed null and void. This was dire news, if not unexpected. The Scots had created a king, as was their right, but if the rest of the world turned its back on him, Scotland could not survive. From a personal point of view, Robert was racked with guilt over his deed at Greyfriars and, for the rest of his life, he would try to atone for this great sin.

In England, Edward was stunned with disbelief at the actions of Robert Bruce (for that was who he remained as far as the English Court was concerned). Edward had become suspicious of him over the last few months, but even he would not have expected sacrilege and usurpation. He had conceded much to Bruce in the past, forgiving his misguided behaviour, and this was how that upstart now repaid his kindness. The King of England had been made a fool, and the people responsible would all go the way of Wallace. Edward was consumed with more anger than ever before and, old age not withstanding, the veteran campaigner prepared to go to war yet again. Action was swift. He appointed the Earl of Pembroke, Aymer de Valence, to lead an initial force of 3000 men with specific instructions to lay waste the land and everything that lived upon it. All was to be carried out under the menacing dragon banner, which signalled that no quarter was to be given and that the army was free from any bounds of chivalry. With the exception of churchmen, hanging without trial was the fate for all men who had collaborated with Bruce, whatever their rank. Pembroke was certainly the appropriate man to carry out these orders for he was John Comyn's brother-in-law and on his route north was joined by many of Comyn's family or his sympathisers. Edward would follow with the Prince of Wales and another army once the carnage was under way.

As Armageddon loomed over King Robert, he made preparations for the defence of his new realm as best he could. The recurring nightmare of the last ten years was about to begin all over again - this time with Bruce taking the place of Wallace. But history could not be allowed to repeat itself and Scotland's new leader would have to succeed where others had failed. He traversed the country mobilising support and taking over some castles in the north to cover his back during the inevitable frontal assault. Apart from his home ground in the southwest, much of the south was enemy territory, so Lothian was out of bounds as usual. The Church was eager to participate where it could, and not just in matters spiritual. Bishop Wishart was active around his Glasgow diocese, taking Kirkintilloch castle with no trouble. This was partly due to the employment of siege weapons, an unusual luxury for the Scots, but on this occasion specially made from wood supplied by the English themselves: the bell tower of Glasgow Cathedral would have to wait for its repairs! Wishart then headed east and in Fife *comme homme de guerre*, like a man of war, he overcame Cupar castle.

Above: *Slezer's seventeenth century drawing of St Mungo's Cathedral, Glasgow.*

Left: The Arms of Aymer de Valence, Earl of Pembroke.

Unfortunately for the crusading Bishop, his period of adventure was to be short-lived, as Pembroke was hot on his heels. The English fighting machine had blazed its way up through the Lowlands and by the start of June had reached Perth, taking it effortlessly. Wishart was captured whilst still in Fife and Bishop Lamberton was taken at Scotlandwell near the town of Kinross, where he had been encouraging the people to join their king. Both the head of Scotland's Church and the Bishop of Glasgow were spared the penalty of death owing to their holy positions, but they did not escape abuse and punishment. They were sent south in chains, along with Abbot Henry of Scone, to spend years of incarceration in England. Although the loss of these powerful

men and their friendship was a severe blow to Robert's morale, co-operation from the Church was already well-established and assured for all time. As Pembroke continued his iron grip on Scotland, all eyes turned towards King Robert as they awaited his next move. By now he had consolidated his support in the central Highlands but, with little over 4000 men, still could not match Pembroke's forces, which had been doubled with recruits from north of the border.

Upon hearing of Pembroke's occupation of Perth, the king headed south and, in the late afternoon of June 18, approached its walls. With no siege weaponry to hand Robert threw down the gauntlet and challenged Pembroke to come out and fight. He knew Pembroke and, holding him in high esteem, expected a challenge to be respectfully met. However, Aymer de Valence was not his own man on this occasion and declined the challenge, claiming it was too late in the day to do battle, but he would comply tomorrow. The new King of Scots naïvely thought he understood his adversaries, and perhaps did not realise how determined Pembroke was to carry out Edward's orders. He withdrew to the north of the town and camped along the River Almond, near Methven. Fully expecting his challenge to be met the next day, Robert did not think to secure his camp in any way. He had chosen a safe spot on high ground, with a nearby wood for cover, but his men slept haphazardly and unprotected.

The River Almond, near Methven, Perthshire, where King Robert may have camped before his ambush by the Earl of Pembroke.

Right: *The Earl of Pembroke falls upon the unsuspecting Scots camp at the so-called Battle of Methven. Most who were not captured or killed fled the scene, including King Robert himself.*

The flight west

Before the next day had dawned, the king's camp was suddenly wakened by the approach of thundering hooves and the shouts of men out for blood and revenge. Pembroke had left the safety of Perth in the dead of night and fallen upon the unsuspecting king. There was chaos and panic as Robert and his scattered force tried to gather their armour and horses in the half-light, while English cavalry continued its assault. The king himself made it to his horse and was surrounded by his faithful supporters. They tried to fight their way out as the English, in their desperation to capture Robert, unhorsed the king no less than three times. But for the strength and courage of his friends, his fight would surely have ended there and then. King Robert faced the awful truth of the situation and realised that they could not win here and that if Scotland were to survive, he must desert the field and leave his army to fight their way out as best they could. With a small group gathered around him, they cut their way through the English ranks in a tight formation and headed west.

Although described as a battle, what happened at Methven was little more than a dishonourable rout. Pembroke had shown a complete contempt for the knightly code and had given Robert a stern signal of the style of warfare he would now be forced to fight.

The Battle of Methven had taught King Robert a timely lesson. It was as well for his cause that he had been forced to withdraw, humiliating though the circumstances were. If he had fought Pembroke and won, he would have gone on to face the main English army, commanded by Edward, and undoubtedly lost. The day when the Scots would have the ability to face the English across an open field was years away, and there was much to do in preparation for that day. It seemed an impossible task and, as the king fled from disaster, his mind must have been in turmoil. Robert had left many friends behind, all of them loyal supporters who were willing to die for Scotland. However justified his reasons, he, their king, had left them in the hands of the English. Any who did not escape were certain to die, and most significantly amongst them were Sir Christopher Seton, the king's own brother-in-law, who was the first to swear fealty to him at Dumfries, and brave Sir Alexander Scrymgeour, the king's standard bearer. In due course they were mercilessly hanged and beheaded. Only one person, a young man of noble rank, was spared and he was Thomas Randolph, King Robert's own nephew through his mother's first marriage. He was too much of a catch to dispense with, and was converted to the English cause.

However, all was not lost and Robert could be thankful for the company of those who did escape with him: James Douglas who was never far from the king's side; Gilbert de la Haye, the High Constable and chief protector of the king's person; Neil Campbell, Chief of his clan; and Edward Bruce, the king's brash younger brother. Behind them were a few hundred survivors who made their way in the leading group's general direction. It was not a long ride into the mountainous protection of Argyll, and they galloped swiftly down the wide and lush Strathearn towards Loch Earn. Today, the approach from this direction would bring us to St. Fillans at the east end of the Loch, and it was the protection of this Celtic saint with whom the king would find great comfort. There were many places in the area associated with the sixth century saint, and Robert was certain in his hour of need and in the fastness of the West Highlands, that it was the old Celtic Church from which he could draw strength and support. In the eleventh century, Saint Margaret had introduced the Church of Rome to Scotland, relegating the Celtic Church to peripheral areas where it still survived. The king and his diminutive fighting force turned northwest at Lochearnhead up Glen Ogle and into Glen Dochart. The terrain was increasingly wild, but better the hostility of the elements than that of Pembroke's ravaging army.

Below: King Robert fled west through Strathfillan in search of the safety and isolation of the Highlands and Islands.

Less than two months after the Battle of Methven, King Robert came to a halt in Strathfillan at the shrine of the Saint. Here it was that he was given absolution by the Abbot of Inchaffray, with his men as witnesses. The guilt of his sacrilege continued to torment him, and he wished those who would follow him to be in no doubt about how seriously he took his responsibilities as king.

At some point during this time, the king ordered that all his female relatives should be brought from Kildrummy Castle, where they had been staying, to be with him. Since the excommunication, King Edward had ordered that all women associated with Robert Bruce, if caught, could be assaulted or murdered without reproach. That being the case, Robert would rather they received his personal protection and suffer the inconveniences of life on the run, than trust their care to others. He had given the responsibility of their safe conduct to his favourite brother, Nigel, and it was he who brought the king's wife, Elizabeth, his daughter, Marjorie, two of his sisters, Mary and Christian, and she who had crowned him, Isabel, Countess of Buchan, to him before he went any further. There is no doubt that the presence of these women would have caused a hindrance to their progress, and it is thought that the king may even have contemplated fleeing with them to Norway, where another of his sisters was Queen. However tempting a prospect this was, Bruce did not shirk his duty and continued his westward journey up Strathfillan towards Tyndrum.

Route of Robert I after Methven – 1306

Above: *Strathfillan, where King Robert suffered his second defeat at the hands of the MacDougalls, proving that not even the Highlands were safe from his enemies.*

✗ Site of Battle

His destination was Macdonald territory, where he could find help from the Lord of the Isles, but he would have to pass through hostile country in order to get to Angus og Macdonald. He was perhaps in more danger now than before, simply because of the unpredictability of enemies amongst his own countrymen. The Comyns had many family ties in the north and it was impossible to know when or how they would wish to exact their revenge. The king and his party had a good geographical knowledge of the area and had to be wary of the clans who inhabited each Glen. Around August 11 they made their way along a narrow pass at Dail Righ before reaching the head of Strathfillan. Then, without warning, screams and shouts could be heard coming from the hills above them. The noise got louder and before the king had a chance to rally his men, they found themselves at the centre of a savage attack from all sides as fierce Highlanders, MacDougalls, descended upon them. Under the command of John MacDougall of Lorne, they had been following

the king's progress for days, waiting for the right moment to pounce. As a cousin of murdered John Comyn, MacDougall could hardly ignore the chance to get even, and in his own territory.

Once again, the king came close to losing his life. In attempts to pull him from his horse the clansmen furiously grabbed at him, one of them snatching a brooch from his shoulder, as he bravely held them off. His men fought as best they could within the confines of the pass and most of them managed to stay with their mounts. Concerned that he had put the women in this dangerous situation, the priority for the king was to surround them and find a way of breaking out. He formed up an arrowhead formation, and, with the women inside, they charged their way out with sheer brute force. The king's brooch was MacDougall's only prize that day, and the Brooch of Lorne, as it became known, has been proudly kept by the Lords of Lorne ever since.

The king could not have had a worse start to his reign. His forces, such as they had been, were greatly depleted. Only a few hundred men and horses had survived Methven, and now just a handful of those remained. Robert had few enough options as it was, but now he would have to rethink his original plan to head west. Having brought the women all the way from Kildrummy, he decided that the only choice was for them to return. Far from having the ability to protect them, it was he, the king, who had become a liability. Everyone who stayed with him put their lives at risk, so from now on he and his closest capable friends would go on alone and by foot. After an emotional farewell to Elizabeth and Marjorie, his brother Nigel and the Earl of Atholl accompanied them, the other ladies and all the horses back to Aberdeenshire. From Kildrummy, once it was safe, they should be sent further north to Orkney where within the domain of the King of Norway, they would be safe.

Dispensing with their heavy chain mail and armed only with dirks, King Robert, James Douglas, Neil Campbell, Gilbert de la Haye and Edward Bruce disappeared together into the mountains. They had a kingdom to win back and went in search of help - or a miracle - to achieve it.

Left: Dunnet Head, the most northerly point on the Scottish mainland, guards the Pentland Firth, with Orkney beyond. In August, 1306, King Robert's queen, Elizabeth and daughter, Marjorie, were bound for the safety of Orkney, which was part of the Kingdom of Norway.

Below: King Robert and his followers headed away from MacDougall territory via Balquhidder Glen.

A view towards the hills on the east side of Loch Lomond, where King Robert hid before his night time crossing by boat to the western shore.

Route of Robert I to Kintyre - 1306

Dail Righ

Balquhidder Glen

Craigroyston

Bute

Kintyre

Carradale

Arran

Dunaverty Castle

In search of strength

For a medieval king, the story of Robert I is very well documented, but we shall never know for certain what happened throughout much of the dark months from September 1306 to his return early in the following year. We do know that in order to survive this period, he must have possessed extraordinary powers of endurance to overcome the physical hardships of a fugitive king, exposed to the harsh elements of winter. But the King of Scots did more than just survive, he came back fighting with renewed vigour and strength. What began here was his emergence from privileged, feudal superior to seasoned military leader able to combine skills learnt in the tourney ground with imagination to adapt to circumstances. His failures at Methven and Dail Righ had proved his unreadiness for the deregulated war in which he was now engaged with his enemies, both English and Scottish.

The king was forced to change his plans after Dail Righ. The MacDougalls would take every opportunity to harry his small group as long as they were in their territory. They abandoned their westward course and headed south, back down Glen Ogle towards Balquhidder. From there, the journey continued southwards and they arrived on the eastern shore of Loch Lomond. Here they were still in MacDougall country and concealed themselves in a hillside cave at Craigroyston above the Loch until they could find the means to cross. They found a small abandoned boat and, through the blackness of a moonless night, made their crossing two by two. Once on the west side, they were safely in the lands of the Earl of Lennox, a loyal supporter of the king. Robert did not know if Lennox had survived Methven, or if his lands had been given to another. He remained cautious, and his little group remained hidden. They foraged for food and even survived on raw meat for fear that smoke from a fire would reveal their presence.

The plan was now to head southwest towards Kintyre. Macdonald territory stretched as far south as this, and hopefully the king could reach the Lord of the Isles by this route. They would have to pass through the Campbell lands on Bute and as Neil Campbell, their chief, was with them the king should not be hindered in his quest. Transport by water had to be the quickest way of reaching their destination and Campbell himself had been sent on ahead to discreetly arrange for a ship. As the king followed on behind, his party inadvertently found themselves in the midst of a deer hunt, but were relieved to find it led by the Earl of Lennox. He too had escaped capture at Methven and, making his way home, had been forced to hide out on his own land.

Their hopes raised now that they had found some support, after proper rest and sustenance, they continued their journey, Lennox escorting them to where Campbell had moored a galley. Sailing from Loch Long out into the Firth of Clyde and around the southern tip of the Isle of Bute, they approached Kintyre through the Kilbrannan Sound. They pulled into Carradale and, on foot, made for the castle at Dunaverty, which the king had made sure was in safe hands before he had been crowned. Continuing the journey down Kintyre on foot, they discovered that Angus og Macdonald had heard of their approach and was already there waiting for them. Given that Angus knew of his coming, they could be sure that the English were also aware of King Robert's voyage to Kintyre. They would not have long at Dunaverty before the enemy were in pursuit. Sure enough on or around September 22, Sir John Menteith arrived to attack the castle, only to find that the king had already left. He and his following had already departed with the implication that he had taken to the sea once again, this time fleeing the country. From this moment King Robert disappeared from the history books and his course until the following February is unknown.

Some think that the king never left his realm before returning to the mainland; however, from the Mull of Kintyre, the most likely place to which he would go was Rathlin Island and possibly on to the Irish mainland. The king had close family connections with Ireland, particularly on his mother's side through the Earldom of Carrick, and he was married to the Earl of Ulster's daughter. Although Ireland owed allegiance to the English crown, Robert would find much sympathy there and it is likely that for the next few weeks he began to co-ordinate the campaign of his return.

Below: The site of Dunaverty Castle on the southernmost tip of the Mull of Kintyre. With nowhere left to run, King Robert's only way out was over the sea to Ireland or the Isles.

Looking out over the islands of Rhum and Eigg from the mainland. King Robert sailed through these waters in search of support for his return.

Possible route of Robert I - winter 1306 / 1307

Canna

Barra Kisimul Castle

Rhum

Eigg

Castle Tioram

Coll

Tiree

Possible route through the Hebrides

Last recorded route of Robert I in 1306

Islay

Rathlin

Dunaverty

Ulster

King Robert did not remain detached from his kingdom and, in fact, sent men across to his territory to gather information and money from his Carrick tenants. Then he set about building his strength. While two of his brothers, Thomas and Alexander along with James the High Steward, ventured into Northern Ireland to raise men and arms, the king himself looked to the Hebrides for support. Of course, the Lord of the Isles was the most influential man here, and his power surpassed even that of the king. In the Highlands and Islands, the people did the bidding of their chief, not the king. Fortunately for Robert, Angus Macdonald was on his side and willing to commit Islesmen and ships to Scotland's cause. Confident of gaining more support in the Western Isles, King Robert left Rathlin and headed north towards the territory of Christina Macdonald of Garmoran. Based at Castle Tioram, Christina was Lady, in her own right, of vast tracts in the northwest, including Moidart, Arisaig and Knoydart on the mainland and Gigha, Rhum and Eigg amongst other islands. He was hopeful for her support, not least because they were distantly related thanks to his large family.

Christina took him under her wing and, as the winter months continued, she escorted him around the Hebrides and up into northern territories rarely visited by Scottish kings, gathering vital support. Steady progress had been made and the king must have been heartened by the numbers now willing to join his cause. But then news arrived of events concerning his family, and Robert soon began to wonder whether the fight was worth continuing, and if it could ever be won.

Left: *St. Duthac's chapel, Tain, scene of the shameful capture of Bruce's queen and daughter.*

Above: *The remains of Kildrummy Castle, Aberdeenshire, once the mightiest fortress in the north of Scotland.*

A king in despair

Throughout these weeks, engaged with plans as he was, the king's mind must have wandered to thoughts of his family. Being aware of the English army's unstoppable vengance, he must have been anxious about their safety. One can hardly imagine the anguish and helplessness as he received word of their fate. Sir Robert Boyd, whom the king had last seen leaving Dail Righ with his wife and daughter, arrived at Castle Tioram with dire news. Their party had successfully reached Kildrummy Castle, and were safely inside when they learned that Pembroke was not far away, in Aberdeen. Kildrummy was the mightiest stronghold in the north, but Nigel Bruce then realised that the English were gathering a significant array of siege machinery to specifically target this castle. With reinforcements from Edward's army, Kildrummy was too vulnerable for the women to stay and Nigel decided to send them further north, as King Robert had intended, towards Orkney. He sent them on their way with the Earl of Atholl and stayed at the castle, in preparation for a lengthy siege.

Kildrummy Castle nestles within a gorge along Upper Strathdon and such was its strength that it was impregnable to a besieging army. For days the walls were battered from every accessible direction and it withstood every blow. Only treachery from within would destroy Kildrummy and that betrayal came from a greedy blacksmith, who, tempted by rewards of gold, started a fire inside the castle. Much of the internal structure was wood, and the fire spread too quickly to extinguish. Soon the gates were weak enough for the English to breach and it was all over. The blacksmith, Osborne, was indeed given his reward - gold, molten, poured down his throat. Nigel Bruce was taken to Berwick and there, without trial, along with other survivors of the siege, was hanged and beheaded.

The Earl of Atholl and the women had made fair progress to the north, but they too were met by treachery. They had reached Tain, on the south bank of the Dornoch Firth and considered themselves safely beyond the grasp of England. However, the Earl of Ross, who was a Comyn ally, went in pursuit of them and, as they sought sanctuary in the tiny chapel of St. Duthac, they were captured and sent south to Edward. Satisfied that Pembroke was adequately carrying out his orders, the English king had decided to stay at Lanercost Priory in Northumberland.

He sent the Earl of Atholl to his death in London, and the fact that no-one of his rank had been executed for more than 200 years did not save Atholl. Edward's response to the protests of many sympathetic English nobles was to hang the earl from a higher gallows than ordinary men. Now he turned to King Robert's closest relatives, and with the intention of luring him back into the fight he planned special punishments for the women. For her part in crowning King Robert, a special cage, to be hanged from the walls of Berwick Castle, was constructed for Isabel of Buchan and for four years all who passed below gazed upon her. For being the wife of Neil Campbell, a similar fate awaited Mary Bruce, the king's sister, but this time upon the walls of Roxburgh Castle. Worse still, was the treatment of Robert's daughter Marjorie. Guilty of nothing but being his daughter, this twelve year-old princess was caged in the Tower of London. Only later did Edward give in to the pleas of his own wife, to move the girl to a convent. Compassion was shown to another of Robert's sisters, Christian. She was Sir Christopher Seton's widow, and in sympathy was sent to Sixhills nunnery in Lincolnshire. Finally, one might have expected Elizabeth de Burgh to face the harshest treatment but, as Edward's goddaughter, she was let off lightly, being imprisoned in a Holderness manor house, north of the River Humber. To add to this, Edward had sent a fleet of galleys up the western seas to search for Robert. It seemed that he would not rest until vengeance was complete.

The bearer of this news, Robert Boyd, had managed to escape after the fall of Kildrummy and had come in search of the king. We need hardly imagine the despair he must have felt. Since becoming king everything he did had turned into a disaster and those associated with him had faced death, torture and imprisonment. He had asked too much of his friends and family and all, without exception, had suffered because of him. As eloquently written by John Fordun, the 14th century historian:

"Great was the task that Robert Bruce took upon himself and unbearable the burdens upon his shoulders. His mishaps, flights and dangers; hardships and weariness; hunger and thirst; watchings and fastings; nakedness and cold; snares and banishment; the seizing, imprisoning, slaughter and downfall of his near ones and - even more - his dear ones no-one now living, I think, recollects or is equal to rehearsing."

Left: *In one of the most shamefully unchivalrous acts of the war, Isabel of Buchan was caged outside the walls of Berwick castle. Her suffering is represented here in a painting by Stewart Carmichael, completed in 1908.*

Above: *King Robert's most famous legend: he contemplates his predicament, while drawing inspiration from a spider.*

Towards the end of 1306, Robert must have spent many occasions in seclusion contemplating his future. It was around this time that the famous story of the spider, with which Robert the Bruce is universally connected, was born. Searching for inspiration, the king, while at rest in a cave, watched a humble spider attempting to construct its web. It could not attach to the slippery cave walls, and the spider kept swinging backwards and forwards until it found some purchase. It did not care how many times it tried and failed, it just carried on relentlessly. Such was the king's inspiration and such was his philosophy, as he demonstrated for the rest of his life. It is understood that the story of the spider was created by Walter Scott, some 500 years after the event, in his *'Tales of a Grandfather'*. However, in the Douglas family archives, a history book refers to a somewhat different story of the spider some 200 years before Scott. In this earlier account, the incident happened to James Douglas who relayed it to his king:

"Sir I being somewhat solitarie in the fields seriouslie contemplating of your affaires and casting my eyes aboutt, I spied a spider clymbing by his webb to the height of an trie, and at 12 several times I perceived his web broke, and the spider fel to the ground. But the 13 tyme he attempted and clambe up the tree without difficultie. Soe Sir, although fortune hath shewn hir self adverse towards you in 12 severall battles and encounters whereby your Majestie is driven to this exigence, as to take the Hebrides for your refuge My advise is to follow the example of the spider..."

As this moment of history was not recorded, we shall never know the truth, but it is a powerful tale, and one which inspired not just Robert the Bruce, but generations of others since, who have overcome adversity against overwhelming odds.

The long awaited return

Now ready to restart his quest the king, wary of Edward's ships, returned to Rathlin Island. He now had a very respectable force of his own, even without his loyal supporters from the mainland. The year had turned and it was January 1307. With his eyes turned due east towards his castle at Turnberry, now in the hands of Henry Percy of Northumberland, the king finalised plans for his return, and the return of Scotland to the Scots once and for all.

From the shore beneath the formidable battlements of Turnberry Castle, fifteen galleys could be seen looming out of the night from a misty western sea. Seen, that is, by only one man who was expecting their arrival. It was the middle of February, and Cuthbert, King Robert's spy, watched as the first galley came to a halt on the beach in front of him. Two men alighted - the king and James Douglas. This was the start of their campaign to regain the mainland, but plans had gone awry and they urgently reconsidered their objectives for the night.

Since leaving Rathlin Island, the king had meticulously planned his comeback. His first mission to the mainland had to succeed if the English were to understand the seriousness of his intentions. Even more important was that he gather support amongst the Scottish population and that they believe him to be capable of defeating the English. He had started with confidence,

firstly sending Douglas and Robert Boyd across to Arran to prepare the way for himself and his force of 33 galleys, bristling with Islesmen and Highlanders. The east side of Arran provided an excellent base to launch his campaign: Douglas, Boyd and a small strike team made a successful attack on the timely arrival of supply boats in Brodick Bay laden with arms and food to be delivered to the English-held Brodick Castle. Upon receiving the news that all was well, the king set out for Arran, arriving on the western shore of the island at Drumadoon Bay. His next move was to send his spy, Cuthbert, across to the Ayrshire coast and, on an appointed day, if it was safe to cross, he would light a beacon on the beach at Maidens, out of sight and just to the north of Turnberry Castle. It is often thought that the king watched for this signal from Brodick Castle, but even assuming that he had defeated the English garrison, he could not have seen any activity at Maidens or Turnberry from Brodick Bay: it is more likely that Kildonan Castle on the south-east tip of Arran was where he received the signal.

Return of Robert I to mainland - February 1307

Kintyre
Arran
Brodick Castle
Drumadoon Bay
Kildonan Castle
Dunaverty Castle
Maidens
Turnberry Castle

Kildonan Castle, Arran, is in sight of the Carrick coast; it is probably from here that Bruce left for the mainland to restart his campaign for the kingdom.

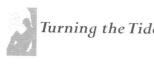

Above: The lighthouse at Turnberry stands on top of the castle ruins. Here King Robert set foot on the mainland once more, to win his country back.

While Cuthbert was on his way, the king also sent out his two youngest brothers, Thomas and Alexander, to Galloway with their recruits from Ireland in a fleet of 18 galleys. Their destination was Loch Ryan, tucked inside the Mull of Galloway. From there they would move inland to attack the main supply route through Ayrshire from Carlisle, thus hindering retaliation against the king's attack from the sea. Tragically, the plan went horribly wrong when the young Bruces' expedition was halted by an attack from Macdowall of Galloway, an English ally. Most who were not killed were taken captive, with several Irish leaders receiving immediate execution. The king's brothers were sent to Carlisle to face Edward and an all too familiar fate. Once again, following in the steps of their older brother, Nigel, they were drawn, hanged and beheaded without trial. Robert did not yet know it, but he had only one brother left.

The king must have assumed that his brothers and Cuthbert had achieved some success, when he finally spotted the faint flames of a beacon emanating from the coastline he knew intimately from boyhood. Without delay, he put his plan into action and, setting out with his fleet at dusk, he at last made for home. It was dark when the galleys beached on the shore, and it was then that the king received news that all had not gone well: Cuthbert had not been ready to send the signal. He did not know about the disaster of the Galloway expedition, but he was more concerned about the immediate situation and that someone else had lit the beacon. It appeared, however, that no one had any knowledge of the king's presence, though the Carrick countryside was awash with English soldiers and Turnberry itself was too well guarded to be taken that night. It was too late to turn back now, and improvisation would be the key to success. They still had the advantage of surprise, but King Robert decided not to aim for the castle, disheartening though that was for him. Instead, the 200-strong English garrison who were housed outside the castle walls became his target. In the style of Wallace at the Barns of Ayr, and against the ethics of his own training, he fell upon the unsuspecting barracks with his agile Highlanders who were bred for just this kind of silent cut-and-thrust work.

His first act as guerrilla leader had gone smoothly with none of the garrison surviving and no casualties on his own side. Disappointingly, he had not been able to coax Percy out of the castle, which remained safely in English hands. The king had started the day hoping that by the end of it he would be directing his campaign for the kingdom from within the walls of his mother's home. But in reality, he would have no roof over his head that night and decided to waste no time at Turnberry. Collecting all the weapons and armour they could carry, he and his men disappeared into the Carrick hills, from where they would mount their next assault. Although he had been a fugitive for eight months, the king had never been in as much danger as he was now. He had returned to stake his claim and had made his presence known, but he had no islands on which to hide out. He was in the thick of enemy territory and the people were too frightened to rise up even if their king had returned. The only real hope for Robert was that Edward was not long for this world and, when his end came, the English grip on Scotland would slacken.

Word of King Robert's attack at Turnberry spread very quickly and, as stories developed, his success there became exaggerated. Before long the entire southwest had become a fortress from which 'King Hob', one of his English nicknames, could not escape. He was soon surrounded on all sides by both English and Scots enemies: The Earl of Pembroke was in the southeast, Macdowall of Galloway and Robert Clifford were to the south, John MacDougall of Lorne was to the north at Ayr, and John de Botetourt covered Nithsdale to the east. But the king was, so far at least, well protected in the hills and woods and soon help began to trickle through. Then one day a woman arrived at the king's camp, a former mistress of Robert's, known as Christian of Carrick. She brought with her men and supplies, and the awful news of his brothers' fate. Since the English had an iron grasp on the southwest, the king must have guessed that the Galloway adventure had failed, but until now he had not known the terrible outcome. In a state of shock, the King had felt this anguish and guilt once before, when word of the rest of his family's fate had reached him in the Hebrides. But he had made the decision to fight on, and all of those who went with him knew the risks involved.

The enemy's net continued to tighten around the king and his camp, as he tried desperately to find a way out of the trap. But then events took a turn and King Robert soon found new hope in his campaign.

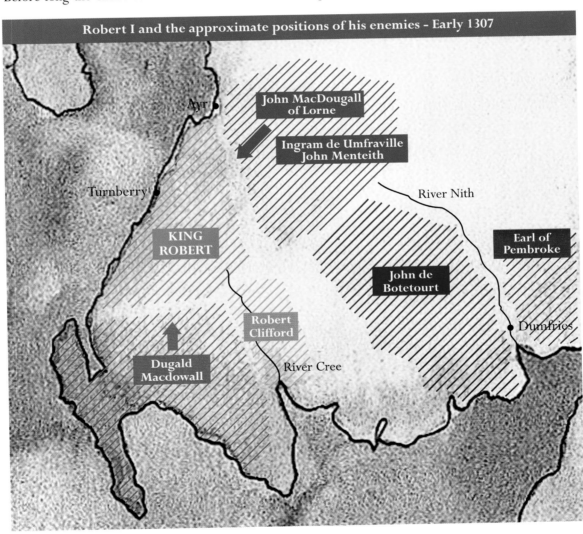

Robert I and the approximate positions of his enemies - Early 1307

Above: *King Robert holds off an attack by the Macdowalls.*

A spring of success

Around the hills of Carrick, Robert kept his men constantly on the move, making sure that no two nights were spent in the same place. Guards were on constant alert all around the camp wherever they stopped. The half-hearted regime which led to disaster at Methven would not be repeated again.

The king's vigilance paid off, for on one moonlit night they were approached by several hundred of Macdowall's men. We do not know the exact location of the events which followed but, having defeated the Galloway expedition of his brothers, this vile chief was hungry for a third Bruce scalp. But before they were anywhere near his camp, the king was ready for them. He positioned his own men out of sight, on the opposite side of the riverside path on which the enemy was approaching. While they laid in wait, Robert himself and Gilbert de la Haye, his High Constable went ahead down to the river bank where the king had previously noticed a narrow ford. They could hear the muffled sound of men and horses, the outline of which soon appeared out of the darkness. Ordering de la Haye back to stay with the others, and move forward on his signal, the king stood at the foot of the ford waiting to tempt the Macdowalls across. As they saw this lone figure on the other side of the river, the

urge to attack was too strong and they piled into the water, soon realising that they would have to cross in single file. Robert was able to take them on one by one, as they waded through the river. Having dispatched several of them by his own sword, the king called back to his men who rushed down the bank, causing the Macdowalls to turn and flee whence they had come.

While the king's adventures in the forest continued, James Douglas had parted company to spy out his own lands around Douglas Castle to the north and west of them. Since it had been given to Robert Clifford, it was crawling with English soldiers, but with Easter approaching, James decided to capitalise on the festivities. On Palm Sunday the garrison had left the safety of the castle to attend a service in the nearby church. In disguise as local peasants, Douglas and his handful of men fell upon the unsuspecting English and charged into the unprotected castle. They discovered that a banquet was being prepared for the returning garrison, which they did not waste. They ate what they could themselves, piled up all that was left in the cellar along with the castle's stocks of grain and wine, and set it all alight. "Douglas's Larder" was how the fire that consumed Douglas Castle became known.

Word of these activities soon reached Edward. Barely alive as he was, the persistence of the Scots constantly brought him back from the brink. Still at Lanercost, he sent word to Pembroke demanding that Bruce be pursued to the end of the earth and captured at all costs. The defeat of the Macdowalls and Douglas's Larder were minor victories, but strength grew from these events, as Wallace had shown at Lanark after his wife's death ten years before. By April 1307 King Robert, with little more than 300 men, had shifted his base south into Galloway, hiding out in Glen Trool. Meanwhile Pembroke, learning of Robert's whereabouts, prepared to leave Carlisle with a colourful array of 1,500 heavy cavalry. Impressive, perhaps, but totally inappropriate for the rock-pitted hills and glens of Galloway. Glen Trool is one of the most magnificent valleys in the southwest, with Loch Trool carved beautifully out of its head. Pembroke approached the loch from the east hoping to surprise the king's camp beyond. But the track between the mountains on the southern side of the glen and the marshy ground around the loch was very narrow for the heavy warhorses making it impossible for them to charge. They had learned nothing from Stirling Bridge and, despite their superior strength and numbers, were vulnerable and exposed. As they reached the steeps of Mulldonach, cries from above them half-way up the mountain alerted Pembroke, but before he could take action, King Robert had launched his attack. Holding their position, the Scots bombarded the English cavalry with rocks and stones, pushing them on to the marshes, and then pursuing them down the hill, until they scattered in all directions. Pembroke himself escaped back to Carlisle, and the king's first major victory since his return was secure. His reputation as the successor to Wallace was growing with every blow, and many began to join his cause, bringing much-needed armour and weapons.

Robert's confidence was now such that he felt he could move more openly through the hills. He made his way north towards Ayr hoping to conquer more of the southwest. He halted just east of Kilmarnock in a town called Galston, and planned his next move. Once again, though, the target came to him. The disgraced Pembroke had been forced by an increasingly agitated Edward to turn around and finish what he had started. Rallying more strength to his vastly diminished forces, he set out north once again, making for Ayr from where he would attack Robert's growing army.

The view east in Glen Trool, Kirkcudbrightshire, where King Robert had his first major victory over the English.

Above: Loudoun Hill, Ayrshire, where both Wallace and later King Robert defeated an English force.

Route of Robert I through southwest - spring 1307

✕ Site of Battle

Rising to the challenge, King Robert began to make plans. Knowing the land well, he moved his men due east to an imposing landmark known as Loudoun Hill. Rising up through gentle rolling plains, this prominent volcanic plug dominates all that surrounds it. For Robert it had all the natural features necessary to exploit a large army, and the potential for a few man-made ones. On May 10, Pembroke's army advanced on Galston, to find a handful of Robert's men taking flight towards Loudoun Hill. The chase was on, as the English fell for the bait and charged towards them. The Scots, on light horse, managed to stay ahead of their foe and led them straight into the king's trap. The highway ahead ran to the south of the big rock. It was wide enough for an army, but on either side of them, the boggy conditions would not allow them to deviate from their present course. There was still no sign of the main Scots army, now doubled in size, but they were biding their time, and before long the English understood why. The front line of heavy horse abruptly found itself collapsing into a grass-covered ditch, and those who managed to stumble across encountered another ditch several yards ahead. The whole highway had been pitted with these man-made traps and the Scots, ahead of them, knew exactly how to pick their way through.

With confusion running through the English ranks, King Robert's main attack came from around the back of Loudoun Hill, as his infantry charged into the floundering English horse. To reinforce his assault, he sent his own light cavalry, gathered since Glen Trool, around the back to hold them in from the south. Once again Aymer de Valence, Earl of Pembroke, escaped with his life to Bothwell Castle, but he had been doubly humiliated. For Robert it was a fitting revenge for Methven. He kept up the pressure, attacking a force under Roul de Monthermer, the Earl of Gloucester and pursuing him to Ayr Castle, which had remained in English hands.

It is remarkable that, after only three months, Robert had turned back the tide of failure. He still had a mountain to climb, but his enemies were now demoralised, recognising the new king's determination. Soon after Loudoun Hill, Alexander Abernethy, a Scots lord who had deserted to the English side wrote: *"I hear that Bruce never had the good will of his own followers or of the people generally so much with him as now. May it please God to prolong King Edward's life, for men say openly that when he is gone the victory will go to Bruce."*

The effect of all this talk was enough to stir Edward from his bed, and take the fight to Robert in person. Forgetting his human weakness, the King of England called every capable Englishman to arms and, at the beginning of July, took to his horse for the last time. Leading his army north from Carlisle, he got no further than Burgh by Sands, and, at the age of 69, died on English soil. It was July 10 and, cursing Scotland in his last breath, he made an extraordinary request to the Prince of Wales, who was by his side. He did not wish to be buried just yet, but asked that the flesh be boiled from his bones, and that they be carried forward into Scotland until it was finally conquered. Even in death, Edward I refused to accept defeat but, being of a different character, the new King of England completely ignored his father's wishes, turned the army around and headed south to Westminster, where he promptly buried the late king. On his simple tomb an apt description of this most remarkable king was carved: "Hammer of the Scots". What a fitting tribute to all those thousands of Scots who sacrificed themselves for freedom, that he never achieved his ambition.

Civil strife

The English retreat south could not have come at a better time for Robert. The war was by no means over and he needed time to win the support of his own people so that he could fight England with the whole country behind him. The new king of England, no matter whether perceptibly weaker than his predecessor, was still a Plantagenet and would not easily give in to Scottish resistance. Edward II was not made of the same war-like mettle as his father and, although he enjoyed outdoor pursuits such as horseriding, it was not in the context of combat, making him no match for Robert Bruce. Aged only 23, Edward was tall, good looking and not yet married. He was not unpopular amongst the ordinary people, but on ascending the throne he soon became hated by the nobles, placing his personal interests and close friends above kingly duties. He was extravagant and preferred the company of men to that of women showering his court favourites, notably Piers Gaveston, with wealth and power.

Below and right: The monument and inscription at Burgh-by-Sands, Cumbria, to King Edward I; he finally breathed his last at this bleak spot on the Solway marshes.

KING EDWARD I MONUMENT (BUILT 1685)
EDWARD I FOUGHT A LONG, BITTER CAMPAIGN TO CONQUER SCOTLAND.
OLD AND SICK HE MADE CAMP ON THESE MARSHES WHILST
PREPARING TO SUBDUE HIS ENEMY ROBERT THE BRUCE.
EDWARD DIED HERE ON JULY 7 1307.

All these distractions brought a welcome reprieve to the King of Scots. His efforts over the last few months had to some extent made him master of the southwest, but he still had many enemies at home. Pembroke had been ordered to stay behind with a modest force covering central Scotland along the river Clyde. The English still occupied all the main castles in Scotland, and many Scots Comyn supporters refused to recognise Bruce as their king. Robert needed the opportunity to confront these people without the fear of a hostile English army at his back. For the first time in his life he was on the offensive and the pace at which he threw himself into this quest surprised everyone. He immediately pushed south into Galloway, scattering the Macdowalls and forcing many to escape over the border into Cumbria. At the end of September 1307, the king turned around and blazed his way north to confront his enemies there. The Earl of Ross, who had betrayed Robert's wife, and John Comyn, the son of his old rival, were holding out against him. The king left James Douglas in charge of the southwest, where he admirably continued his king's work, extending the southern conquest into areas even Robert had thought unattainable. Claiming back his own Douglasdale, he pressed eastwards into Selkirk Forest, taking Jedburgh with little effort.

The king, meanwhile, was making steady progress towards the Comyn and Ross territories of the north. Slipping through the English defences, he crossed the Clyde at Glasgow and headed up towards the Great Glen. However, always concerned to cover his back, he decided to confront the MacDougalls before going any futher. Supported by the Lord of the Isles, who sailed up Loch Linnhe with his galleys, they together squeezed John of Lorne into submission. Without crossing swords they forced him into a truce which he accepted in the short term at least. It was now October and, with unstoppable momentum, the king progressed up the Great Glen making the Comyn castle of Inverlochy, at the southern end of this long fault line, the first of his targets. Seizing Inverlochy, Robert then began his policy of destroying all castles in Scotland once they were back under his control, no matter how great they were. In fact, the more important the stronghold, the more imperative it was that the English should not be allowed to retake it. Besieging castles was a time-consuming effort that the Scots could ill afford so it was far better to remove the stronghold altogether.

Below: Inverlochy Castle, Inverness-shire, stands on the shores of Loch Linnhe below the bulk of Ben Nevis.

Right: Loch Ness and the Great Glen provided no obstacle to King Robert's march north.

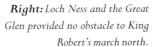

Above: The substantial remains of Urquhart Castle, Inverness-shire, look out over Loch Ness.

After a long march up Loch Ness, the king surrounded Urquhart Castle surprising William, Earl of Ross, who was holding it on behalf of the English. As much as Robert desired revenge on the man who had handed his family over to Edward's justice, he was more concerned to unite his kingdom. Without striking a blow against Ross, and much as it pained him to do so, the king promised him clemency if he surrendered peacefully. The earl, seeing the size and extent of the king's army did not take much persuading, and, as with John MacDougall of Lorne, agreed a truce until summer of the following year. Interestingly, both the earl and MacDougall immediately wrote letters to King Edward II, explaining their actions and stating that they were waiting for aid from the English king, whereupon they would end their truce. So Robert's back was secure for now, but for how long? He ended his trek up the Great Glen and arrived at Inverness.

Not everyone in the north was hostile towards him and indeed he found considerable support in the form of David Murray, the Bishop of Moray. There were few enough Bishops around to give him support as it was, with Wishart and Lamberton in English prisons. As it transpired, before the king's months in exile, he had asked Murray to raise help in the northeast, knowing the men of Moray to be of independent minds and unlikely to be beholden to the Comyns in the north. The bishop had been busy, for Robert arrived in Inverness to find him with considerable support ready to take the castle, which they did, once again razing its battlements to the ground. Then heading eastwards, they destroyed Nairn and attempted to assail Elgin Castle. This was the only stronghold which eluded the king, but he decided that enough had been achieved, and with most of his adversaries dealt with he now turned his attention to the real enemy - the Comyns.

With his small army, still of little more than 700 men, the king ventured east towards Inverurie to confront the Earl of Buchan, cousin of the dead John Comyn, but matters suddenly took a turn for the worst when Robert fell seriously ill. The details of the king's illness are sadly lacking but this was the first incidence of a recurring disease which plagued him for the rest of his life. The king had exhausted himself and, although still only 33 years old, it was inevitable that the harsh living and unsustainable pace of his campaign would take its toll somehow. A cold winter was approaching, and Robert's condition did not improve, so with Edward Bruce taking charge, the king was placed on a litter and carried into the protection of a wood at Slioch, a few miles north of Inverurie, near Huntly. The Earl of Buchan was aware of their presence and advanced on them deploying his men around the edge of the wood. It was Christmas Day, and the ground was frozen with snow. The king's party stayed under cover of the trees and it was impossible for the Earl to know their position and numbers. He resorted to firing arrows at random into the trees to no avail. Robert co-ordinated his defence by making use of their camouflage, moving his men about over a number of days and keeping the Earl of Buchan guessing. Buchan soon tired of the situation and decided to retreat until he could build up his own forces. He withdrew while keeping an eye on the king's position.

As the year turned and 1308 arrived, the situation for Robert deteriorated. His closest comrades remained faithfully at his side, but the rest of his men began to doubt whether their king would survive the cold winter. Provisions were dwindling and there was talk of desertion, but Edward, Robert's brother, decided to take control of the situation before it came to that. He ordered that the king should be placed in his litter and that they all confidently march out of the woods and retreat into the Strathbogie hills. This masterful operation took Buchan so by surprise that he simply let them go on their way. Throughout the next few weeks, despite the freezing winter conditions, the king made a steady recovery and he and his men came down from the hills and camped at Inverurie, waiting to see what Buchan would do next. The Earl had not been idle, but had gathered more support from the south, including English recruits led by Sir John Mowbray. At some point in the spring, on an uncertain date, John Comyn, the Earl of Buchan, assembled his force of 1000 men at Old Meldrum, just north of Inverurie. The king, who had been resting, bounded into action and, although he still required support on his horse, he and his bold army marched confidently north to rendezvous at last with Buchan.

The events that followed at Old Meldrum could hardly be described as a battle, although The Battle of Inverurie is how it became known. Such was Robert's military success since returning to the mainland that his reputation preceded him. Buchan's men thought the king to be on his death bed, so when they saw him approach at the head of an army, they turned and fled. Their leaders could not fight without them, so Buchan and Mowbray did the same escaping north to Fyvie. Spurring forward, Robert gave chase, his men cutting down all those that they caught up with. The king may have been encouraged by his success, but he was not yet well enough for the cut and thrust of heavy campaigning. He placed his brother in command of the army with orders to destroy Comyn's lands of the northeast, so that they be left in no doubt as to who ruled Scotland now. In the days that followed, land was burned and the population was cut down in what became known as the 'Herschip' or harrying of Buchan.

The Norman motte at Inverurie Bass, Aberdeenshire; near here, King Robert defeated the Earl of Buchan at Old Meldrum.

Above: *The view west along the Pass of Brander. Above the road on the right is Ben Cruachan, where Douglas came over the top to lead a counter-attack on MacDougall.*

Master of his own people

It was July 1308 and, as the king's conquest of the north took hold, James Douglas' campaign in the south had also made an impact. In fact the Black Douglas, as he became known to his terrified English victims, had gained quite a reputation for his 'cloak and dagger' attacks. The king needed him by his side once again, so he ordered him to come north and he arrived with a very important prisoner. In the aftermath of the Battle of Methven, Robert's nephew, Thomas Randolph, had been captured by the English but spared execution. Like Douglas, Randolph was a young man with considerable military talent, perhaps the reason for sparing him. He had grown sympathetic to his captors who had persuaded him that his uncle had fled the country, only to return to fight a coward's war, by stealth and without honour. Whilst raiding in Selkirk Forest, Douglas had apprehended this proud youth and took him on the long journey north to be reunited with his uncle. The king kept a close rein on him and, over time, Randolph realised his attitude to be mistaken.

King Robert now felt that he could confidently leave the northeast. Aberdeen, which had for long been in English hands, had fallen thanks to its people taking the lead from their king. Now the Scots could return to trading with Europe through one of their richest east coast ports. All Robert needed next was to secure his western seaboard, which meant tackling MacDougall in the northwest, and Macdowall in Galloway. The latter adversary had not been entirely conquered after the king's raid into their territory following Glen Trool, and now they were regaining their strength. He sent his formidable brother, Edward Bruce, to face them while he himself and James Douglas contemplated how MacDougall of Lorne could be brought to heel.

It was mid-August by the time the king's forces reached MacDougall's territory in Argyll. He sent scouts ahead to assess the lie of the land and how MacDougall was going to oppose him. From Dalmally the king skirted the northern end of Loch Awe and approached the Pass of Brander. A treacherously narrow track was all that separated Loch Awe from the dizzy heights of Ben Cruachan on its north side. The king waited at the jaws of the Pass as his scouts returned with news that thousands of MacDougall's men were at the other end, blocking its exit. Not only that, but as many again were deployed up the slopes of the Ben, lying in wait for Robert and his men. Was MacDougall really naïve enough to think that Bruce would fall for the trick at Dail Righ again? He clearly made no allowance for the fact that King Robert was now a battle-hardened guerrilla leader. In response to this, the king sent James Douglas over the top of Ben Cruachan from the north, ready to pounce on the ambush from above.

Ready at last to repay John of Lorne for his hostility, the king and his force began to make their way up the Pass as if nothing was suspected. Before they drew level with the MacDougalls on the hillside, Robert signalled to Douglas to begin their attack. From the tops of the Ben came a barrage of arrows and rocks, and the startled MacDougalls turned around to find themselves the victims of an ambush. As the assault went on from above, the king's men left the narrow track to assail them from below, squeezing the panic-stricken Highlanders in the middle of a relentless attack. Witnessing all from a galley on Loch Awe, John MacDougall made his escape to the western sea and eventually to England. The king, meanwhile, continued the pursuit out of the Pass of Brander towards the west coast, plundering MacDougall land until he reached Dunstaffnage Castle. There he laid siege until Alexander, John of Lorne's father, surrendered it and himself to the king's mercy. Knowing that John could return at any time, Robert decided to hold the man's father hostage to prevent any further trouble.

While his brother triumphed in the north, Edward Bruce, as expected, had run a brutal campaign in Galloway but, just as MacDougall had escaped to England, Dugald Macdowall had also managed to slip through the Bruces' fingers. He had accumulated a significant army, including English support from Sir Ingram de Umfraville. Together, at the end of June, they attempted to defeat the smaller Scots force on the banks of the River Dee near Dalbeattie, but the younger Bruce led such a vicious offensive that Macdowall and the rest were scattered, fleeing in all directions. They found sanctuary in English-held Buittle Castle and from there they eventually fled Scotland. Edward had cleansed the southwest of the enemy for the time being, but its castles remained firmly in English hands. Caerlaverock, Lochmaben, Dumfries, Ayr and others would need retaking by the king on another occasion, but for now Edward Bruce had carried out his orders.

Following victory in the Pass of Brander, Robert marched back up the Great Glen towards Moray to confront William, Earl of Ross, once again. With the king's main opposition in the north of Scotland now effectively crushed, the earl was out on his own. The period of truce was now up, Edward II had not responded to his request for help and he realised that any attempt to resist King Robert would be futile. In October 1308, in a ceremony at Auldearn near Nairn, the king, with fury in his heart, accepted the unconditional surrender and allegiance of the Earl of Ross, betrayer of his wife and daughter. The earl, to his credit, thereafter served his king consistently well.

King Robert had won his country over and, although he was not without enemies, he was now the undisputed king. Scotland had not been in such a position since the days of Alexander III. The civil war was over but there was still work to do: the real enemy had to be faced and the king, still an excommunicate, needed international recognition that he was the legitimate sovereign of his land. For now, all that seemed a long way off.

Below: Much of Dunstaffnage Castle, Argyll, on its rocky promontory, survives from King Robert's day.

Unrest in England

Despite the English presence in Scotland, the cataclysmic changes there seemed to go unnoticed in England. Throughout 1308, Edward II had created annoying distractions for his nobles by his behaviour towards his court favourite, Gaveston. England had suddenly lurched from its instinctive aggression towards other nations to internal division and argument over who held the reins of power. Early in that year Edward had married Isabella of France but, at twelve years old, she was of no interest to him and did not yet show any sign of the influential rôle she was to play in later years. As the daughter of Philip the Fair, King of France, her presence at the English court strengthened the relationship between their two countries, and further alienated Scotland. Whatever the King of Scots did to claim it, Edward still believed that Scotland belonged to him.

All this suited King Robert well. He could now pursue the second phase of his quest to win Scotland unchallenged from the south. Before the end of the year, he received a tremendous boost to his cause from the King of France. It appears that Philip, anxious for peace between Scotland and England had, despite his daughter's marriage, sent a letter to Robert re-affirming the ancient alliance between the French and the Scots. He also requested help for a Crusade, to which it was clearly impossible for Scotland to respond. Nevertheless, the letter inspired Robert to arrange his first parliament as king, held at St. Andrews in March 1309. Out of this was sent a reply that, as soon as Scotland had been returned to its rightful liberties, it would gladly join the King of France in a Holy Crusade. This two-day parliament was heavily attended and also, to the surprise of all, by none other than William Lamberton, Bishop of St. Andrews. King Edward had finally taken the Scottish situation seriously, and had released Lamberton to act as an intermediary for negotiations towards a truce.

The main outcome of events at St. Andrews was confirmation that Robert was to be accepted as rightful King of Scots, and that the disastrous reign of John Balliol was proclaimed null and void. Needless to say, this whole concept was rejected by Edward II out of hand, but Robert would not give way on the issue of independence and make the same mistake as Balliol. He was king of an independent kingdom and, in that position, was answerable only to God. Peace negotiations ended there and then.

All this tough talk of resistance by King Robert excited the Plantaganet blood in Edward's veins and, having come to an agreement with his nobles which pushed Piers Gaveston out of the way, he ordered them to arms. He would, at last, respond to the calls for help from all the English-garrisoned castles in Scotland and send an army to help them out. So, in the autumn

Above: A contemporary image of Edward II and his wife, Queen Isabella.

of 1309, two separate hosts arrived in Berwick and Carlisle ready for invasion. But their commanders, Sir John Segrave and Sir Robert Clifford, had bitter memories of previous wasted campaigns and, after considering the prospects of a hard winter on the march, decided not to cross the border. With the absence of Longshanks holding their leash, they clearly had no incentive to move and even agreed a truce with the Scots. This went on until the summer of the following year, all of which gave King Robert valuable time to travel his country, accepting allegiances and establishing himself as undoubted ruler.

By sharp comparison, King Edward's position of authority continued to be undermined. The relationship between France and England had soured and Philip was making demands on his son-in-law. Edward's young queen, Isabella, had informed her father of the indifference with which she was being treated and, in turn, Edward learned of the blossoming friendship between Scotland and France. It appears that Philip had deceived Edward by sending him copies of correspondence to Robert Bruce, Earl of Carrick, whilst the real letters were titled Robert Bruce, King of Scots. As a consequence of all this, Philip decided to summon the English king to France to give homage for all lands held there of the French crown. There was no greater humiliation for an English king than to be reminded that he was not Lord Superior over all his domains. In order to avoid Philip's summons, Edward decided to turn his attentions north and mount an invasion of Scotland himself, over three years after his father had expected him to carry his remains forward and complete his conquest. However, it was a different Scotland to which he was returning: one which was now united in its resistance to English rule.

So, in September 1310, Edward invaded Scotland from Berwick, marching up through the borders via Roxburgh, Jedburgh and ending up in Biggar one month later. Accompanying him as always was Piers Gaveston; presumably Edward considered the Scottish expedition less of a risk to his favourite's safety than him remaining in England. Edward naïvely waited in the central Lowlands expecting the King of Scots to meet the challenge. However, the Lowlands were deserted, for King Robert had retreated behind the Highland line and most of the populace had fled in front of the invading army. With his armed host growing impatient and hungry, Edward decided to head west into the Clyde Valley where they fared little better. By now, Robert had sent down small divisions of footmen under James Douglas, whose job it was to harry the English flanks. They successfully picked away at the fraying edges of the dispirited army until Edward came to cross the Clyde at Dumbarton. There he had expected to find John MacDougall, who had been sent up from England to join forces. But here too

he was disappointed, as MacDougall's fleet had been blocked by the Lord of the Isles. Robert's efforts to gain control of the western sea had now paid off.

Edward faced no other alternative but to change direction and head east. Realising that the English were on the retreat, Robert now set in motion his own imaginative war game. He sent more infantry south to continue intimidating the English extremities. Then, when Edward had finally had enough at the end of October, he left Scotland whence he had come, and stayed in Berwick until the campaigning season of the following year. As he crossed the border, King Robert came south with his whole army and led an attack on English sympathisers in Lothian. On hearing this news, Edward immediately turned north again to confront the invisible Scots, but found the countryside deserted. For his next strategic trick, at around Christmas, Robert put out rumours that he was going to attack the Isle of Man, which currently belonged to the English crown. Edward, who had ships along the east coast of Scotland, sent these around to the west to make sure that Man remained safe. No sooner had they sailed away, than in came the Scottish supply ships to the east coast ports, having returned from Europe laden with much needed food and arms. King Robert, meanwhile, was not to be found anywhere near the Isle of Man!

For the next six months, this cat and mouse game continued, as the English tried to root out the Scots and tempt them into battle. But the King of Scots did not rise to the bait and refused at all costs to get involved in any form of pitched battle with the main English host. The fights he had won with Pembroke in previous years were at less significant odds and he was not yet

Above: Traprain Law, East Lothian. This part of the Lowlands was the scene of a devastating attack by King Robert.

Above: *An impression of Scarborough Castle around 1350; in 1312 Edward II hid Piers Gaveston here from his enemies before the place was besieged and Gaveston captured.*

Right: *Earlier, Gaveston was placed in Bamburgh Castle for safety.*

ready to gamble with victory over the whole of England. Finally, in June 1311, Edward gave up this fruitless chase and went south, leaving Gaveston at Bamburgh Castle. It was now that King Robert launched his first attack on northern England. Eager to rebuild Scotland's foodstocks following years of invasion, the prime objective was to loot cattle so, in August, he crossed into Cumbria and devastated the land as far as Haltwhistle. The English population were not slaughtered, perhaps a measure of Robert's control over his men, and casualties only occurred when resistance was offered. He then returned home and, realising that resistance had been negligible, decided to invade eastern England the following month. Entering Northumbria over the Cheviots, he marched deep into the county devastating the land before turning north again at Corbridge. Once again, the people of northern England were to suffer the backlash of Scottish anger and were given no protection by their king in far-off London.

Edward did have his excuses. Tensions were rising in England due to the continuing wrangle over Gaveston and the power he was holding over Edward. The nobles and barons had put pressure on the king to send him from the court and, having agreed, Edward deceived them, deciding instead to hide Gaveston in Scarborough Castle. The king had moved himself to York in an attempt to raise an army and, while he did, Scarborough was besieged and Piers Gaveston captured and later executed by the Earl of Lancaster. For the first time in his life, Edward experienced genuine rage and civil war broke out between the king and Lancaster.

Right: *Lanercost Priory, where much of the anti-Scots propaganda was written and which King Robert raided on his route east.*

Hadrian's Wall, along the route of which King Robert led an attack of English towns.

Once again, King Robert had time on his hands and in July 1312, he decided to launch another major invasion into northern England while the opportunity was there. His route was similar to that of the previous year, across the Solway Firth, but this time it was more ferocious and unforgiving. He destroyed Lanercost Priory, where the English chronicles of this war were being written. Following the line of Hadrian's Wall, he swept through Hexham and Corbridge, sending his brother and Douglas on into County Durham. Resistance, as before, had been feeble and the local populace resorted to paying blackmail to the Scots king, in order that he agree to leave them alone and agree a truce. This became an effective way for Scotland to replenish its broken treasury and, mercenary though it may seem, it was considered merely compensation for the years of ravaged land brought about by countless English invasions.

Below: King Robert's castle at Loch Doon was originally built on a loch islet, but in 1935 was moved and rebuilt on the loch shore when construction of a dam raised the water level.

Cleansing the castles

King Robert returned home and immediately arranged a parliament to be held in Inverness on 29 October 1312. Present on this occasion were envoys from the king of Norway who were there to renegotiate the Treaty of Perth, which had followed the Battle of Largs back in 1266. Since then, healthy relations between the two countries had soured and Robert was anxious to strengthen international co-operation. The Treaty of Inverness underlined their 46 year-old friendship and guaranteed support from northern Europe.

Also under discussion here was how to deal with the English-occupied castles, most of which were now south of the Highland line. A strange situation existed where English garrisons were cowering behind the walls of these impregnable fortresses and without the main English army they were useless. However, as long as they existed to replenish and supply invading armies with men and arms, Scotland would not be free. Since 1309, there had been a continuing campaign of winning over some of the less important castles, such as Bruce's ancestral stronghold at Loch Doon in the southwest. There had been nothing clever in this as it been largely achieved by starving out the garrisons. But the Scots could ill afford the time it took to sit around and wait for the castle in question to surrender, and siege weapons on the scale used by the English themselves were too expensive,

so a positive policy for regaining them had to be adopted, although the eventual result would be a negative one of razing them to the ground. To take the mightiest strongholds in the land such as Edinburgh, Stirling and Roxburgh, the king would have to apply his imagination.

King Robert's campaign to cleanse the castles is a remarkable story of ingenuity, daredevil tactics and sheer brute force. Following his parliament at Inverness, the king moved south towards Perth. There he left Thomas Randolph, who had now been made Earl of Moray, together with the Earl of Atholl, to set up a siege outside the walls of the city. With them in place, he headed south at a cracking pace to attack the castle at unsuspecting Berwick. In the dead of night the king, James Douglas and a lightly-dressed strike team attempted to scale the walls of the town using rope-ladders and grappling hooks. Unfortunately, the attempt failed when a dog was roused by the clanking of iron hooks over the wall. Robert did not linger at Berwick; there was little point once their presence had been revealed. He headed back to Perth, having succeeded at the technique if not at gaining a castle. This was the first occasion that rope-ladders had been used for such a purpose; the next time, it would work.

Above: *King Robert landed at Ramsey Bay on the Isle of Man in 1313, to claim it back from England.*

Left: *Rushen Castle on the south of the island was quickly taken.*

It was now January 1313 and, on his return to Perth, the king was now hungry for success. The River Tay flows to the east of the town, which was itself heavily defended by a wall around its perimeter. The other exposed sides were surrounded by a man-made moat, which became the focus for Robert's plans. Carefully surveying the depth of the moat and the height of the wall, the king then ordered the conspicuous withdrawal of the entire siege. As soon as he and his men were out of sight, they set up camp in a nearby wood, and began preparing more rope ladders. After a week had elapsed, when the garrison had let down their guard, Robert and his men returned to the banks of the moat on a moonless night. Stripping off most of their clothing and carrying only rope-ladders and dirks, they descended into the water at its shallowest point. Wading through the ice-cold water up to their shoulders, they made it across and managed to ascend the walls with no alarm being raised. Once they were all safely on top of the battlements, there was no longer any need for stealth and the king ordered their descent into the town, half of them guarding the walls to prevent escape. By dawn Perth and its castle belonged to the king, who received the surrender of its governor Sir William Oliphant. As had become typical, Robert spared those who did not resist, many of whom were Scots and, with orders to destroy all fortifications, the king moved to the far southwest to tackle all those castles along the Solway Firth which were served by Carlisle. Dugald Macdowall was still around, opposing the king and presently holding Dumfries against him. When the castle eventually fell, once starved of provisions, Robert forgave Macdowall for betraying his brothers

and accepted his allegiance. He required the support of this powerful chief, not the alienation of his clan, certain had he ordered his execution. On the whole the king's policy of clemency towards his enemies had a positive outcome, but on this occasion the independent-minded Macdowall fled the scene and took up arms with the English once again.

By the end of March 1313 all other main castles in the south west, including Caerlaverock, had fallen. The mightiest of all the castles - Stirling - still eluded the king so, sending his brother north to prepare a siege, Robert himself decided on another target. He had previously threatened the Isle of Man, but had not made a serious attempt to retrieve it. It belonged to the Scots Crown but since 1290 had been in English hands and a valuable supply base for their invasions. In May the king, with help from Angus Macdonald's fleet, sailed into Ramsey Bay. By the end of that month, Robert had marched overland to the south of the island, stopping off at Douglas on the way and ending up at Castletown where on June 12, after a brief siege, he took Rushen Castle. Later that year, the king added 'Lord of the Isle of Man' to the growing list of Thomas Randolph's titles, but the island was not Scottish for long and, twenty years later, it was taken back by the English in whose hands it has remained ever since.

Meanwhile, back on the mainland, Edward Bruce was growing impatient with the lack of progress on his siege of Stirling Castle. He could find no way of breaching its defences and it was too well-provisioned to be starved into submission. On

June 23, Midsummer's Day, there came about the most significant bargain in Scottish history. Sir Philip Mowbray, the castle governer who could himself see no end to the situation, laid down a challenge to Bruce; that if by Midsummer's Day of the following year, an English army did not arrive to end the Scot's siege and rescue the English garrison, Mowbray would surrender to Bruce. Without considering the consequences or consulting his brother, Bruce accepted and set in train an unstoppable challenge to England's honour. Following his return from the Isle of Man, the king arrived on the scene to find the fate of his country hanging in the balance thanks to the short-sighted pride of his brother. No English king could ignore a gauntlet thrown down so blatantly and never before had they had so much time to prepare for a predetermined date: 23 June, 1314.

For the first time since his fight back had begun, the king was not in control of his campaign. He would have to face the most formidable army in Europe under conditions which he had been determined to avoid. But he wasted no time in rising to the challenge and made his first task the completion of cleansing the castles. They must be rendered useless for the approaching army and the principal ones were in the southeast, through which King Edward would undoubtedly march to get to Stirling. In September Linlithgow fell easily, and not at the king's hands. A folk hero by the name of William Bunnock jammed his hay wagon under the portcullis and attacked the garrison from inside the castle with assistance from eight armed men who were concealed under the hay. Early in the following year, 1314, James Douglas prepared to take the mighty Roxburgh Castle, located high up on a promontory squeezed between the Rivers Tweed and Teviot. Douglas had always looked for opportunities to attack the English when they were distracted by other events and religious celebrations had proved the most successful. Here was no exception and in February, on the night of Shrove Tuesday, he made his move. The men of the castle garrison were all contained within the Great Hall, making merry before Lent began. Covering themselves so they would be mistaken for cattle, Douglas and his men crawled up the path, way below the lofty walls of the castle. They unfurled their rope-ladders and scaled the walls in the usual fashion. With only one or two men posted around the walls, they had no problem reaching the Hall and overpowering the intoxicated English. With the operation complete, the whole castle was dismantled.

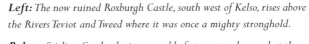

Left: *The now ruined Roxburgh Castle, south west of Kelso, rises above the Rivers Teviot and Tweed where it was once a mighty stronghold.*

Below: *Stirling Castle; the impregnable fortress stands guard at the gateway to the Highlands.*

Inspired by the achievements of Douglas, Thomas Randolph attempted to upstage him with the unthinkable: the taking of Edinburgh Castle, a fortress as impregnable as Stirling. These two men were ever vying to be accepted as the King's champion, and the ongoing competition between them ensured much success for the Scottish cause. Randolph had been besieging the castle for weeks, had not wanted to make the same mistake as Edward Bruce and had received news of the Douglas success. Amongst Randolph's own men were skilled rock climbers from the north and all he needed was local knowledge about the castle. The resourceful Randolph began to search for assistance amongst the people of Edinburgh and he found one William Francis, son of a watchhouse keeper who had served high up on castle rock.

He knew the castle and its crag well from the days when, unknown to his father, he would scale down the rock to visit his lover in the town. He made rope-ladders to the correct length and, on the dark night of March 14 thirty men, Randolph included, began the deadly ascent up the north face of the rock. The rest of his men went around to the east porch to create a distraction for the guards. The climbers made it over the wall, took the defenders by surprise from behind and opened the east porch. The rest of the Scots swarmed through the gate and into the fortress, leaving the English completely defenceless.

Following the capture of Edinburgh Castle, King Robert reluctantly ordered its destruction. Only the tiny chapel at its summit, dedicated to St. Margaret, would be spared. That he had demolished so many fine castles in his own land must have brought sorrow to the king, but castles could be rebuilt and in the future they would be. Now he turned his sights on Stirling and the prospect of a confrontation on a scale not seen since Stirling Bridge 17 years before.

Left: *St. Margaret's chapel is the only building within the walls of Edinburgh Castle to survive from the fourteenth century.*

Below: *The formidable task of scaling Edinburgh Castle rock can be seen from this photo of the north face.*

Part 4. 1314 – 1330
THE PRICE OF FREEDOM

"See approach proud Edward's power"

The king began preparing his men for battle and searched out the land around Stirling. The Scots would have the upper hand if they chose the battle site. The task was to prevent the English army from reaching Stirling Castle and Robert eventually found some ideal ground to the south of the town. A little village with the name of Bannockburn provided excellent opportunities for his plans.

Above: The view towards Stirling Castle from the fields of Bannockburn.

As the Scots cleared the land and chose their battle site, King Edward had indeed risen to the challenge. Both the English and the Scots were well aware that the whole affair was about more than rescuing the garrison at Stirling Castle: it was about English national pride. The bargain between Edward Bruce and Sir Philip Mowbray gave Edward the excuse he needed to end King Robert's run of success, and the whole of England rose to the occasion with characteristic fervour. The civil war came to an end as all the differences of the past were buried and the murderers of Gaveston forgiven. How much more satisfying it would be to destroy the Scots rather than each other. The English could boast the upper hand in just about every respect: numbers; equipment; wealth and international support. Only one thing was lacking; the brilliance and intelligence of a natural leader.

By the end of 1313, Edward's preparations for the invasion were well under way. Just before Christmas, eight earls and eighty-seven barons, mainly from the northern counties of England, were commanded to call their vassals to arms. Invitations to join in and claim the spoils of victory were sent out to the most accomplished knights from France, Germany and the Low Countries. The Earl of Ulster, King Robert's father-in-law, eagerly joined the English campaign despite his own daughter's imprisonment for the previous eight years. A significant number of troops was raised from Ulster, as from Wales. However, the greatest number of infantry came from England and the emphasis on footmen rather than heavy horse indicates at least some appreciation of the nature of warfare in Scotland. Their orders were to arrive at Berwick no later than 10 June 1314 and, as that date approached, the size and scale of the forthcoming invasion became more and more apparent. Berwick was, in fact, too small a location for the amassing army and instead they chose Wark on Tweed to set up camp. Coincidentally, the site where the English launched their first invasion eighteen years previously would now serve the same purpose for their tenth.

By the appointed date, the largest army ever raised by England had gathered. There were 15,000 spearmen, 3,000 Welsh longbowmen and 2,500 armoured cavalry. Technically speaking, this was far more than was necessary to raise the siege of Stirling Castle. The infantry was arranged into 10 divisions, with the vanguard led by the Earls of Gloucester and Hereford. Serving with them were the veterans of many Scottish campaigns: The Earl of Pembroke, Sir Robert Clifford; Sir Henry Beaumont; Sir Hugh Despenser, Sir Marmaduke Tweng and a great crusader from France, Sir Giles D'Argentan. We must not forget that also serving King Edward were Scots still opposed to Robert. Among them were John Comyn junior and a previous Guardian of Scotland, Sir Ingram de Umfraville. The English baggage train alone was impressive. Ships laden with food had been sent up to Leith and over 200 horse and oxen-drawn wagons had been commandeered for transporting provisions for the army. They also carried the possessions of English nobles who had been promised Scottish estates and would move in once the inevitable victory had been achieved.

The Scottish army could not have been more different from that which gathered at Wark. Traditionally, King Robert would have formed his army in the same feudal way as his English counterpart, but he had learned much over the last seven years, and many of those who were ready to fight at his side would do so voluntarily. Soon after Randolph had taken Edinburgh Castle in March 1314, the king had begun to rally his army. From April onwards he based himself in the forest of Torwood, between Falkirk and Stirling, south of his intended battlesite. Here he was well protected by what was then thick woodland through

which ran an ancient Roman road. He would have plenty of warning of the approaching English army as this was the route they would have to come. As his army began to accumulate, Robert began to calculate how he would deploy his troops. It was obvious from the start that he was not going to have anywhere near the numbers of his enemy, and in ordinary pitched battle terms that would mean certain failure. But as long as battle was fought on his terms and he chose the battle site, inferiority of numbers need not be a disadvantage.

He divided his infantry into four divisions: The first was a vanguard of 500 men which would be commanded by Thomas Randolph. Since he had become Earl of Moray, most of his troops had come from this earldom and also from around Inverness. Edward Bruce would lead the second division, which was made up of 1,000 men from the northeast and from Galloway. Division three numbered approximately 1,500 and was commanded by Walter Stewart, who had become High Steward since his father, James, had died five years previously. Most of the troops from this division came from the Steward's lands around Renfrewshire and Lanark and also included recruits from the Borders. However, Walter was young and was put under the watchful eye of James Douglas. Finally, the largest division was led by the King. This force of 2,000 consisted of men from the earldom of Carrick and, following his late arrival, all the Highlanders and Islesmen with Angus Macdonald. No one knew the fighting capabilities of these men better than the king, and only he could ensure that they fought with the discipline required in a pitched battle.

King Robert's Commanders

Possible breakdown of Scottish divisions at the Battle of Bannockburn.

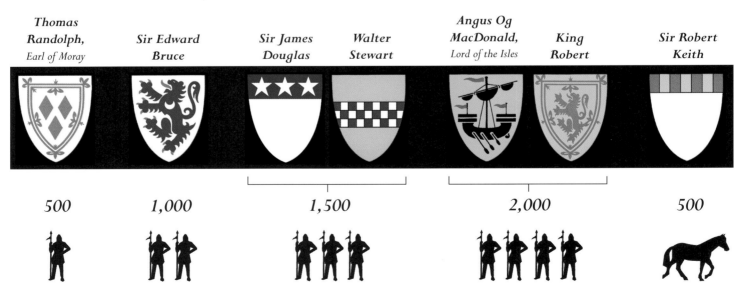

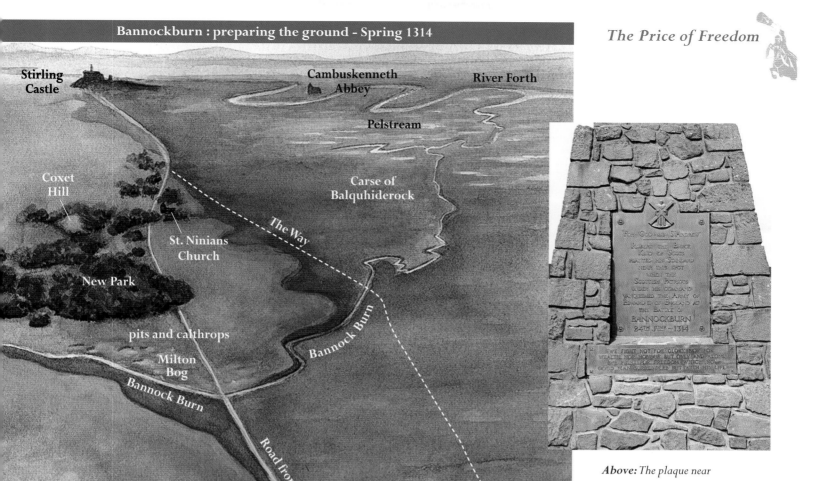

Stirling Castle

Coxet Hill

New Park

St. Ninians Church

pits and calthrops

Milton Bog

Bannock Burn

Bannock Burn

The Way

Cambuskenneth Abbey

Pelstream

River Forth

Carse of Balquhiderock

Bannock Burn

Road from Falkirk

Above: The plaque near Bannockburn Heritage Centre commemorating the battle.

The Scots simply could not match the vast numbers of heavy cavalry in the English ranks, but they could muster 500 agile light horse, which could be far more effective if deployed in the correct way. Although the sum total of the king's army was only 5-6,000 men, for the first time it was an army united in its cause. Men of different rank, from all corners of Scotland, stood shoulder to shoulder for no other reason than to fight for their freedom, and leading them was a man who had fought consistently for that one principle since taking the crown 8 years previously. He may have been King of Scots, but when it came to the battlefield he took no position of privilege. Over the coming weeks he began to train his men. He himself had not fought a pitched battle on this scale before, but he recalled the well-known tactics used by Wallace. The schiltron was an effective formation for holding back a cavalry charge, but it was largely defensive. To win this battle the Scots would have to attack the English, not simply hold them off, so Robert adapted the schiltrons so that they could advance into the enemy. This would suit the aptitude of his foot soldiers, most of whom would prefer a running battle.

Once the king knew his own capabilities and had some indication of the scale of his foe, he set about preparing the battle ground. The Roman road which cut through Torwood ran straight up to Stirling, but along its route to the east the ground became increasingly marshy as it crossed the Bannock Burn. To the west of the road, the hills and forest of Torwood continued into the New Park, a royal hunting forest established by Alexander III. There was therefore little option for the English army but to approach Stirling along that road or perhaps just to the east of it where the village of Bannockburn was located and where a less significant road known as the Public Way crossed the carse. Moving his army north out of the Torwood he planned to make his stand on the edge of the New Park, where rising ground was backed by thick woodland. Opposite him and across the road to the east was a plateau of farmland which ran into the Carse of Balquhiderock, a vast area of marshy ground embraced on three sides by the Bannock and Pelstream Burns. Either side of the road, just north of where it crossed the Bannock Burn, the king ordered the digging of shallow pits. Covered over with grass, these would handicap the English cavalry if they attempted to leave the road on to the open ground. Strewn between the pits the Scots scattered calthrops, small four-pronged weapons with one prong faced upwards, to disable the English horses. The Scots set up their supply base in the relatively safe Cambuskenneth Abbey, on the north bank of the River Forth.

On June 22, King Robert sent Douglas and Sir Robert Keith south into the Torwood to wait for the approaching English army. They returned that evening with the news that King Edward had reached Falkirk where his army had set up camp for the night.

Bannockburn – "Now's the day"
Events of 23 June

Edward's army had set out from Wark on 17 June, marching up through Lauderdale towards Edinburgh, where they met the supply ships which had docked at Leith. On 22 June, with the deadline for relieving Stirling now only a day away, the army made a brisk journey to Falkirk. It was a blazing hot, dusty day and they were exhausted by the time they camped that evening. As midnight passed, it was now 23 June and the duration of Sir Philip Mowbray's bargain was now up. At first light the English host began the final leg of its journey and, as they approached Torwood, they were met by Mowbray, who had managed to slip away from the Castle and bring Edward vital news about the deployment of Scots divisions. From high up on the rock of Stirling he had, to an extent, been able to observe the movements of the Scottish army. This could be to the English advantage, assuming they knew how to interpret the information.

The Scots had also risen early in anticipation of the English advance. King Robert now knew the size and scale of his opposition from the reports brought back to him from Douglas and Keith. Those two men had been alarmed at the prospects of facing 20,000 men with their own meagre 5,500. How could they expect to overpower an army that outnumbered them four to one? The king told them to keep their doubts to themselves and to inform the ranks that the English were approaching in great numbers, but were disorganised and leaderless.

Robert had already positioned his divisions the night before. Division one, the vanguard under Randolph, had been sent north towards St Ninian's Kirk to cover the Public Way if the English did attempt to cross the Carse. Divisions two and three, under Douglas and Edward Bruce, stood astride the entrance to the New Park and the king himself, with the fourth and largest division, covered their rear just inside the trees at a place known as the Borestone. Sir Robert Keith and his precious light cavalry were kept back in the trees to be used at an appropriate time. Making the most of every last man, the king ordered the camp followers, craftsmen and late arrivers to stay out of site behind Coxet Hill, to the west of them. Known as the 'small folk', they were either too poorly-equipped or not well-enough trained to participate in the main battle. However, by 23 June, their numbers had grown to about 2,000 and they could serve a useful purpose at some stage of the battle.

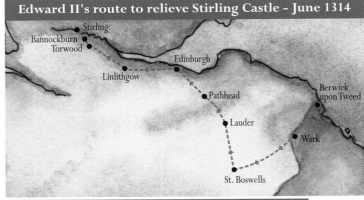

Edward II's route to relieve Stirling Castle - June 1314

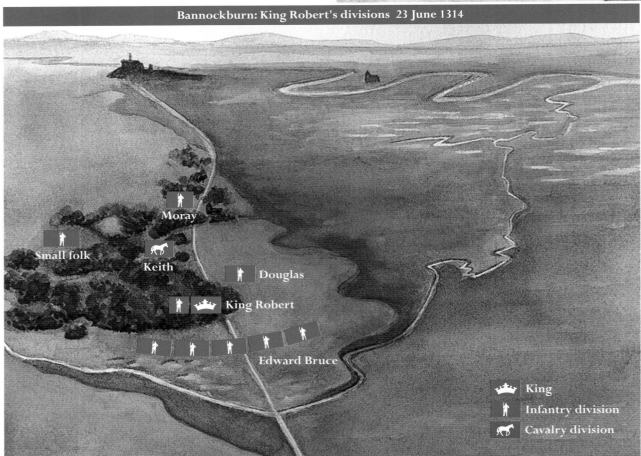

Bannockburn: King Robert's divisions 23 June 1314

As the day wore on, all Scots eyes turned towards the south east. As the morning sunshine gained strength, the glistening armour and heraldic banners of the formidable English vanguard could be seen emerging from the Torwood. They did not deviate from the main road, as they were heading directly towards the main Scots positions in the New Park and needed to cross a ford at the Bannock Burn. King Edward was holding back with the main army, but behind the vanguard came 600 of the armoured cavalry which began to peel off from the rest and head towards the Public Way. It appears that the English strategy was to attack from the front whilst the cavalry went around to the Scots rear thus preventing their escape.

Mounted on a robust Highland pony, King Robert rode amongst his front line offering encouragement and ordering them to hold back as the vanguard began to cross the ford. Out ahead of the field was Sir Henry de Bohun, the young nephew of the Earl of Hereford, attired in full battle dress and sitting astride an enormous charger. He spotted the King of Scots with the golden circlet around his helmet and prepared to charge him. Winner of countless tournaments as he had been, Robert was taken aback by the challenge as he was ill-prepared for a joust! He was without armour and had no lance, but turning his pony around and running away would send all the wrong messages to his men. Taking the battle axe at his side, he rode

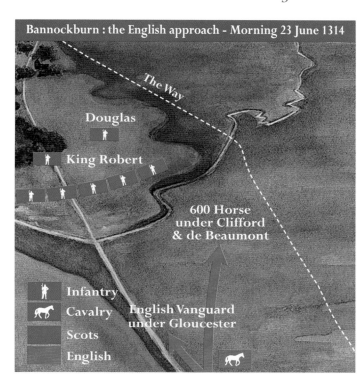

Bannockburn : the English approach - Morning 23 June 1314

forward towards the young knight who by now was nearly upon him. Pulling to one side and rising up in his stirrups, he wrong–footed de Bohun and brought his axe crashing down so hard through the knight's helmet and skull that it sheared off leaving the king with the wooden shaft in his hand.

Above: *King Robert slays Henry de Bohun on the first day of the Battle of Bannockburn.*

As de Bohun toppled to the ground, the Scots became too excited to hold themselves back and they charged towards the approaching English. The vanguard was already struggling to negotiate the pits and calthrops as the Scots clashed headlong into them, causing panic and confusion. The English were forced back across the Burn and King Robert recalled his unruly Scots. He had not intended battle to be joined at that point, but he had been partly responsible. When his commanders berated him for risking his life in such a way he responded with the words *"Alas, I have broken my good battle–axe"*. His mind was on other matters as his attention turned to those 600 English horse, which by now had made steady progress along the Public Way. Thomas Randolph, in command of the division covering that route, had left his post to be with the king, who sharply reminded him of his duty. Pointing towards the English he proclaimed to Randolph that *"A rose from thy chaplet has fallen"*. Annoyed that he had disappointed his king, Randolph dashed towards his division and arranged the men into a schiltron. He led them to a point where they would intercept the English and waited.

Below: The English vanguard advances, but falls foul of the Scots pits and calthrops.

Bannockburn : First encounters - Morning/Afternoon 23 June 1314

Moray's Schiltron

Clifford & de Beaumont

English Vanguard turns back

Infantry
Cavalry
Schiltron
Scots
English

Moray's schiltron holds firm against the might of England's cavalry on the first day of the Battle of Bannockburn.

Upon seeing a body of infantry standing like lambs for the slaughter, the leaders of the English horse, Sir Robert Clifford and Sir Henry Beaumont ordered a charge towards the schiltron - 600 horse against 500 men! However frightening a sight it must have been, Randolph's men stood firm in their hedgehog formation, as the English attacked them from all sides. But they could not breech the the wall of spears and many brave knights were impaled in the attempt. In the end, they resorted to riding past and throwing their weapons into the schiltron, which still stood firm. By now, King Robert and James Douglas were becoming concerned over Randolph's efforts. From a distance, all they could see was a mass of cavalry enveloping the schiltron, which could have been disintegrating for all they knew. Douglas was impatient to go to their aid, but Robert held him back, insisting that they stand firm here in case the vanguard returned to attack them. They need not have worried about Randolph, as with the diminishing cavalry numbers, the Scots schiltron began to press forward from its position. The weeks spent training this formation to become mobile had paid off, as the English horse was pushed back, forced to flee in all directions. The Scots had won an important psychological battle, as for the first time infantry had overcome the strength of cavalry in a pitched battle, proving that King Robert's strategy could work.

It was now early afternoon and the English commanders had returned to the main army and King Edward, who were still waiting in Torwood. Having made little progress so far, it was clear that they were not going achieve much on that day, and the rest of the army needed rest and water. The dilemma was where to camp that night which would put them in a strong position for the following day. Despite being advised to stay put within the shelter of Torwood, Edward decided that the whole army should cross the Bannock Burn further to the east and camp on the Carse of Balquhiderock. If the Scots forces had equalled their own, the English might be vulnerable to attack in this position. But he was confident that with his numbers, the King of Scots could not successfully lead an attack against them. So, as the afternoon wore on, the English slowly moved out and prepared themselves for an uncomfortable night on the Carse.

Meanwhile, King Robert was holding his own Council of War as he and his commanders watched the English army in its entirety move out in front of them. He was urged to abandon any further confrontation with the English and withdraw his army into the west to fight his guerrilla war as he had done up to now. But the king would not be put off. The morale of his men was high since the victory of Randolph's schiltron and his own triumph over de Bohun, and now king Robert watched the English in disbelief as they marched out on to the unstable ground of the Carse, surrounded by the waters of the Pelstream and Bannock Burn. This was all too much of a gift to the Scots, and their king would not turn away from the golden opportunity to free his country.

Bannockburn : the English camp - Evening 23 June 1314

King Edward II & main English army camp on the Carse

Bannockburn – "Let us do or die!"
Events of 24 June

King Robert had planned a dawn offensive. Not only would the English be taken aback, but in the early morning the height of the tide on the two burns would ensure that the English were trapped. Not all had gone the king's way, as during the night the Scots supply base at Cambuskenneth had been attacked by the Earl of Atholl. He was one of the many Scots nobles who had fought for the English, and been accepted back by Robert in return for his loyalty. But a family grudge against Edward Bruce had caused him to turncoat once more and as a result the Scots had lost their supplies.

On the morning of 24 June, the sun arose into a clear sky, indicating another long, hot day. The king stirred his men to action but before ordering them into their formations, he ordered that Mass be celebrated. It was St John the Baptist's day and they would need God's protection as well as strength and courage to fight well. The army could not win the day on empty stomachs so they took time to eat and then formed up into their divisions. To complete the ceremonies, the king promoted both Walter Stewart and James Douglas to knighthood and, following this, the entire army received the blessing by Maurice, Abbot of Inchaffray who held the holy relics of Saint Columba in the Monymusk reliquary. Then, before they moved off, the king gave a speech attributed to him by Bernard, Abbot of Arbroath. From personal experience, he spoke with great emotion:

"My lords, my people, accustomed to enjoy that full freedom for which in times gone by the kings of Scotland have fought many a battle! For eight years or more I have struggled with much labour for my right to the kingdom and for honourable liberty. I have lost brothers, friends and kinsmen. Your own kinsmen have been made captive, and bishops and priests are locked in prison. Our country's nobility has poured forth its blood in war. Those barons you can see before you, clad in mail, are bent upon destroying me and obliterating my kingdom, nay, our whole nation. They do not believe that we can survive. They glory in their warhorses and equipment. For us, the name of the Lord must be our hope of victory in battle."

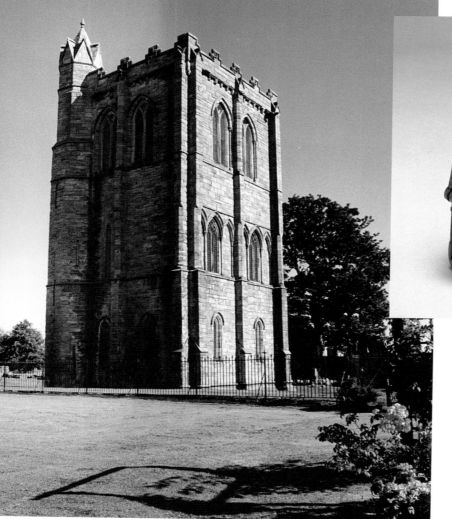

Above: *The Monymusk Reliquary contained the holy relics of Saint Columba and was carried at Bannockburn by the Abbot of Inchaffray.*

Left: *Cambuskenneth Abbey, site of the Scots supply base which was raided on the eve of the battle.*

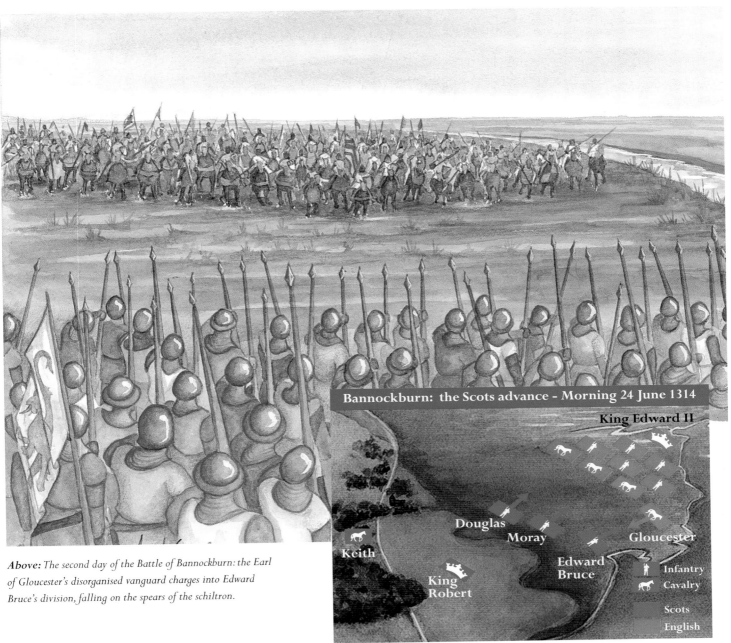

Bannockburn: the Scots advance – Morning 24 June 1314

King Edward II

Douglas

Moray

Gloucester

Keith

King Robert

Edward Bruce

Infantry

Cavalry

Scots

English

Above: The second day of the Battle of Bannockburn: the Earl of Gloucester's disorganised vanguard charges into Edward Bruce's division, falling on the spears of the schiltron.

As the day broke, the Scots began to move out of the New Park and on to the Carse. The four divisions would march out one after the other, each in schiltron formation. Edward Bruce led his division first, advancing to the right next to the Bannock Burn. Behind him and to his left were echeloned the divisions of Randolph and Douglas. Bringing up the rear, but remaining on the edge of the New Park was the king's division of 2,000. Keith and the 500 light horse held their position behind the king in the Park as did the 'small folk' of camp followers and late arrivals, hidden behind the Coxet Hill.

The English, meanwhile, who had been unaware of the Scots movements, awoke to see them moving down from the New Park ready to attack. King Edward was clearly surprised to see the Scots apparently inviting the English to join them in battle. To offer themselves thus, on open ground when they were so outnumbered was clearly suicidal. To Edward's further disbelief,

the Scots halted and knelt in prayer. Thinking this to be a sign of surrender, the English King proclaimed: *"Those men kneel to ask for mercy"*. However, Sir Ingram de Umfraville, who was close by Edward and knew King Robert well added *"You are right; they ask for mercy, but not from you. They ask it from God."* Edward had been advised to delay the battle, but now his hand was forced. With that, Edward ordered the call to arms and the English moved in complete disorder to prepare themselves. Immediately facing Edward Bruce's division, next to the Bannock Burn, was the Earl of Gloucester's vanguard. He caused his men to mount up in such a panic that he failed to put on his own surcoat identifying himself. Without judging the strength of the first schiltron, they charged forward with a velocity that caused most of them to founder on the bristling wall of spears. Gloucester himself perished unrecognised at the front of his men.

Bannockburn: the battle climax - 24 June 1314

Longbow

King Edward II

Douglas

Moray

King Robert

Edward Bruce

Keith

Infantry
Cavalry
Scots
English

Not much time had passed and by now the three Scots divisions had come up to engage with most of the English front line. Although they were great in number, the English had very little room in which to manœuvre and found themselves fighting on an extremely narrow front. Most of their infantry and bowmen were wasted at the back, unable to find room to fire their arrows on the enemy, and the heavy cavalry failing to find a firm footing on the soft, marshy ground of the Carse. Now the Scots brought the full weight of their schiltrons to bear as they pressed slowly, relentlessly forward, all but flattening the field in front of them, pushing those behind into the Bannock Burn itself. No-one seemed to be in command of the English host, but eventually somebody managed to deploy a detachment of longbowmen over the Pelstream Burn on to some high ground. Within minutes they were dropping their yard-long shafts on top of Douglas's left flank and would have caused great carnage, as happened at Falkirk, had King Robert not acted swiftly. At last he had a job for the light cavalry and, from his position at the back, he signalled to Sir Robert Keith to spur forward and scatter the English longbow. The lightly-armed horsemen were there in no time, and the bowmen fled in all directions.

By mid-morning, some parts of the schiltrons were beginning to waver through sheer exhaustion, as the English fought feverishly to hold their ground. Now King Robert was ready to send his own division forward. The battle had not yet been won and these were the last of his men. With the words; *"My hope is constant in thee"*, the Macdonald motto ever since, he commanded Angus og Macdonald to advance with the Highlanders and islesmen. Driving forward to the left of Douglas's weakened schiltron, the final division gave the entire Scots fighting machine added impetus. Realising that victory was in sight they shouted as one; *"on them, on them, they fail"*. With nowhere left to go, the screaming, floundering Englishmen and horses tumbled backwards into the Bannock Burn to either drown or make their escape in any direction they could.

Leadership from the English commanders had been non-existent although King Edward had fought gallantly alongside his men. But those surrounding him soon realised that their cause was lost and their main concern was to get the king to safety. Pembroke and D'Argentan dragged his horse around and pushed through their own men towards the Pelstream Burn. The ebb of the tide had provided a relatively easy crossing and, surrounded by a body of 500 horse, Edward made his escape north towards Stirling Castle. The rest of his army was left to defend itself as best it could, but the attention of all on the battlefield was very quickly drawn to the fluttering banner of three lions, as it disappeared into the horizon. Once the King was in safety, Giles d' Argentan took his leave and returned to the battlefield. He would not flee like a coward and, setting his lance at the Scots spears, he charged headlong to his death. Then, to the surprise of everybody, the 'small folk' came rushing out from behind the Coxet Hill and ran towards the Carse shouting in triumph and waving their primitive weapons. The English took them to be reinforcements and soon abandoned their fight. There followed a rout, as the schiltrons broke off their attack to pursue the fleeing army.

Edward, meanwhile had been refused entrance into the Castle by Sir Philip Mowbray, who in lowering the drawbridge would have also let in the Scots. The King of England had to turn about and head southwest, around the back of the Scots, towards Torwood. Hotly pursued by Sir James Douglas, he eventually made it to Dunbar, where he escaped on a boat to Berwick. Many of the remaining army, nobles amongst them, surrendered to the Scots. King Robert's army had been victorious in a battle which no-one, including themselves, had expected them to fight, let alone win. The king himself had been an inspiration, taking full advantage of weaknesses exposed by the opposing army. Unlike King Edward, he had kept absolute control over his men, maintaining discipline to the very end.

Below: *The English are pushed into the Bannock Burn as the Scots schiltrons surge forward.*

Bannockburn: the battle climax - 24 June 1314

King Edward

Keith

King Robert

Douglas

Moray

Edward Bruce

Small folk

Scots

English

In the aftermath of battle, King Robert also displayed humble qualities of decency and benevolence when it came to dealing with the vanquished army. The dead were given Christian burials and the remains of Sir Robert Clifford, who had perished, and the Earl of Gloucester, Robert's cousin, were returned to their homes. Many significant men had been taken captive and would be exchanged for Scots prisoners in England. Until then, they were treated with respect as guests of the king, and not shackled away in dungeons. King Robert became internationally respected for his generous spirit.

How fared Scotland now?

Bannockburn is always recognised as the point at which Scotland regained her freedom, and this was true in terms of English occupation. However, the war was far from over and England did not accept defeat or Scotland's independent status for a long time to come.

By their victory on 24 June 1314, the Scots had gained considerable material wealth, for not only had they captured so many great nobles, but they now possessed the contents of their entire baggage train. It is said that the whole population benefitted from the value of these goods which amounted to £200,000, or nearer £50 million today. But the immediate concern for Robert was the return of his family, friends and all other Scots imprisoned in England. Amongst their own most valuable prisoners was the Earl of Hereford, who had commanded the English vanguard along with the deceased Earl of Gloucester. He had fled to the southwest following the battle, and headed for the safety of Bothwell Castle. However, its governor Walter FitzGilbert, who had been supporting the English, changed sides and after receiving Hereford made him his prisoner. The ransom from Hereford alone brought the return of the 15 most important Scottish captives. Amongst them were Robert's wife Elizabeth, parted from him for eight years, his daughter Marjorie, now a young woman of 20 and the Bishop of Glasgow, old and sick but grateful to be free. The brave Mary Bruce and Isabel of Buchan, who endured great suffering, had contrasting fortunes. Both had been released from their encaged confinement in 1310 and 1312 respectively, but only Mary was returned to Scotland. From 1314, the whereabouts of Isabel is a mystery as she seems to have disappeared from recorded history.

Below: This most famous statue of King Robert was unveiled at Bannockburn by the Queen in 1964.

The occupation of Scotland's castles by English or English-sympathising garrisons was definitely over. Stirling had yielded soon after Bannockburn and only Berwick remained in English hands, although Edward I's destruction of the town and massacre of its citizens had put an end to its reputation as Scotland's premier sea port. The Scots finally saw an end to year after year of invasion. The status of Scotland was no longer as high as it had been in the days of King Alexander III, and 18 years of being ravaged by war had taken its toll on the land and the prosperity of its people. As King of Scots, Robert saw it as his duty to achieve that prosperity at any cost. Although he had won acclaim amongst other European nations as a fair and Christian king, he was still an excommunicate, and Edward of England was determined that Scotland should not be recognised as an independent nation. Robert's objective was acknowledgement from England and Rome that he was the legitimate King of Scots.

Following his flight from Bannockburn, Edward II had returned to the south of England, where he could recover from his defeat and consider his next move. Edward by no means carried the support of his lords who had not expected the humiliation that Bannockburn brought. Resentment was growing amongst English nobles who expected the rewards of victory, not the impoverishment of defeat. The English king had to earn the loyalty of those who fought for him and they were not used

to failure. So forgetful had Edward been of his responsibilities, that he had even left his Great Seal behind on the Bannockburn battlefield. He did not stoop to ask for it back and no thanks were given when King Robert retrieved it and graciously returned it to his English counterpart.

There was only one way for the King of Scots to remind Edward that Scotland was a force to be reckoned with - invasion of England. Ironically, peace could only be brought about through a policy of aggression. Once again, the people of northern England would have to brace themselves for further Scottish attacks, which would be carried out with more confidence than ever before. Less than two months after Bannockburn the king sent his brother Edward with James Douglas and Sir John de Soules to lead an invasion into Northumberland. In fact, they went deeper into England than ever before if only to test how far they could go without being resisted. They reached down into Yorkshire, plundering towns and villages, demanding blackmail and burning the land. While the raiding went on, King Robert was continuing to strengthen his power and influence over Scottish nobles. Since the eleventh century the great Norman families of Scotland, including the Bruces, had paid homage to English kings for estates owned in England. The inconsistent behaviour of these nobles throughout the war had shown that this was no longer a sustainable situation.

Above: The River North Tyne is seen here just
south of Bellingham, Northumberland.

Robert I's campaign to resume the Lordship of Tynedale

Deadwater
N. Tyne
Wark on Tyne
Haltwhistle
Corbridge
Newcastle
Hexham
S. Tyne
Carlisle

Route of the River North & South Tyne
Route of Robert I

A parliament held at Cambuskenneth Abbey in November pronounced the most significant reforms of land ownership in medieval Scotland. All Scots swearing allegiance to King Robert should give up their English lands or face disinheritance from their Scottish lands. It was a question of choice between nationalities, and an oath of allegiance to the King of Scots had to be absolute. All Scots of landowning rank, whether having fought for or against Scotland at Bannockburn, must declare their allegiance to Robert alone within a year, or forfeit their Scottish lands and title.

Never seeming to tire, and with official business over, the king rounded off his triumphant year with another raid into England. He concentrated his invasion along the River Tyne, east of Newcastle, targeting Hexham and Corbridge. Tynedale was a lordship previously belonging to the King of Scots. Robert seized it back for Scotland and received the homage of the local inhabitants. More raids were carried out at the beginning of 1315 but, however devastating to the people of northern England, these attacks still did not provoke any response from Edward. He seemed oblivious to the needs and protection of the northern half of his country. Most of England's wealth and population existed in the south, untouched and unaffected by Scottish invasions. Robert would have to consider another alternative to stir Edward and he found it across the Irish Sea.

Ireland had been occupied by the English throughout the Scottish war and had become a significant supply base for invasions to Scotland. King Robert's success in overthrowing the Anglo-Norman regime in Scotland and their subsequent defeat at Bannockburn had given encouragement to other Celtic nations. If Ireland could rid itself of its English occupation with help from Scotland, Edward would face a threat from the west which he could not ignore, and the King of Scots would finally have some leverage over him. Ireland was divided into sub-kingdoms, as ancient Scotland had been, and its kings, although subdued by the English invasion, still ruled over their people. Robert sent messages of goodwill to the kings of Ireland reminding them of their shared ancestry and, in his own words, *"to negotiate with you in our name about permanently strengthening and maintaining inviolate the special friendship between us and you, so that with God's will our nation may be able to recover her ancient liberty."* Such was King Robert's reputation for success in these matters that he received a positive response almost immediately. Edward Bruce was invited to become High King of all Ireland and rid them of the English, which seemed an ideal opportunity for Robert's increasingly ambitious brother.

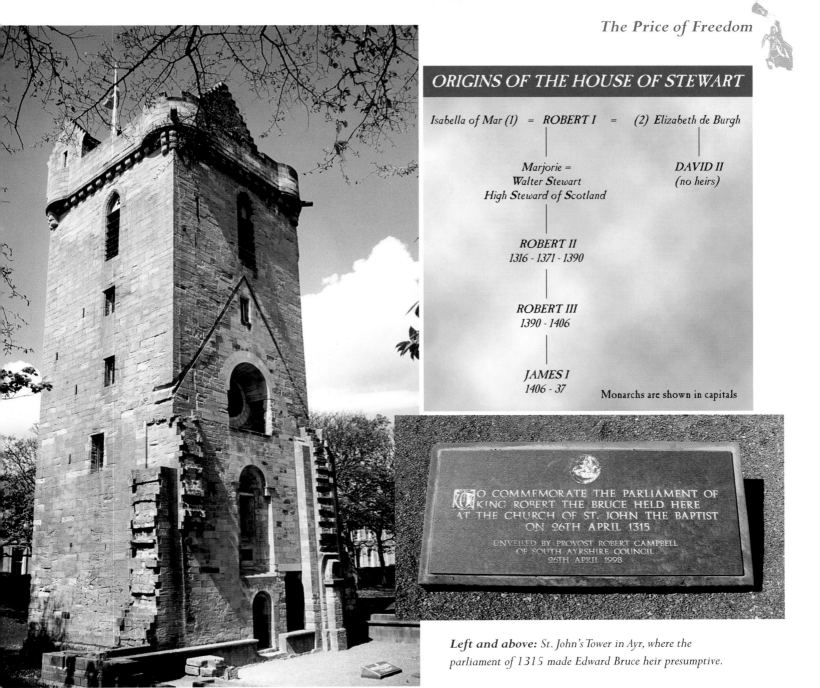

ORIGINS OF THE HOUSE OF STEWART

Isabella of Mar (1) = **ROBERT I** = *(2) Elizabeth de Burgh*

Marjorie =
Walter Stewart
High Steward of Scotland

DAVID II
(no heirs)

ROBERT II
1316 - 1371 - 1390

ROBERT III
1390 - 1406

JAMES I
1406 - 37

Monarchs are shown in capitals

TO COMMEMORATE THE PARLIAMENT OF
KING ROBERT THE BRUCE HELD HERE
AT THE CHURCH OF ST. JOHN THE BAPTIST
ON 26TH APRIL 1315
UNVEILED BY PROVOST ROBERT CAMPBELL
OF SOUTH AYRSHIRE COUNCIL
26TH APRIL 1998

Left and above: *St. John's Tower in Ayr, where the parliament of 1315 made Edward Bruce heir presumptive.*

Before the Scots could invest in their Irish adventure, one further matter had to be settled - the succession to the throne. Should anything happen to King Robert, the next in line had to be established and, to this end, a parliament was held at Ayr in April 1315. In the absence of any male heirs, Marjorie Bruce should succeed her father, but medieval Scotland required more than a 20 year-old woman to rule it. Robert and his queen, Elizabeth, had been parted for most of their married life and had as yet to produce any children. It was therefore decided that Edward Bruce should become heir presumptive until King Robert, or Marjorie from a future marriage provided a prince for Scotland. Shortly after this parliament, Marjorie, by her father's arrangement, married Walter Stewart. The house of the High Steward had always been strong supporters of the Bruce family, and young Walter had been a hero at Bannockburn. The seeds were sown for the beginning of the great royal house of Stewart.

High hopes for Ireland

Towards the end of May 1315, Edward Bruce set off for Ireland. He had been given a significant force of 6,000 men, even more than the king himself had led at Bannockburn. To keep his headstrong brother in check, Robert also sent his level-headed nephew, Thomas Randolph. They arrived at Larne on 26 May and quickly made their presence felt amongst the Norman-Irish nobles of Ulster. Blazing his way south, Edward arrived in Dundalk one month later and pushed further down towards Dublin. He defeated a host of English commanders in minor battles over the next six months: at Connor, the Earl of Ulster; at Kenlis, Roger Mortimer; and in February 1316, the Lord Lieutenant of Ireland, Edmund Butler, at Skerries. Less than a year after landing on Ireland, Edward was crowned High King of Ireland at Dundalk. It was 2 May, 1316.

Meanwhile, the effects of the Irish expedition were already being felt elsewhere and, as anticipated, the King of England was having to respond. The Welsh were expecting the new Irish king to come and restore their liberty as he had done Ireland's, so they came out in rebellion against England. Edward II had now been distracted from a campaign in Europe and from raising forces against a new Scottish offensive. While his brother was keeping up the pressure in Ireland, King Robert was busy at home. He finally put an end to the annoying opposition of John of Lorne by winning over the men of Argyll. Sailing out into the Hebrides to challenge MacDougall once again, the King of Scots took his ships through the shortcut at the top of Kintyre at Tarbert. But there was no water here and the galleys were dragged over land with the help of felled trees and a good easterly wind. Not since Magnus Barelegs 200 years before had this feat been attempted, and its accomplishment resulted in MacDougall's men flocking to King Robert's banner. John MacDougall fled to England for good, where he remained until his death three years later.

With Edward of England preoccupied with Wales and Ireland, Robert once again turned his attention to Border country and planned a serious offensive, not only on the countryside, but on the northern strongholds. In July 1315 he led an assault on Carlisle Castle, attacking it 'English-style' with siege weapons. But the defence by its governor, Andrew Harclay, was too thorough for the Scots, and the land around the castle base was too marshy to support heavy weapons. Not even James Douglas and his famous rope-ladders got the better of the defenders, as his men were picked off as they reached the top of the battlements. King Robert could have achieved more by staying with his traditional policy of winning castles by stealth and cunning, a method which had a one hundred percent success rate. After only ten days, he withdrew his men and returned home. He did not have much more luck at Berwick, when early in 1316, he and Douglas attempted to surprise the garrison at night. Their attack was foiled by the appearance of the moon as they approached the walls, and the town of Berwick still eluded the Scottish king.

Above: Carlisle Castle today.

Left: This facsimile of the Carlisle City Charter of 1316 shows Andrew Harclay defending Carlisle from the attack by King Robert.

Carrickfergus Castle, Co. Antrim, where King Robert landed to fight the English in Ireland.

Right: *The tomb of Marjorie Bruce, wife of Walter Stewart, in Paisley Abbey.*

James Douglas remained in the Borders to harry and intimidate Berwickshire, his adventures there adding to his reputation as the Black Douglas. King Robert had received tragic news further north and left Douglas to it. Not long after her marriage, Marjorie had conceived a child which was expected in March of that year. Whilst out riding, she had been violently thrown from her horse and was killed instantly. The baby, a boy, was cut from her body and, although badly disabled following the experience, had miraculously survived. Edward Bruce remained heir, but Robert Stewart, a tiny scrap of humanity, would one day inherit Scotland and all her troubles. King Robert had felt responsible for his daughter's suffering over the years and was greatly saddened by her death.

He immediately threw himself into another English invasion, which again pushed a long way south and ended up on the east coast before the return north. Towards the end of 1316, word arrived from Ireland that Edward Bruce was in need of his brother's assistance. The Norman barons in Ireland had not given up without a fight, and the High King of Ireland needed a boost to his campaign. King Robert decided that he himself could leave his realm without any serious worries. Once again there were civil disputes in England between Edward II and his nobles, so it was not likely that Scotland was under threat for a while yet. Putting the reins of power into the capable hands of Douglas and Walter Stewart, the king made preparations to leave. Before he left, further sad news came from Glasgow when the old Bishop, Robert Wishart, finally passed away in November.

With an impressive army behind him, the king arrived at Carrickfergus at the beginning of 1317, where he met his brother for the first time since Edward had become king. They agreed that they would march their combined forces through the whole of Ireland to make their presence known and for Edward to introduce himself to the five provinces of his new country, as was traditional of the High King. The experience of power placed at his disposal had clearly consumed the King of Scots brother, and from the beginning, his campaign lacked discipline and organisation. Edward spurred off ahead with the vanguard, leaving his brother to bring up the rear. Within no time, this vulnerability had been seized upon by Robert's father-in-law, the Earl of Ulster, who made ready to pounce on the King of Scots exposed division as he passed by. But the astute king sensed an ambush and, keeping his experienced army in close formation, fought off the Anglo-Irish attack, forcing the Earl to withdraw to Dublin. Robert pursued him, but found the town so well defended that he left them to it, heading south towards Munster. There he was assured that there would be more support for an uprising against the English.

Above: Whyte's Castle, Athy, County Kildare. In 1316 Edward Bruce overcame an English force at nearby Ardscull.

It was clear, though, that the King of Scots was not fully prepared for the ways of the Irish. This was not Scotland and he could not take control of events. Moving into the west, he had reached the River Shannon only to find his army facing a native Irish clan which was feuding with one of the Irish chieftains amongst his own forces. He had no wish to involve himself in the civil disputes of Irish clans when he was there to rid them of English occupation. He withdrew his army before any confrontation. His foray into Western Ireland had been in vain. There was no support there and with the English reforming their strength, it was time to retire north to his Ulster base and rejoin his brother. Robert's timing had been bad, as they were now hindered by a famine which had spread throughout the south west of Ireland, caused by a year of worsening climate. Progress was very slow and desperate, as they were held back by sickness and starvation. Finally they reached Ulster and with a new Lord Lieutenant of Ireland, Roger Mortimer, having been appointed from England, the King of Scots decided to cut his losses and return home. With its internal feuds, it was obvious that Ireland would take many days to be won yet. Taking a few of his men and Thomas Randolph with him, the king returned home and by May 1317 was back on Scottish soil. It had been an odd diversion for King Robert. He could have spent those lost weeks more usefully in his own country, but it had created a valuable distraction for England.

Robert I's campaign route in Ireland - February-April 1317

- - - - ▶ Scots journey South
- - - - ▶ Scots journey North

A war on diplomacy

At last the King of Scots could return home and continue his battle to secure a lasting peace, and acceptance of himself and Scotland as a legitimate king and nation. However, while Robert had been away, Edward of England had been making overtures to the new Pope in Rome, John XXII, keeping the pressure on the Vatican to uphold the excommunication. The Scots would have to double their efforts to counter the English diplomatic effort. Rome was concerned that the Christian countries of Europe were not committed enough to fighting the infidel in the Holy Land, and that England especially was always too preoccupied with its military campaigns at home to care about the Crusades. Regardless of the failure of their military conquest, the English argument seemed to be that if the Scots would only accept the English King as their overlord, and stop rising up in arms against England, Edward would gladly devote more of his time and effort into fighting the infidel. With Scotland being outside the protection of Holy Church, they were unable to effectively fight their corner. But the result of all this was pressure from the Pope for both countries to agree a truce and a few months after his return from Ireland, King Robert received emissaries from Rome carrying letters urging his co-operation.

The attempts to lull Scotland into a truce foundered almost immediately, and all because of the way in which both kings had been addressed. Edward had been given his due title of illustrious king of England, whereas Robert had been titled "*the noble Robert Bruce, acting as King of Scots.*" Of course there was no way that this was acceptable and the letters were never opened. The emissaries were politely sent away with the reply that until such correspondence was correctly addressed, the king could not respond to it; after all there were other men in Scotland called Robert Bruce. Further attempts were made to engage Robert in a truce, none of them giving him his due as King of Scots. Until he was able to gain peace on terms which would benefit Scotland, there would be no truce. Instead he would continue to threaten the north of England and win back all that belonged to his kingdom. He turned his attention on Berwick once again and made preparations to attack the English-held town. It was still a worthy prize if the Scots could regain it, and it was clear that King Edward was not going to assist the garrison and population in its defence.

By the beginning of 1318, the Scots had set up camp a few miles from Berwick, and prepared to besiege the town's walls. There was always an element of luck in winning over these strongholds and the Scots had never been lucky with Berwick. However, on this occasion, good fortune arrived in the form of an English citizen of Berwick bearing a grudge against the soldiers of the town. Peter Spalding sent word to the Scots that he could get them into the town, over an an exposed section of the wall. King Robert decided that, as this was a rare opportunity, he would take the man at his word. On 1 April, the walls of Berwick were successfully scaled by Randolph and Douglas and the town was swarming with Scots. The king had ordered a quiet takeover of Berwick, but the enthusiasm of his men had raised the alarm and many of the citizens had made it to the safety of the castle. King Robert besieged it for a few days, cutting off its supplies, whereupon it surrendered. For the first time in his campaign to regain Scottish strongholds, King Robert did not destroy a castle. It proves the high esteem in which Berwick was held by the Scots, that they were prepared to preserve it and defend it against the might of an English attack, which there would inevitably be.

Berwick from Tweedmouth; In 1318, King Robert besieged and captured the town.

Mitford Castle, one of many Northumberland strongholds that King Robert seized in his campaign to attract attention from Edward II.

The king left his son-in-law, Walter Stewart, in charge of strengthening the town and he himself led an army into northern England. This invasion was particularily vicious and perhaps indicates King Robert's impatience over the King of England's lack of interest in the north. In Northumberland, he seized the castles of Wark, Harbottle along the Coquet valley and Mitford, near Morpeth before striking into Yorkshire yet again. On his way down, he burned the land before arriving at Ripon and exacting blackmail, finally returning with hostages from the town.

The result of this summer of activity was a step backwards for Scotland's spiritual cause. Robert's deeds in England had been reported to the new Pope who himself further endorsed the excommunication on the King of Scots, though now it also applied to all who supported him and his cause. Meanwhile, his brother continued to keep the English busy in Ireland. There had been much activity on the high seas between Ireland and Wales, resulting in defeat of the Scottish fleet and the cutting off of supplies to Edward Bruce. However, the High King had managed to mobilise Irish national support and in October 1318,

having assembled a new army with some troops from his brother, Edward prepared for an assault on Dundalk. As on so many other occasions, he charged in with no real strategy, but this time it would be his undoing. He had arranged his army into three divisions but sent each one after the other without proper overall command. The new English Lord Lieutenant, Richard Clare, had deployed his vastly superior army in front of the approaching Scots and Irish, outside Dundalk. The High King's forces were so disorganised that their numbers were wasted. The first division was defeated before the second arrived to reinforce it, and both were obliterated before the final one, led by Edward Bruce himself, showed up.

Despite the pleas of his commanders to withdraw, Edward was determined that he would not turn and run, and so ordered a charge into the enemy. The King of Scots' only surviving brother perished on that battlefield, bringing to an end any further hopes of co-operation with Ireland. Yet, at the same time, that country was no longer of any use to the English, who had lost coherent command of most of its provinces.

Renewed conflict

The news of the High King of Ireland's death cannot have surprised King Robert that much. Edward's impetuous behaviour was such that it was only a matter of time before he threw himself carelessly into his own death. The King of Scots would surely have been saddened by the loss of his last brother: all four of them had been victims of this war. Of immediate concern to Scotland however, was the succession to the throne, and now that the heir apparent was dead, agreement had to be made on who should next be king. Queen Elizabeth, now approaching 40, had still not brought forth a son and it was feared that she was past the age of bearing children. The infant Robert Stewart was the logical choice, and a parliament was called at Scone to settle the succession. On 3 December, 1318, the king's two year-old grandson became heir to the throne, with Thomas Randolph to act as regent should he still be a minor when the time came. Also in this parliament, the king sought to prepare the whole of Scotland for continuing conflict with England. They still had to be prepared at any time to face their southern neighbour, whether in attack or defence, and every man of fighting age had to arm himself for such an event.

Below: *Edward II moved north to York, where he left his queen, Isabella, behind the safety of its walls. Her safety, however, was soon threatened, as Douglas and Moray headed south for an attempted abduction.*

It was the beginning of 1319, and there had been no serious conflict between England and Scotland on their own territories since Bannockburn five years previously. By now, though, the situation had altered and the conditions for hostilities had returned. From the English point of view, they had much to avenge, if somewhat belatedly. There had been countless invasions by the Scots into northern England who had recently taken back Berwick upon Tweed. That alone was enough to finally stir Edward II from his southern lair. The English king could relax over any further trouble in Ireland, and the ongoing dispute between himself and the Earl of Lancaster, the executioner of Piers Gaveston, had subsided for the moment. Edward II marched north to York, bringing with him his queen, Isabella, now a woman of 25. They had grown closer since Gaveston's death, as was evident by the birth of a son, Edward, to Isabella in 1312. Edward then marched on to Newcastle, where an army of 8,000 had assembled in preparation for an assault on Berwick. Making their way north, the English host, with an impressive array of siege weapons, arrived outside the walls of Berwick as a fleet of English ships sailed up the east coast into the River Tweed. Young Walter Stewart prepared town and castle for the inevitable onslaught and Edward surrounded the walls with his troops and siege weapons, far greater in numbers than was necessary for the task.

Throughout September 1319, the English assailed the walls of Berwick. Walter Stewart's defence of the town was admirable, for not only did he hold out against the assault, but he launched an effective counter attack on the English below. To begin with Edward's troops attempted to scale the walls, keeping the Scots occupied along their full length while the English ships approached, thus completing the attack from all sides. Stewart's men successfully held the battlements, and even ventured out to burn the ships once it was evident that they could not reach the walls. Following their failure to conquer the town, the English then brought up their siege weapons. This time they would attempt to go under the walls, by digging away at their foundations under the protection of the 'sow'. This giant canopied vehicle, underneath which men were protected, moved into position, as the Scots fired catapults towards it. Before the English could get to work on the walls, a huge stone went crashing through the sow's canopy, rendering all those beneath it defenceless. Despite their consistent failure, the English onslaught over the walls continued, and Berwick's brave defenders became depleted. The castle garrison, shut away in case the walls had been breached, was brought out as a last resort. Time was running out for the Scots who now needed rescuing by their king.

Robert did not have the numbers to successfully attack the English encampment at Berwick, and Edward had so successfully protected his troops that there was no way of reaching the town. The King of Scots worked on a plan to draw Edward and his army away from Berwick, and a threat to Queen Isabella, still at York, was a tempting prospect. King Edward's obsession with Berwick meant that the north of England, as far south as York, was unprotected. So while the King of England's back was turned, King Robert sent his two most able men, Douglas and Randolph, with an army to that great city to kidnap Isabella.

Their journey south was hardly secretive and word of the plot went ahead of the Scots. Without delay, the queen was sent to Nottingham and the citizens of York, led by its Archbishop, decided that in the absence of an army, they would defend themselves. They learned that the Scots were not that great in number and approaching York via Boroughbridge. The Archbishop boldly marched out with a humble army, largely consisting of clergy, and approached the Scots encampment at Myton on Swale, just east of Boroughbridge. They advanced in complete disorder, with no strategy at all, coming up on the Scots to find them preparing for attack in schiltron formation. Douglas and Randolph were equally prepared to fight men of God on the battlefield, as they were trained soldiers. However, the reputation of Douglas preceded him, and the 'divine' army of York lost their nerve. In blind panic, they fled in all directions, hotly pursued by the Scots. There was utter carnage that day in the event which became known as the 'Chapter of Myton', because of the hundreds of clergy who were slain.

Edward II attacks Berwick; Scots invade England - September 1319

English route north
Possible Scots route south

Above: The clergy of York, later known as the Chapter of Myton, march out to challenge the approaching Scots.

The Scots may not have achieved their objective at York, but the event caused a stir in Berwick, and soon the English were divided as to the course of action. Edward did not really care about the plight of his northern subjects, and was insistent on remaining at Berwick. However, the nobles with lands in the north were otherwise inclined and soon withdrew their forces from the siege. Edward had to follow suit, but kept the remaining army intact to trap the Scots as they returned north. Douglas, however, had slipped passed them without Edward even realising.

Towards the end of 1319, Douglas invaded the northwest of England yet again, and the cumulative effect of this aggressive activity at last caused Edward to agree to a two-year truce, effective from the beginning of 1320. This was all very well, but Edward would still not concede over the question of Scottish Independence. Whilst having agreed a truce, the King of England in a two-faced deal persuaded the Pope to continue condemning King Robert. As a result the pope ordered *"Robert Bruce, governing the Kingdom of Scotland"* to come to the papal court and answer for his deeds and those of his countrymen. As before, Robert did not respond, due to the use of this title and once again the Pope reissued the excommunication. It was all depressingly familiar to the King of Scots: no sooner had he gained the upper hand, when Edward destroyed his progress. A new approach was required to the quest for a permanent solution, and the latest truce now gave him time. If military success was not enough to convince the Pope of Scotland's right, then the collective voice of the Scottish people could be. They would speak for their king and the world would listen.

Below: Looking north from the bridge over the River Swale towards the field where the 'Chapter of Myton' was fought.

"For Freedom Alone"

In March 1320, a Great Council gathered at Newbattle Abbey, just south of Edinburgh. It was decided here that the entire community of the realm, earls, barons and freeholders, would put their seals to a letter asserting Scotland's ancient liberties, and the duty of their king to defend them. The content of the letter was agreed at Newbattle, and written by the King's Chancellor, Bernard de Linton, who was Abbot of Arbroath. The result was a diplomatic masterpiece which stands alone amongst all other written documents of the age and has been revered down the centuries.

'The Declaration of Arbroath', as it became known, began by explaining the origins of Scotland and how for centuries it had enjoyed freedom without interference from its aggressive southern neighbour. It went on to tell of how God and Saint Andrew had preserved Scotland and *"Thus our nation under their protection did indeed live in freedom and peace up to the time when that mighty prince the King of the English, Edward, the father of the one who reigns today, when our kingdom had no head and our people harboured no malice or treachery and were then unused to wars or invasions, came in the guise of a friend and ally to harass them as an enemy."*

The letter then pays tribute to King Robert, stating that *"from these countless evils we have been set free, by the help of HimWho though He afflicts yet heals and restores, by our most tireless Prince, King and Lord, the Lord Robert. He, that his people and his heritage might be delivered out of the hands of our enemies, met toil and fatigue, hunger and peril ... and bore them cheerfully"*. They followed this, however, with a warning to their king. At a time when feudalism had reached its peak, the Declaration was an extraordinary example of what the people of a nation expected of their king. They made it clear that *"if he should give up what he has begun, and agree to make us or our kingdom subject to the King of England or the English, we should exert ourselves at once to drive him out as our enemy and a subverter of his own rights and ours."* Then, with words that have rung down the centuries, they justified their call for independence: *"for, as long as but a hundred of us remain alive, never will we on any conditions be brought under English rule. It is in truth not for glory, nor riches, nor honours that we are fighting, but for freedom - for that alone, which no honest man gives up but with life itself."*

It did not end with those words, but went on to state that as the Pope had no real cause for prejudice against the Scots, he

The present-day buildings of Newbattle Abbey, Midlothian. The content of the Declaration of Arbroath was agreed here at a Great Council.

Above: *The Declaration of Arbroath, 1320: one of the few documents, and the most significant, to survive from Scotland's medieval past.*

should ask Edward to leave them alone: *"May it please you to admonish and exhort the King of the English, who ought to be satisfied with what belongs to him since England used once to be enough for seven kings or more, to leave us Scots in peace, who live in this poor little Scotland, beyond which there is no dwelling-place at all, and covet nothing but our own."*

Then, knowing the Pope's devotion to the Crusades, they offered themselves to fight his cause, when no longer defending themselves against the English *"who for false reasons pretend that they cannot go to the help of the Holy Land because of wars they have on hand with their neighbours. The real reason that prevents them is*

that in making war on their smaller neighbours they find quicker profit and weaker resistance. But how cheerfully our Lord the King and we too would go there if the King of the English would leave us in peace..."

Finally, the letter put it to the Pope that he should not believe all of England's propaganda: *"But if your Holiness puts too much faith in the tales the English tell and will not give sincere belief to all this, nor refrain from favouring them to our prejudice, then the slaughter of bodies, the perdition of souls, and all other misfortunes that will follow, inflicted by them on us and by us on them, will, we believe, be surely laid by the Most High to your charge."*

The letter was sealed and issued at Arbroath Abbey on 6 April 1320, although complications over safely sending it to the Pope meant it did not reach him until the end of June. However, the effect of the Declaration of Arbroath on the Pontiff was profound and he immediately turned on King Edward II, no longer calling for a truce, but for a permanent end to the war. Such was the attitude of the English that it would be several years before any kind of agreement was reached, but the Declaration had been perfectly judged, and became the turning point in the campaign for recognition of Scottish nationhood.

Despite the apparent unity shown by all who put their names to the Declaration, some of these nobles were conspiring against King Robert at the very time that it was being considered by the Pope. It was the first internal threat to his position since the parliament of 1309, where all in Scotland unequivocally accepted Robert as King of Scots. A plot to overthrow the Bruce dynasty was revealed through gossip by the Countess of Strathearn. It appeared that the old rivalries of the pre-war years, when Bruce the Competitor fought Balliol for the throne, had not gone away. Sir William Soules, son of one of the many other contenders, was the figurehead of the plot, and his family had Comyn connections and Balliol sympathies. The Soules conspiracy was discovered and foiled within days of becoming a reality, when Soules himself was caught mustering a small force at Berwick. In August 1320 the 'Black Parliament' as it became known tried Soules and the Countess, herself a Comyn, and convicted them for treason, sentencing them both to perpetual imprisonment. It seems likely that Soules had been coerced into the plot by other conspirators, notably Roger Mowbray and David Brechin. They were found guilty

and some condemned to execution. The time had passed when acts of clemency were made to those who opposed the king. The likes of Brechin had fought for the English at Bannockburn and then been accepted into the king's peace. There could be no more forgiving of traitors who had already had the chance to prove their loyalty to King Robert. The Black Parliament had been a test of discipline and saw an end to the old family rivalries, at least for that generation.

While the Soules Conspiracy had been a threat to the House of Bruce, other events that year appeared to safeguard its future. Although in her 40th year, Queen Elizabeth put an end to speculation that she was barren by giving birth to a child, a girl called Margaret. She and Robert had been married for eighteen years, eight of them being spent imprisoned in England. Now, at last, she was capable of producing an heir, whatever the risk to her health at that time of life.

In the spring of 1321, the Northumberland castle of Bamburgh was the setting for negotiations to create a lasting peace between England and Scotland. Unfortunately, the English remained obstinate and their envoys refused to accept anything less than a settlement which included English overlordship. Whatever Edward II had intended to gain from these talks, he only made sure that conflict would continue across the border until he admitted defeat. However, without the use of a single blow, the Declaration of Arbroath signalled the beginning of the end to England's credible claims over Scotland.

Arbroath Abbey, Angus, where the Declaration of Arbroath was sealed by the Earls, barons and freeholders of Scotland.

Right: *The High Altar of the Abbey.*

In 1322, King Robert's men assembled at Culross, Fife, seen here from the south bank of the Forth.

England's unworthy king

Although peace negotiations at Bamburgh had come to nothing, there was still an effective truce in place until the end of 1321. However, during this year King Robert sought to make the disputes in England work to his advantage. Once again, the Earl of Lancaster, together with the Earl of Hereford, had risen up in arms against Edward II. This foolish king, who had learned nothing from his disastrous relationship with Piers Gaveston, now had a new court favourite. Hugh Despenser had been dealt the same privileges as Gaveston, much to the resentment of Lancaster and Hereford. Having already clashed with the king, these two earls joined forces to attack Edward once again.

King Robert was to drive a harder wedge between the opponents by siding with Lancaster, who had promised Scotland its independence if he was given support to overthrow King Edward. However this did not prevent Robert resuming his campaign to intimidate northern England following the end of the truce. At the beginning of 1322, the Scots embarked on a three-pronged assault into England, reaching down to Hartlepool, Ripon and Darlington. The army assembled by Lancaster did nothing to oppose the Scots, as the earl was more interested in confronting his own king. Edward had risen to the challenge, raised his own army and went north to deal with the two dissident earls who were based at Pontefract. Upon hearing of the king's approach, Lancaster and Hereford fled north towards the Scots in the hope of gaining their support. Unfortunately for them Andrew Harclay, the governor of Carlisle, had gathered together an army in the north east and, in support of King Edward, rode south to confront the earls. At Boroughbridge, Harclay soundly defeated their army in an encounter which killed Hereford and brought Lancaster to his knees. The earl was handed over to the king, and in revenge for the execution of Gaveston, Edward had Lancaster beheaded without trial.

Above: *The modern bridge at Boroughbridge, where Harclay defeated Lancaster in 1322.*

The King of England clearly felt that all his troubles were behind him and, believing himself invincible, he declared that he would lead another campaign to Scotland. This time he really would raise the greatest army ever to set foot there. It was all tediously familiar and strange, to say the least, that both Edward II and his father never learned that the size of their army did not determine the success of their campaign. Time and again, thousands of men had been led north and wasted, either by starvation or by the use of bad military tactics. Nevertheless, in August 1322, the English king once again set foot over the border and, predictably to anyone other than Edward, found the entire Lowlands devoid of life and the land laid waste. King Robert had put his scorched earth policy into action well ahead of the English advance, and had even managed his own invasion into England and back, as Edward was marching north.

As the English army picked its way through the barren Lowlands, growing hungrier by the day, Robert was assembling an army of considerable strength at Culross in Fife. However, he did not intend to oppose Edward on this occasion, but waited for his inevitable retreat. After a month, the English king turned his army south. He had reached Edinburgh, but the failure of his supply ships to arrive at Leith due to bad weather meant that he could not sustain his men.

In October, as the last remnants of Edward's starving, straggling army disappeared over the border, Robert blazed his way south and entered England over the Solway Firth in the west. This was no usual raid, but an attempt to reach Edward himself, who had stopped at Rievaulx Abbey. The Scots army marched down the Eden valley towards north Yorkshire, and at a cracking pace had reached Northallerton by 12 October. Now, for once, Robert would confront King Edward on his own territory. The English, however, were not unprepared for such an encounter and had positioned a considerable army at Old Byland on the top of Sutton Bank, just west of Rievaulx. King Robert set out to attack the Abbey, but he came face to face with the English and would have to confront them if he was to capture Edward. The English forces were commanded by John of Brittany, the Earl of Richmond, who had deployed his army on the summit of Sutton Bank. To attack, the Scots would have to ascend a pathway up a steep incline. King Robert planned to assail the English from two directions, sending Douglas and Randolph conspicuously up the path, while holding back a division of Highlanders to scale the cliffs on the side of the hill and attack the English flank.

Despite the bombardment of arrows and rocks from above, the Scots reached the enemy under the momentum of an almighty charge. Before they reached the top of the hill, Robert ordered his Highlanders to begin their ascent. They came over the summit and the English were engaged on two fronts. Richmond and his army became disorientated and fled in all directions. The Earl himself and several knights were captured to be ransomed later for a considerable sum. Without delay, King Robert pressed on to Rievaulx, only to find that Edward had eluded him. Word of the battle had reached him and he escaped to Bridlington, once again leaving behind the Great Seal of England as he had done at Bannockburn. Staying at the Abbey to gather the spoils, Robert sent Walter Stewart off in pursuit of Edward. However, the King of England managed to stay ahead in the chase and decided to make for the safety of York, where he could not be reached. The Scots stayed in the area for a while, ending their campaign in Beverley and returning home at the beginning of November.

Right: *Rievaulx Abbey, N.Yorks., where Edward II stayed while the Scots fought at Sutton Bank.*

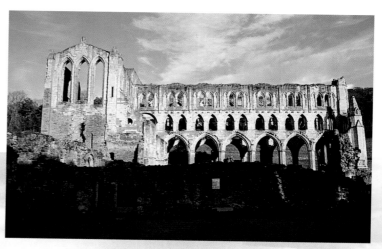

Below: *Sutton Bank, N.Yorks., today a compelling view for visitors was, in 1322, the scene of an encounter between the forces of King Robert and the Earl of Richmond.*

Above: Byland Abbey, near the site of King Robert's victory over Richmond.

If King Edward had managed to escape with his life, he had certainly not done so with his reputation intact. A king hounded in his own country by an invader was an ordeal undergone by Kings of Scots, not of England. Edward may have crushed his rebellious barons, but his competence as monarch was seriously called into question by his fatuous invasion of Scotland followed by the Battle of Old Byland and its aftermath. There were plenty of nobles who were sick of conflict with Scotland year after year and sought to bring about an end to the war. Andrew Harclay was one such man and, as Governor of Carlisle, he had borne the brunt of attacks by the Scots since 1314. His influence in the north had grown since he had defeated Edward's enemy, the Earl of Lancaster, at the Battle of Boroughbridge. Harclay had been rewarded with the Earldom of Carlisle and was made Warden of the West March. At the turn of 1323, Harclay crossed the border for a secret meeting with King Robert at Lochmaben Castle. They agreed between them to draw up a treaty which would end hostilities for good. The words of this treaty maintained that the kingdoms of England and Scotland would be distinct and separate, each having its own king *"of its own nation"* and governed according to its own laws, customs and rules. It was an ambitious scheme which, should Edward II accept it, also included the payment into the English treasury of 40,000 marks by King Robert.

By his actions, Harclay had taken a tremendous risk to his position, as all these negotiations had been done without the permission of the English crown. Harclay returned to his earldom and prepared to take his proposals to the King of England. But Edward had already received word of Harclay's plans and was enraged that his own royal prerogative had been over-ridden on such an important issue. Knowing that Harclay had considerable support in northern England, Edward had him quietly arrested

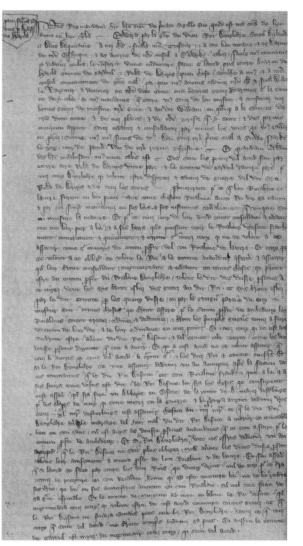

Above: The "Treaty" of Andrew Harclay, which became his death warrant. Many of its principles were eventually agreed between England and Scotland.

and put on trial for treason. However sensible the initiative was, and as well-meaning as he had been, the Earl of Carlisle was stripped of his title and condemned to death. Before suffering the cruel fate of traitors, he stood on the scaffold and told onlookers that it would be better for the communities of both kingdoms that each king possess his kingdom freely and peacefully, without homage, rather than that every year there should be so much slaughter, burning and depradation. Then, on 2 March, 1323, Andrew Harclay bravely went to his death.

Edward had lost a loyal and capable commander who, by taking the initiative, had simply shown up Edward's inability to rule. If England's king coveted Scotland, then he should at least have the means and the ability to conquer it. Edward had proved himself to be incapable, and should have left the Scots in peace. But Harclay's efforts had not been wasted, and precipitated an open change of attitude amongst England's nobility. He should perhaps not have acted independently, as his view was shared by others of his rank. Two months after his execution, a truce was underway between England and Scotland.

A change in fortunes

Andrew Harclay had been such an able defender of northern England that Edward was forced to consider a truce with the Scots, lest they over-run Carlisle. The King of England had misjudged the situation once again, as there was no equal to Harclay who could take his place. In May 1323 a thirteen-year truce was agreed by the government of England and representatives of King Robert at talks held at Bishopthorpe just south of York. It was confirmed by Robert himself in the following month at Berwick. The agreement did not solve the question of Scottish sovereignty, but it effectively brought an end to the war. The acceptance of an independent Scotland, although still a few years off, was now a formality.

The terms of the truce brought much-needed stability to the battered borders of England and Scotland, where the construction and repair of all castles was to be halted. Neutral stewardship of the border itself gave the people a security they had not known before. This was achieved by the appointment of 'special wardens', who would arbitrate over border disputes and patrol the border itself. As well as this, Scottish ships trading with Europe were protected from all acts of English piracy. The most significant advantage for the Scots was that King Edward promised not to stand in the way of attempts to raise the excommunication which had been imposed on the entire country. With this in mind, Thomas Randolph was sent to the Pope at the end of 1323 to discover whether Holy Church would consider

the Scots' plea. Randolph had gained quite a reputation for his diplomatic skills and his persuasive techniques did achieve a level of success. He made much of the words in the Declaration of Arbroath, that the Scots would eagerly fight in the Holy Land once freed from the conflict at home. The Pope, however, argued that, as they were all excommunicates, he could not grant them this wish. Randolph argued masterfully that if communications sent to Scotland had been correctly addressed to 'King Robert' and not 'Robert Bruce', then the matter could have been resolved much before now.

The Pope was delighted that a simple change to a title would result in thousands of recruits for his crusade and in January 1324, Robert was formally recognised as King of Scots. Unfortunately the excommunication was not lifted as the English, despite their agreement not to interfere, argued that the Scots had broken a previous truce to occupy Berwick, which they still held. They persuaded the Pope that the Scots should not be given what they desired until the town was handed back, and given the importance of Berwick and the fact that it was a Scottish town, the Scots decided to remain excommunicated.

To remain outside the protection of the Church was an ongoing hindrance for Scotland, but the country's morale was raised when, in May 1324, Queen Elizabeth produced a male heir. For the previous two hundred years, the eldest sons of the Bruce family had been called Robert but, in a change of tradition, they decided to name their son David. The king's grandson was Robert Stewart and, so as not to confuse the two, the next King of Scots was named after David I, who had ruled Scotland in an earlier age of optimism and prosperity. Elizabeth had done very well, bearing four children at an age which had put her own life at risk. Nevertheless, now in her mid-forties, she would never really recover from the traumatic birth of David.

With the prospect of a few years away from strife ahead of him, the king could settle down and rule Scotland in peace for the first time in his eighteen-year reign. He spent these years going some way to reward those who had fought alongside him all those years, to rebuild Scotland's battered economy and to settle down to family life. They could never return to the same prosperity that Scotland enjoyed before the war, and they could no longer depend on raiding into northern England to supplement their supplies of cattle, sheep, grain and other goods. However, the truce allowed trade with Europe to flourish once again and wealth throughout the 1320s began to grow. The king's next priority was to repay everyone who had helped him through the desperate years at the start of his reign. Many had sacrificed

Left: Pope John XXII, to whom the Declaration of Arbroath was sent, receiving emissaries.

River Leven valley, Dunbartonshire, looking north to the West Highlands: nearby, but long since vanished, is the site of King Robert's manor house - his final home.

all to fight for him against immense odds. They had endured the same hardships as himself and had asked for nothing in return. Fortunately, lands and properties from all those nobles who had opposed the king were now available for redistribution. The most significant were the Comyn and Balliol lands of the north east, the MacDougall lands of Argyll and the Macdowall lands of the southwest. These were spread amongst his closest comrades in arms, Douglas and Randolph benefitting particularly well, but also Sir Robert Keith, Gilbert de la Haye, Sir Robert Boyd and Walter Stewart, who had all faithfully stood by him. The Douglas family became a powerful dynasty which dominated Scotland's story for over a hundred years. As a result of their loyalty, Angus og Macdonald and Sir Neil Campbell now extended their Highland domains, making their clans more powerful than ever before, a significant note for the centuries to come.

Most significantly, the king would not forget Scotland's Church. It had constantly gone against the Church of Rome in supporting the King of Scots and his cause. Robert could not have sustained his fight without the financial help and spiritual guidance of the Church which had itself been threatened by takeover from England. Scotland could little afford it, but the king was extremely generous with his rewards. Guilt for the sacrilege committed on the High Altar in Dumfries had remained with him all these years and the Franciscan friars there were to be paid a rent of forty marks a year. Substantial sums of money were given to religious houses all over the country, the most notable being Melrose Abbey. It had been sacked during King Edward's final abortive invasion of Scotland in 1322 and now, in 1326, Robert granted all the revenues collected from Roxburghshire, a generous £2,000, to its restoration. Melrose

was held in high esteem and would become the focus of attention at the end of the king's life.

The time had also come to reward himself in some small way and Robert looked to provide his own family with the comforts of a new home. So many years had been spent in conflict that he did not feel at ease in any of the traditional royal castles, most of which had seen English occupation. So the king set about building a new dwelling for himself and his queen, which would reflect a more peaceful way of life. The place he chose was in the Vale of Leven, northwest of Dumbarton. Robert clearly had a strong affiliation with the west; it had provided a safe haven for him during his most desperate hours and from there he had drawn his most stalwart support. Although the west was now entirely in the hands of his allies, the entrance to the Clyde was the gateway to Scotland from the west and they must for ever guard it against invasion. From here, the king had access to the Isles and ordered the contruction of several ships including his own '*great ship*'. The home that he built was not a well guarded fort, but took the form of an extensive, thatched manor house. Sadly, the buildings are no longer there and the exact location is unknown. It was once thought to have been located on Castlehill, in the days when it was assumed that the king must have lived in a castle. However, the house with its hall, chapel, extensive garden and hunting park was most likely near the site of a farm called the Mains of Cardross. It was near the River Leven enabling his ship easy access to the house.

It is a pity that the house in which King Robert saw out the rest of his life no longer exists, because it would surely have become a national shrine.

Revolution in England

As Scotland was settling its affairs at home, England was once again approaching a state of turmoil. A diplomatic crisis had arisen between England and France which King Edward attempted to solve by sending his wife to negotiate with the new king, her brother, Charles IV. Isabella had grown resentful of Edward's extra-marital activities and saw opportunities in her visit abroad which did not include loyalty to her husband. In response to Edward's neglect of her, Isabella had taken a lover, Sir Roger Mortimer who, along with her son the Prince of Wales, joined her in France to plan an invasion of England with assistance from the French king.

In the spring of 1326, King Robert decided, once again, to take full advantage of England's weakness. Thomas Randolph was sent on his way to France, holding out Scotland's hand of alliance. Negotiations at the French court resulted in the Treaty of Corbeil, which formally renewed the Auld Alliance and meant that Scotland would intervene if England invaded France and vice versa, should England's truce with Scotland be broken. The Scots could afford to feel more confident now that they were no longer alone in the world. A parliament was held in July in which the succession to the Scottish throne was removed from ten year-old Robert Stewart and settled on his uncle, the two year-old David Bruce.

Above: *Berkeley Castle, where Edward II met his horrible death.*

Above: *Edward II's tomb in Gloucester Cathedral.*

Meanwhile, Isabella and Mortimer had been completing their plans to land a fleet in England and in September of the same year they made for the Suffolk coast and landed at Orwell. Edward had been unable to put together an effective army and, upon hearing the news that his wife was approaching London, he and Despenser escaped westward towards Wales ahead of her. Their attempts to reach Ireland were thwarted by bad weather and they were arrested in Glamorgan. To the greater satisfaction of many, Despenser was executed immediately and Edward was imprisoned and forced to abdicate. His son, the fourteen year-old Prince of Wales became king and was crowned on 1 February 1327. Perpetual imprisonment was what Isabella had planned for the disgraced former king, but on two occasions he escaped and was recaptured. Death was therefore the only answer and in attempts to give the impression of death by natural causes, Edward was starved over a period of months. But he had a strong desire to live and would not be broken so, at his final prison at Berkeley castle in Gloucestershire, Edward II was horribly murdered. In order that no mark should be seen on the outside of his body, a red hot poker was forced up his rectum, destroying his bowels from the inside. A shameful and ignominious end for a king.

Stanhope Park, Co. Durham, where Edward III was almost captured by Douglas and Moray.

Right: *The River Wear at Stanhope.*

Three kings called Edward ruled in England while Robert had reigned in Scotland, and on the day of Edward III's coronation, the King of Scots signalled the end of the truce by invading England and attacking Norham castle. In this way, Robert showed his disapproval of the previous king's forced abdication, and also reminded England that the King of Scots desired permanent peace, or hostilities would continue. The English had already broken the truce by acts of piracy on the North Sea. The Scots did not take Norham, but it had the desired effect, as the regents acting on behalf of the young king, but under the control of Isabella and Mortimer, immediately made sure that England held its truce. By now, Robert's health was deteriorating badly but, despite this, in the spring of 1327 he made another invasion of Ireland following a weakened English presence with the death of his own father-in-law, the Earl of Ulster. He forced the nobles there into a truce which prevented them from assisting the English in any campaigns against Scotland.

Despite the apparent peaceful intentions of the English, Isabella was gathering a host at York in the name of her son, in preparation for a Scottish invasion. Included amongst their weapons was a new invention, the gunpowder cannon. The army itself was as great as had been led against Scotland, but the Scots themselves responded swiftly and in a pre-emptive strike made a fierce attack on the north of England. Down they came, led as usual by Douglas and Moray, along the Kielder Gap following the River North Tyne and out into Weardale where they wreaked havoc on the countryside. On 10 July the English army left York, with the young king at its head. They had reached Durham when they could see devastation ahead of them to the north where the Scots had been at work. King Edward III set off in hot pursuit

but, despite their destructive trail, could find no sign of the Scots army. Upon hearing the rumour that the Scots were heading home and would cross the River South Tyne at Haydon Bridge, the English decided to drop the weight of their lengthy baggage train and head off to block their retreat. Their waiting was in vain, as for days there was no sign of the Scots and the weather was deteriorating. Torrential rain began to flood the ground and eventually news arrived that the Scots were much further south and had been waiting for Edward on the south bank of the River Wear near Stanhope.

It was 1 August and Douglas with Moray had positioned their forces on rising ground, while the English army arrived on the north bank to find that the Scots would not vacate their strong position. They proclaimed that *"We are here in your kingdom and have burnt and wasted your country. If you do not like it then come and dislodge us for we shall remain here as long as we please."* Edward's commanders then decided to hold their position, waiting for the Scots to cross the river as they must to return home. Realising the English plan, Douglas waited until dark whereupon he withdrew his men from their camp fires and led them down the bank and across the Wear into Stanhope Park, the Bishop of Durham's hunting forest. On the following night, the Scots fell upon the English camp and almost captured young Edward himself, but for the sacrifice of his servants who died bravely while their king escaped. Douglas and his men melted away into the night and, now that they were on the right side of the river, soon began their journey home. Once again, an English king had been belittled in his own country, and Edward is said to have wept when the news was brought to him that, as he himself wrote *"his enemies had stolen away by night secretly, as if vanquished."* The English withdrew at once to York.

Above: *Alnwick Castle, besieged by Douglas and Moray in 1327.*

Left: *Later characters from William Hole's processional frieze.*

The end in sight

In October 1327 negotiations for peace finally began. English envoys arrived at Norham and King Robert ended the siege, later making for Berwick to compose his terms for peace. Chief amongst his demands were six points:

One, that he have the kingdom of Scotland free, quit and entire, without rendering any kind of homage.

Two, that king Robert's son and heir should be married to the king of England's sister, Joan.

Three, that none should own lands in both England and Scotland.

Four, that the Scots would give military aid to England against her enemies, saving the kingdom of France.

Five, that the King of Scots should pay £20,000 to England.

Six, that King Edward should do everything within his power to get the sentence of excommunication against the people of Scotland raised.

If peace talks were to go ahead, then King Robert would only support them if the English king was prepared to take these terms seriously. There was a startling resemblance between these terms and those put forward in the Harclay treaty in 1323. If the previous English king had listened, and not condemned Harclay, then England could have received a better deal from Scotland.

England was finally coming to terms with the situation, although it was more to do with money than the acceptance of Scotland's independence. As rich a nation as England was, it could no longer afford the yearly campaigns, which had failed on every occasion. King Robert, now returned from Ireland, kept up the pressure and mounted one more English invasion. He repeated his attack on Norham castle, only this time employing the use of special siege engines, and sent Douglas and Moray to confront Alnwick. It was a particularly savage assault on Northumberland, with the intention of all but annexing that county as part of Scotland. It is certainly the case that much of the territory used to be a part of that kingdom, but Robert's motives were more about showing himself as equally capable of overlordship as the English king. At a parliament held in Lincoln, Edward was unable to secure the finances for further campaigns and at last the government of England was left no option but to sue for peace.

While the King of England considered these proposals, Scotland was struck with tragic news. Queen Elizabeth was dead. She had travelled north on a pilgrimage to St Duthac's shrine at Tain, where she had been captured twenty years before. She wanted to give thanks for being returned to her husband, but fell from her horse and had been too weakened from childbearing to survive her injuries. How sad that she did not live long enough to share her husband's final triumph. It had yet to be achieved, for in true Plantagenet style, Edward was only prepared to accept points two and five, regardless of the weakness of his position. It just so happened that they were the ones from which he gained most, namely that he could marry off his sister and the Scots would pay him a lot of money. Perhaps he thought no-one would remember that England had not, in fact, won the war. But Robert was not prepared to negotiate unless the first demand was fulfilled. He must have unequivocal acceptance of himself as King of Scots or talks would achieve nothing.

In November 1327, Edward, always under the advice of his mother, finally succumbed to the weakness of his position and broadly accepted the terms. On 1 March 1328, a Scottish delegation attended an English parliament in York. It was attended by Edward, now sixteen, who issued and approved letters-patent which gave the Scots what they had been fighting for over the last thirty years. The words that the envoys returned to their king must have been music to his ears:

> *"We will and concede for us and all our heirs and successors, by the common council, assent and consent of the prelates, magnates, earls and barons and communities of our realm in our parliament that the kingdom of Scotland shall remain for ever separate in all respects from the kingdom of England, in its entirety, free and in peace, without any kind of subjection, servitude, claim or demand, with its rightful boundaries as they were held and preserved in the times of Alexander of good memory king of Scotland last deceased, to the magnificent prince, the lord Robert, by God's grace illustrious king of Scots, our ally and very dear friend, and to his heirs and successors."*

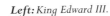

Left: *King Edward III.*

Below: *Clifford's Tower, York. In 1328 a parliament was held at York by the young King Edward III.*

Holyrood Abbey, where King Robert I put his seal to the Treaty of Edinburgh.

Nine days later an English delegation led by the Bishop of Lincoln, Henry Burghersh, arrived in Edinburgh to conclude the treaty in the presence of King Robert at Holyrood Abbey. Unfortunately the king was by now bed-ridden for most of the time as a result of his illness. It was a measure of how he had lived his life that this man, blessed with physical strength and mental stamina, should now be at death's door at the age of 53. But he at least had the satisfaction of seeing peace concluded in his own land. Alongside him was his old friend Bishop William Lamberton who had worked consistently hard behind the scenes to secure independence not only for Scotland, but for her Church. On 17 March 1328 the Treaty of Edinburgh was sealed and approved by the Scottish parliament at Holyrood. On 4 May it was ratified by English parliament at Northampton. It could not have arrived any later for Lamberton, as only two weeks later he died. In one form or another, the treaty accepted all six of Scotland's terms, apart from point three on the issue of landowners, which remained a grey area. It is particularly remarkable how formal and dignified the whole process was. It was almost as if the previous thirty years had not happened. In fact, if Edward's grandfather had abided by the words of the Treaty of Birgham, written thirty eight years before that, then the years of devastation and bloodshed would not have happened. In similar words it had stated that *"The kingdom of Scotland shall remain separate and divided from the kingdom of England by its right boundaries and marches as has hitherto in the past been observed, and that it shall be free in itself and without subjection"*.

Right: *The Treaty of Edinburgh / Northampton, 1328.*

King Robert's six terms were acted upon almost immediately and in the summer of 1328, the marriage of the four year-old prince David to the six year-old princess Joan of the Tower was conducted in Berwick. On the first point of Scottish sovereignty, Edward promised to send all documents in which England claimed overlordship over Scotland north to King Robert. Interestingly, it also seems that there was a willingness to return both the alleged Stone of Destiny and St. Margaret's Holy Rood. Not that the Scots were interested in the former, and Westminster Abbey would not let them go anyway. At last, in October of the same year, the excommunication on all Scots was finally lifted thanks to England's diplomatic efforts. After twenty years in the spiritual wilderness, King Robert had come in from the cold.

The king at peace

King Robert was now free to be the king he had always wanted to be but, unfortunately for him, the illness which had dogged him since his days on the run was now consuming his life. He had dreamt that one day, when his country was free, he would fight a Crusade in the Holy Land. Perhaps it was as well for all Scots that he had chosen not to, as he would not leave home for as long as it was threatened from outside. In this he had shown a selfless devotion to his country that no other king could rival. Many, since his day, have accused Robert Bruce of merely fighting for his crown, but the struggle for Scotland had gone on for 22 years beyond his enthronement at Scone in 1306. He had not run away from his duty and only when he considered the plight of the spider had he questioned whether the fight was worth continuing.

Towards the end of 1328, the king retreated to his new home. He spent a few months at leisure and entertained many visitors, but he was ailing badly and practically ruled Scotland from his bed. There seems to be confusion over the nature of Robert's illness and the details of his symptoms are patchy. It is known that he was afflicted during his long campaign, and that his sickness seemed to come and go. However by 1327 it was serious and eventually fatal. Historians over the centuries have concluded that it was leprosy, but there are considerable arguments against this theory. Firstly, most skin deseases tended to be referred to as leprosy anyway and, secondly, there was never any attempt to isolate the king. Such superstition was attached to this horrifying disease that anyone contracting it, whether king or commoner, would be removed from society. In those months at Cardross, King Robert's son and daughter-in-law were in his presence and it is not possible that the king would have exposed the royal children, let alone his own heir, to leprosy. It seems more likely that the king had developed scurvy or dropsy as a result of his years on the run when he was half-starved and exposed to the harsh elements.

With Christmas out of the way the king began to deteriorate badly. He saw that his life was coming to an end and decided that he would make his own pilgrimage, as his wife had done. He chose to make his final journey down through Carrick to the southwest and St. Ninian's shrine at Whithorn in Galloway. This had always been a special part of the country, where he had spent a happy childhood, where his maternal ancestors had come from and where St. Ninian had first brought Christianity to Scotland in the fifth century. A horse-drawn litter was made to carry the king on this long and uncomfortable pilgrimage, which he began before the winter was over. His route had him taken down the coast of Ayrshire and he eventually reached Whithorn on 1 April. After a few days in prayer at the saint's shrine, he returned via an inland route, which passed Glen Trool. The memory of the battle which began his long campaign for the kingdom more than twenty years before must have brought great comfort to the king as life slipped away from him.

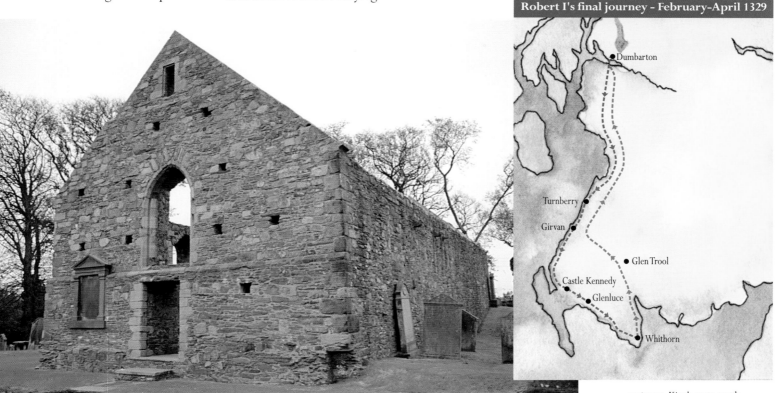

Above: *Whithorn Priory, Wigtonshire, where King Robert prayed at the shrine of St. Ninian.*

Robert I's final journey – February-April 1329

Dumbarton
Turnberry
Girvan
Glen Trool
Castle Kennedy
Glenluce
Whithorn

--➤-- King's route south
--➤-- King's possible route home

Once safely back at Cardross, he called his closest friends to attend him, as he was tired and the end was near. During May he wrote a letter to his son, David, giving him special instructions for the removal of the heart from his body and its burial at Melrose Abbey. But early in June, when his nearest and dearest were gathered around him, he spoke of the crusade on which he had always wished to embark. Confiding in James Douglas on his deathbed, he disclosed that before his heart was buried, it should go on a journey: *"Seeing, therefore, that my body cannot go to achieve what my heart desires, I will send my heart instead of my body, to accomplish my vow."* He entrusted this responsibility to Douglas, knowing him to be his most loyal, trustworthy and capable companion. On 7 June, 1329, Good King Robert passed away. He had cheated death on so many occasions and finally it came, not in battle, not by murder and not by execution, but quietly and at peace.

The king's body was carried with great ceremony to Dunfermline Abbey, which for the last two hundred years had replaced Iona as the traditional place of burial for Scotland's monarchs. There he was laid to rest underneath the choir next to Elizabeth, in a 'fair tomb', which had been made in Paris. Several days before, in accordance with his wishes, Robert's heart was cut from his body and enbalmed. It was placed in a casket and borne around the neck of James Douglas, awaiting its adventure abroad. Much of Dunfermline Abbey, including Robert's tomb, was later destroyed during the Reformation but, in 1819, when part of it was rebuilt, Robert's body was discovered. It was re-interred and marked with a new monumental brass.

Top: *Dunfermline Abbey, Fife, the final resting-place of King Robert I.*

Above: *The King was re-interred beneath the pulpit of the restored Abbey in 1819.*

Above: *Douglas throws the King's heart into battle against the Moors, near Seville.*

After so many years of inspired rule, it seemed hard to believe that the new king was a five year-old boy, with little idea of his destiny. But King David II had the strong arm of Thomas Randolph, Earl of Moray, as his regent and the added privilege of being the first King of Scots to be anointed with Holy oil. His father had achieved more than the removal of his excommunication, but had asked the Pope if future monarchs could be anointed in the same way as their English counterparts. This final acceptance of Scottish sovereignty was granted only days after Robert's death, and made the position of the monarch untouchable. Wars between England and Scotland may come and go, as they did over the centuries, but the legitimacy of the King or Queen of Scots could never be challenged.

In spring of the following year, James Douglas left Scotland on a sea voyage to the Holy land. On his ship, which had been given special protection by King Edward, were a number of knights to accompany him. Their journey took them firstly to Flanders and then on to Spain where they were entertained by Alfonso, the Christian king of Castile and Leon. Douglas was soon caught up with Alfonso's war against the Muslim king of

the Moors, and the Scots were recruited to his army. They went into battle at Tebas de Ardales, near Seville. Douglas was in command of the vanguard and led the attack into the enemy ranks. As imaginative a warrior as he was, Douglas was unfamiliar with Moorish principles of war and did not recognise a cunning feint attack. Without warning the Moors broke off and appeared to flee from the battle. Thinking to have got them on the run, the Scots gave chase leaving their vanguard behind. But they were dangerously exposed and the Moors, not far ahead of them, split their force from side to side and circled back, trapping Douglas and his men in the middle. Then Douglas paused and considered how he might fight his way out of the trap. Perhaps he looked down at the heart chained around his neck and wondered what his late king would have done.

Sir James Douglas took up the chain and, swinging the casket around his head, led a charge straight onto the spears of the waiting enemy. Before he perished, Douglas let go of the casket, and, throwing it in front of his horse he said *"Now pass thou forth in front as thou wast wont to do in battle, and I shall follow, or else die."*

After the battle, the body of Sir James was found lying on top of the casket, and was retrieved by Sir William Keith, a cousin of Douglas. The heart of Robert the Bruce never made it to the Holy Land, as both the casket and its bearer were taken home to Scotland. In accordance with his wishes, the late king's heart was buried at Melrose Abbey where it has remained to this day. Over the subsequent centuries, the Abbey suffered major damage during English invasions and the exact location of Robert's heart is not certain. In 1996, a casket thought most likely to be that of the king's was excavated and examined. Although no further evidence was found, it has been accepted that the position of the heart near to the original altar and the graves of royalty, means it could only be that belonging to Scotland's hero-king. The Good Sir James went home and was buried in St. Bride's chapel, Douglas, his family's ancestral home.

Above: *A new memorial marks the spot at Melrose Abbey, Roxburghshire, where the casket which probably contains King Robert's heart was re-buried in 1998.*

Left: *To the Douglas coat of arms was added the heart of King Robert I.*

St. Bride's Kirk, Douglas, where the Good Sir James was laid to rest after his adventures in Spain.

BIBLIOGRAPHY & FURTHER READING

The author has referred to many publications in writing *Scotland's First War of Independence*. These are listed below along with titles of relevant interest.

Barbour; John - *The Bruce*. Translation first published 1907; reprinted 1996 by Mercat Press, Edinburgh.

Barrow; Geoffrey W. S. - *Robert Bruce and the Community of the Realm of Scotland*. 1988, Edinburgh University Press.

Fawcett; Richard - *Scottish Abbeys and Priories*. 1994, B T Batsford Ltd./Historic Scotland.

Fawcett; Richard - *Scottish Cathedrals*. 1997, B T Batsford Ltd./Historic Scotland.

Fergusson; Sir James - *The Declaration of Arbroath*. 1970, Edinburgh University Press.

Fisher; Andrew - *William Wallace*. 1986, John Donald Publishers Ltd, Edinburgh.

Gray; D. J. - *William Wallace - The King's Enemy*. 1991, Robert Hale Limited, London.

Guest; Ken & Denise - *British Battles*. 1997, English Heritage/HarperCollins Publishers, London.

Hallam; Elizabeth - *Chronicles of the Age of Chivalry*. 1987, Guild Publishing, London.

Hamilton; William, of Gilbertfield - *Blind Harry's Wallace*. Reprinted 1998, Luath Press, Edinburgh.

Kightly; Charles - *Folk Heroes of Britain*. 1982, Thames and Hudson Ltd.

Mackay; James - *William Wallace - Brave Heart*. 1995, Mainstream Publishing, Edinburgh.

McNair Scott; Ronald - *Robert the Bruce - King of Scots*. 1988, Canongate Publishing Ltd., Edinburgh.

P. McNeill & H. MacQueen - *Atlas of Scottish History to 1707*. 1996, The Scottish Medievalists and Dept. of Geography, University of Edinburgh.

Moffat; William - *A History of Scotland - Book Two*. 1985, Oxford University Press.

Prebble; John - *The Lion in the North*. 1973, Penguin Books.

Ross; Stewart - *Monarchs of Scotland*. 1990, Lochar Publishing Ltd., Moffat.

Spankie; Mari - *Bruce's Scotland*. 1994, BBC/Wayland Publishers, Ltd.

Tabraham; Chris - *Scotland's Castles*. 1997, B T Batsford Ltd./Historic Scotland.

Thompson; Pishey - *History and Antiquities of Boston*. First published 1856; reprinted 1997 by Heritage Lincolnshire, Heckington.

Tranter; Nigel - *The Illustrated Portrait of the Border Country*. 1987, Robert Hale Limited, London.

Tranter; Nigel - *The Bruce Trilogy*. 1987, Hodder & Stoughton, London.

Tranter; Nigel - *The Wallace*. 1989, Hodder & Stoughton, London.

N. Tranter & M. Cyprien - *A Traveller's Guide to the Scotland of Robert the Bruce*. 1985, Routledge & Kegan Paul, London.

Guide Books & Pamphlets

Bold; Alan - *Robert the Bruce*. 1988, Pitkin Pictorials.

D. Breeze & G. Munro - *The Stone of Destiny; Symbol of Nationhood*. 1997, Historic Scotland.

Carruth; J. A. - *Heroic Wallace and Bruce*. 1986, Jarrold Colour Publications, Norwich.

King; Elspeth - *Introducing William Wallace*. 1997, Firtree Publishing, Fort William.

Watney; John - *William Wallace - Braveheart*. 1997, Pitkin Guides.

Bannockburn. 1997, National Trust for Scotland.

Freedom is a noble thing; Scottish Independence 1286 - 1329, 1996, Scottish Record Office.

Chronicles

John of Fordun's Chronicle - ed. W. F. Skene 1872.

The Chronicle of Walter Guisborough - ed. H. Rothwell; Royal History Society 1957.

Lanercost Chronicle - ed. J. Stevenson; Maitland Club 1839.

CREDITS AND ACKNOWLEDGEMENTS

The publishers wish to thank the following picture agencies, individuals and institutions
for providing the illustrations on the pages shown below:

Archiv der Hansestadt Lübeck: **56**

Argyll, the Isles, Loch Lomond, Stirling & Trossachs Tourist Board: **84, 85**(upper), **86**(lower)

By Permission of the British Library: **51** - Cott. Claud. D. VI f12v, **73**(lower) - Add 5444, f140b, **79** - Cott. Tib. E. VI f201b

Bord Failte - Irish Tourist Board: **130**(upper)

British Library/Bridgeman Art Library: **27**(left), **147** (left)

Chris Davis: **72**(lower)

Cliché Atelier de photographie du Centre historique des Archives nationales: **36**

Crown Copyright: Reproduced by Permission of Historic Scotland: **65, 67**(right), **rear jacket** heart motif

Cumbria Record Office (Carlisle): **128**(lower)

David Scott - Paisley Museum: **54**(left)

Dennis Coutts: **27**(right)

English Heritage Photographic Library: **107**(upper), **128**(upper)

Murdo MacLeod: **40**(left)

Northern Ireland Tourist Board: **129**(upper)

Isle of Man Tourism: **110**

Lambeth Palace Library/Bridgeman Art Library: **38**

National Library of Scotland/Bridgeman Art Library: **33**

National Library of Scotland: **22**(lower), **40**(right), **58**(lower), **81, 150**

PA News: **8**

© Pitkin Unichrome: **61**(lower), **144**(left)

Reproduced with the permission of the Keeper of the Records of Scotland: **137** - SP13/7, **148**(lower) - SP6/12

Seton Armorial: **68**(right)

Stewart Carmichael - McManus Galleries, Dundee City Council: **91**

Stirling Smith Art Gallery, © Estate of John Duncan. All Rights Reserved, DACS 1999: **Front jacket, 117**(lower)

The Ayrshire and Arran Tourist Board: **26, 109**

The Duke of Buccleuch KT, Bowhill, Selkirk: **80**(right)

The Governing Body of Christ Church, Oxford: **105**

The Master & Fellows of Corpus Christi College, Cambridge: **15**(lower)

The Public Record Office: **28**(lower), **41, 71**(lower)

The Roxburghe Charitable Trust: **16**(right)

The Still Moving Picture Company: **150**(lower)

© The Trustees of the National Museums of Scotland 1999: **Half Title, 35, 81, 120**(right), **125**

UK maps reproduced from the 1986 WH Smith/Philips World Atlas

1:2,000,000 map with the permission of The Controller of Her Majesty's Stationery Office, © Crown Copyright MC 029493

William Hole - The Scottish National Portrait Gallery: **15**(upper), **16** (left), **54**(right), **146**(lower)

William Bell Scott (attr.) - Guildhall Art Gallery, Corporation of London/Bridgeman Art Library: **73**(upper)

Scotland's First War of Independence would not have been possible without the help and permissions of galleries, institutions and individuals in the UK and abroad. In addition, there are a number of individuals and organisations to whom I am especially grateful: I would particularly like to thank author Nigel Tranter for his years of friendship and for sharing his knowledge and enthusiasm over this subject. His advice over the content of text and illustrations has added something special to the book and I feel privileged that he has given so much time to the project. Thanks are also due to Elspeth King of the Stirling Smith Art Gallery who staged the 1997 exhibition on *William Wallace - The Life and Legacy of Scotland's Liberator*, which provided me with additional information and material for this book. Elspeth has been very supportive of this project, and her assistance in its promotion has been invaluable.

Many of the sites visited and photographed for this book are owned and managed by Historic Scotland. The accessibility and care of these places made our task much easier and I would like to thank the many helpful custodians we encountered on our travels. I must also mention Doreen Grove, a Principal Inspector of Ancient Monuments for Historic Scotland, who advised on some details, and Clara Young at the McManus Gallery, Dundee whose help and encouragement was appreciated. The National Trust for Scotland has made the Bannockburn Visitor Centre a focal point for interest in the Battle, and I thank the staff there for their welcome over the years. The assistance of Mairi Stewart at Scottish Native Woods for technical detail is also acknowledged, as is Gordon Casely who was most helpful with heraldic details.

The maps have been meticulously carried out by Darren Bray, whose attention to detail is to be commended. Richmond & Rigg Photography and Swaingrove Ltd. have done an admirable job in printing and enhancing the images. Thanks are also due to Chris Davis for his support with the photography and the project generally. The project management and co-ordination have been carried out by Philip Crome. Finally, we thank Nicholas Russell for his technical assistance in the production of this book.

SUBSCRIBERS

The publishers wish to thank the following people for subscribing to *Scotland's First War of Independence*:

Eric Robert Allan
Anne Boyle
Constance Boyle
Francis Boyle
Duncan Brown
Mr Alexander Cameron
Bruce Casely
Gordon Casely
Mrs Dorothy Chadburn
Ian & Helen Collie
Mr Lindsay Corbett
Miss Joyce Cottle
Mr & Mrs Dick & Jem Clark, Alloa
Mr & Mrs Richard & Fiona Clark & Family, Alloa
Mrs Ann Clark-Jardine & Family, Alloa
Chris Davis
Alex L Dick
Mrs W L Eason-Gibson
Mr & Mrs Jack E Farman
Helen Fenning, Boston
Stan Forrester
Beryl M Jackson
John R & Stephen J Ketteringham
Elspeth King
Sharon B Lake
Myra Lines
Robert Lines
M J Love
Mrs Patricia I Lymer
John MacInnes
I M McGillivray
Mr & Mrs I Medcalf
Mr & Mrs M Medcalf
Miss F A R Murray OBE
Mr Ralph A Ottey
Mr & Mrs T J Sharp
Mr & Mrs David & Margaret Spence
David Start & Ruth Moore, Lincoln
Rosemaree Waite
Beatrice Watson
Marion Watson
R Bruce Weatherstone
Norvel L J Willerton
Alan Wiseman

INDEX